WHAT MAKES YOU HAPPY

By Jimmy Gownley

A Publication of ibooks, inc.

Portions of this book originally appeared in
Amelia Rules! #6-10, published by Renaissance Press

An ibooks, inc. Book

Distributed by Simon & Schuster, Inc.
1230 Avenue of the Americas, New York, NY 10020

ibooks, inc.
24 West 25th Street
New York, NY 10010

The ibooks World Wide Web Site Address is:
http://www.ibooks.net

Visit Amelia and the gang at:
http://www.ameliarules.com

ISBN 0-7434-7909-2
First ibooks, inc. printing April 2004
10 9 8 7 6 5 4 3 2

Original series editor: Michael Cohen

Printed in the U.S.A.

10-04 B&T 14.95

INTRODUCTION

Amelia Rules! is simply one of the best all ages comics I've ever seen. It succeeds on so many different levels, I'm sure anyone who gives it a chance will fall for it hook, line and sinker. Jimmy Gownley understands the full potential of comic book storytelling in a way that few of his peers do, and he wastes no time in getting every ounce of potential out of every square inch of the page. I don't know exactly how he does it, and he does it with astonishing consistency from issue to the next-- so the best I can do is point out a few examples of what I'm talking about.

Take the sequence in *"What Makes You Happy"* which Reggie launches into his hilarious definition of Artisticus Pretentious. Tossing the comic book's cherished panels and word balloons out the window, Gownley combines a graph-paper background, a wickedly funny mock-dictionary definition ("If possible the work should look as if it were done by a deranged toddler."), and wonderfully spare drawings to illustrate the words. *Amelia Rules!* would rule even without such sequences, but, for me, this use of unconventional storytelling techniques is what really makes the series shine.

Here's another example, and one that makes full use of Gownley's considerable talents as writer, illustrator, and computer colorist. In *"Her Three Kisses,"* when Amelia recounts what she picked up from a conversation about her late great aunt Sarah, the reader is treated to a series of tributes to comic book greats, old and new. First we get the traditional comic book approach, but then things cuts loose: the comic book page is invaded by three spot-on comic strip homages to *Peanuts*, *Doonsbury*, and *Dilbert*. In each instance Gownley's quality of line perfectly emulates the source material, and, in a fine example of computer savvy being put to its proper use, the presentation creates the illusion that each strip is freshly clipped from the paper. (Details are always just right in this comic: the *Peanuts* "paper" is yellowed with age.)

But this series knows when to knock the reader out with bravura sequences and when to keep things subtle. Take the page from *"Life During Wartime"* in which Amelia walks home alone. Here we get a mood, an atmosphere, expertly conjured up with a limited color palette, simple, clear narration, and a final panel that is, to a certain extent, the page itself. I love how a border is drawn around the full moon, allowing it to come into the sequence once, then reappear at the end without being drawn a second time. Here's a comic that knows the meaning of "less is more."

All right, then. I'll stop before I spoil any more surprises. Now it's time for you to sit back and enjoy the marvelous comic book gem that is *Amelia Rules!*. And if you find yourself reaching the end and wondering how on earth Jimmy Gownley did it. well, that'll make two of us.

Mark Crilley
Author/Illustrator of the Akiko books

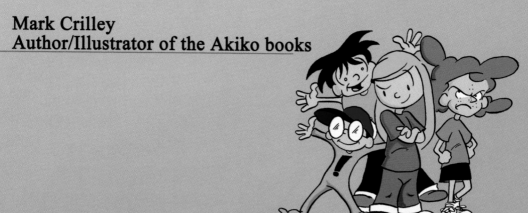

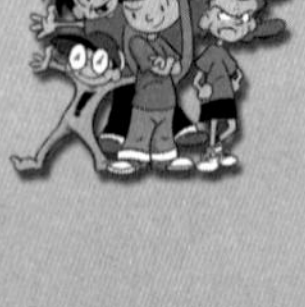

Dedication:

To my beautiful new
baby girls:

Stella Mary and
Anna Elizabeth

and to their wonderful
mother, Karen

You're what makes ME happy.

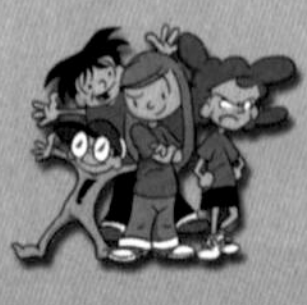

Part ONE

1

"Don't get all mushy, or I'll have to smack you a little."

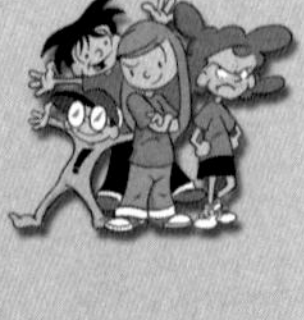

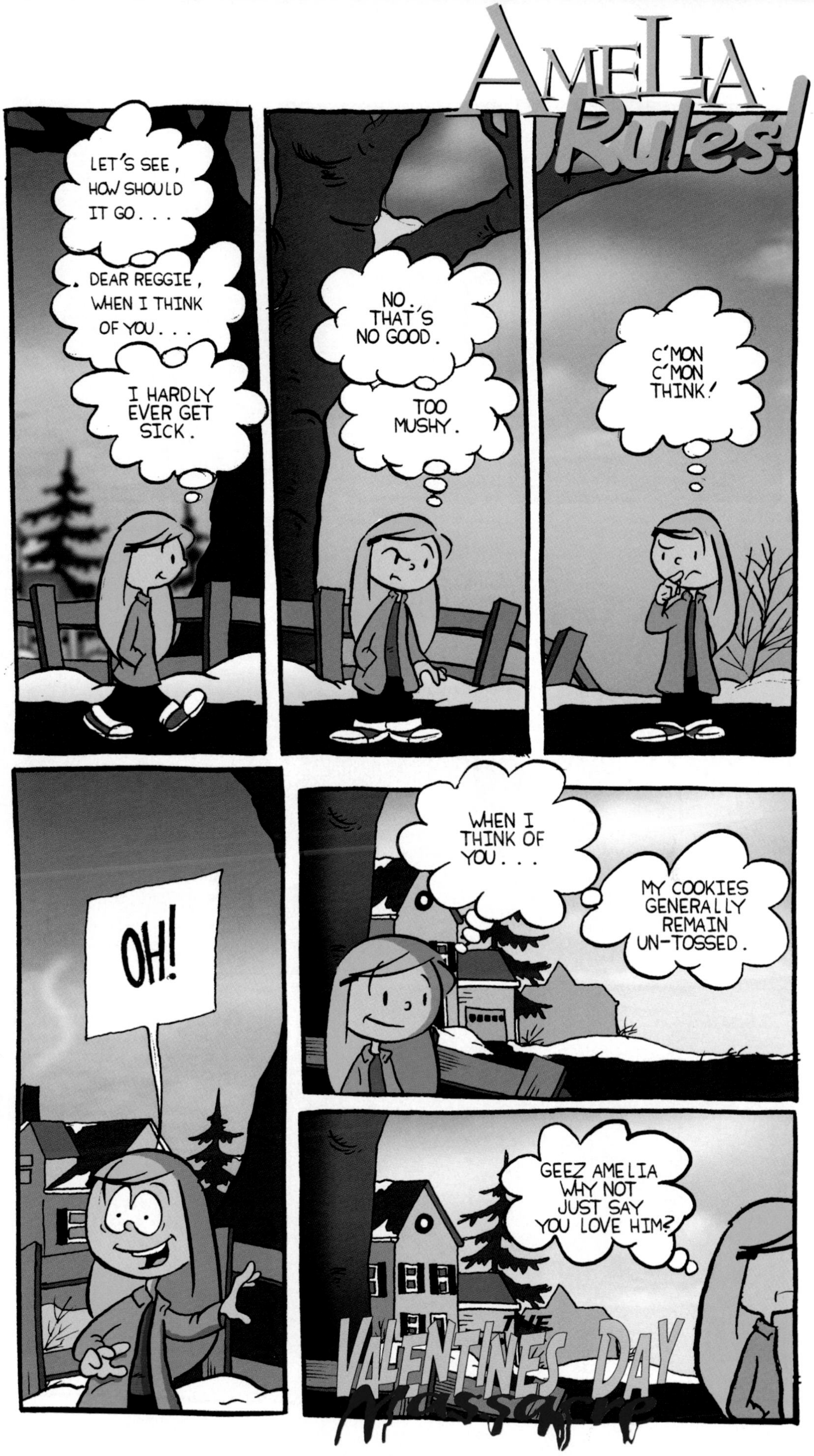
AMELIA Rules!
LET'S SEE, HOW SHOULD IT GO . . .
DEAR REGGIE, WHEN I THINK OF YOU . . .
I HARDLY EVER GET SICK.
NO. THAT'S NO GOOD.
TOO MUSHY.
C'MON C'MON THINK!
OH!
WHEN I THINK OF YOU . . .
MY COOKIES GENERALLY REMAIN UN-TOSSED.
GEEZ AMELIA WHY NOT JUST SAY YOU LOVE HIM?
THE VALENTINES DAY Massacre

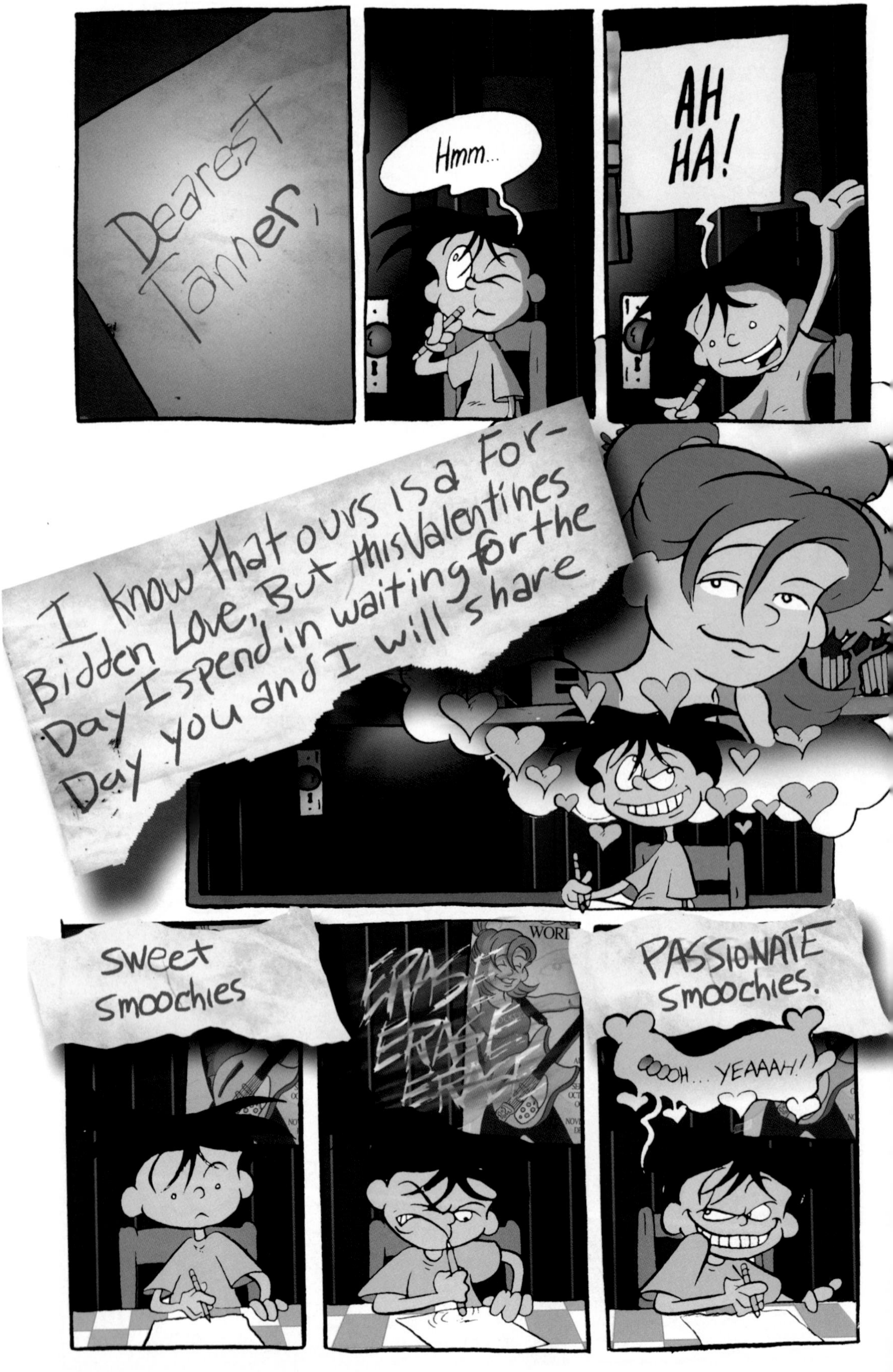

Dearest Tanner,
Hmm...
AH HA!
I know that ours is a For-Bidden Love, But this Valentines Day I spend in waiting for the Day you and I will share
Sweet smoochies
ERASE ERASE ERASE
PASSIONATE smoochies.
OOOOH... YEAAAH!

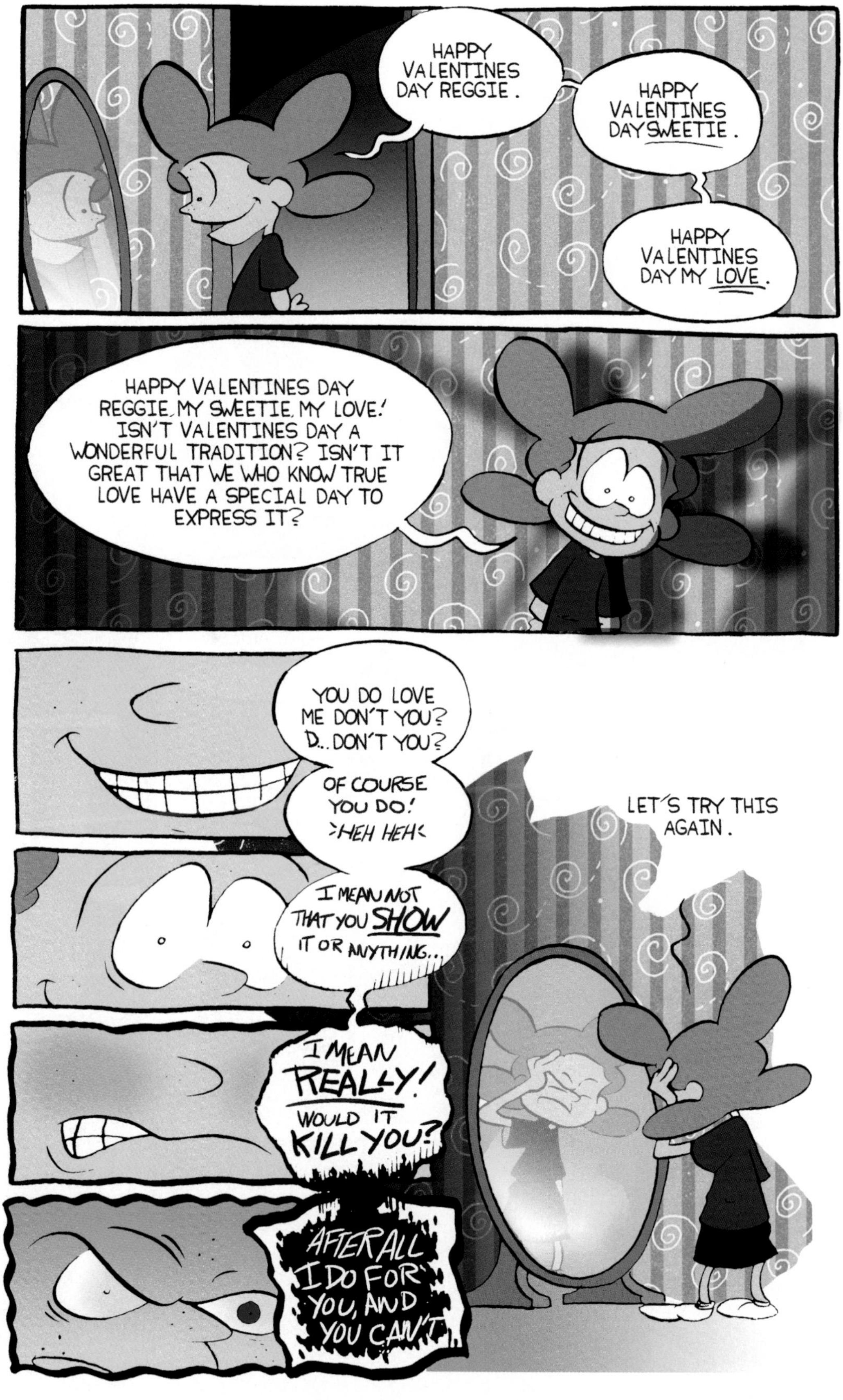

HAPPY VALENTINES DAY REGGIE.
HAPPY VALENTINES DAY SWEETIE.
HAPPY VALENTINES DAY MY LOVE.
HAPPY VALENTINES DAY REGGIE, MY SWEETIE, MY LOVE! ISN'T VALENTINES DAY A WONDERFUL TRADITION? ISN'T IT GREAT THAT WE WHO KNOW TRUE LOVE HAVE A SPECIAL DAY TO EXPRESS IT?
YOU DO LOVE ME DON'T YOU? D...DON'T YOU?
OF COURSE YOU DO! >HEH HEH<
I MEAN NOT THAT YOU SHOW IT OR ANYTHING...
I MEAN REALLY! WOULD IT KILL YOU?
AFTER ALL I DO FOR YOU, AND YOU CAN'T
LET'S TRY THIS AGAIN.

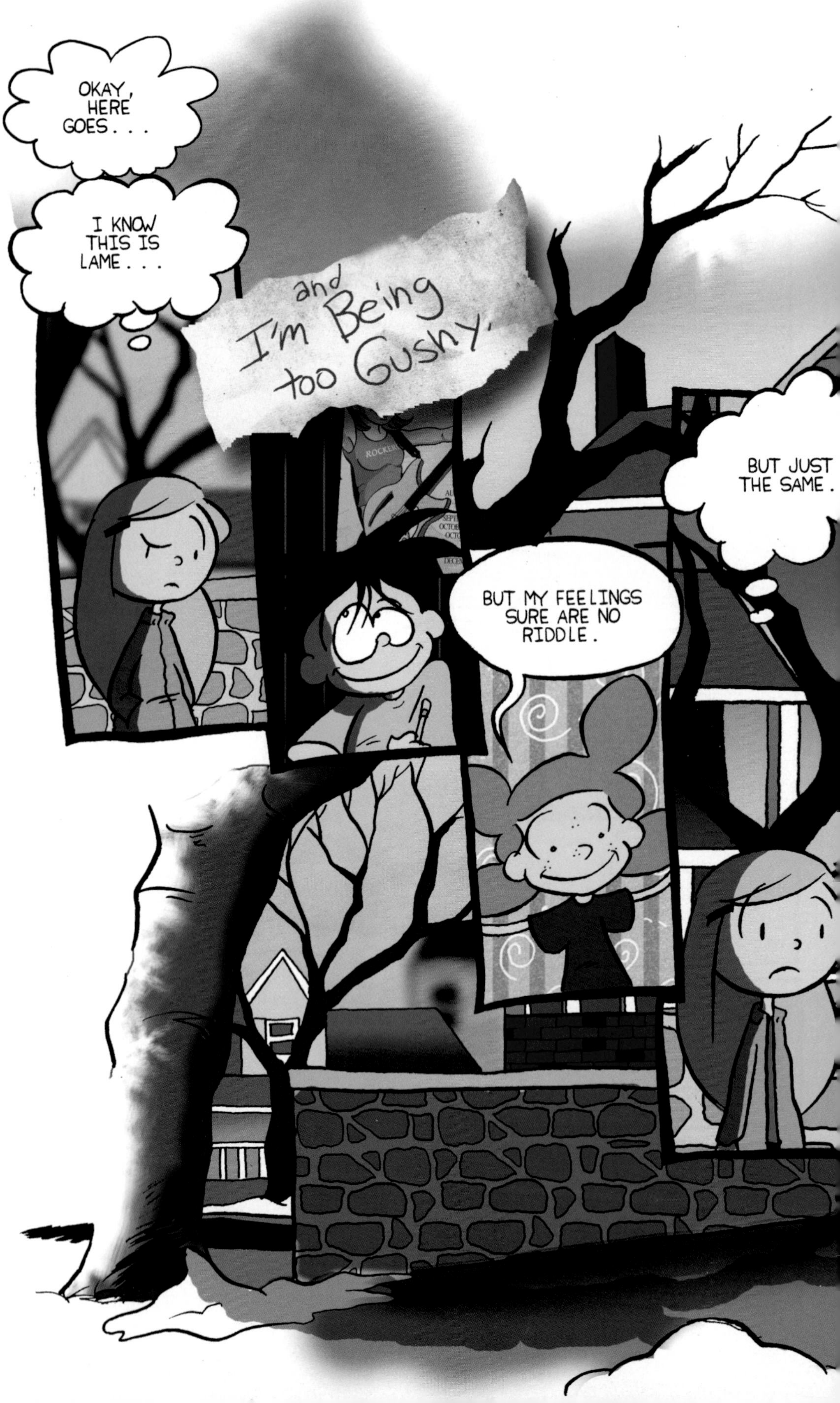
OKAY, HERE GOES . . .
I KNOW THIS IS LAME . . .
and I'm Being too Gushy,
ROCKER
BUT MY FEELINGS SURE ARE NO RIDDLE.
BUT JUST THE SAME .

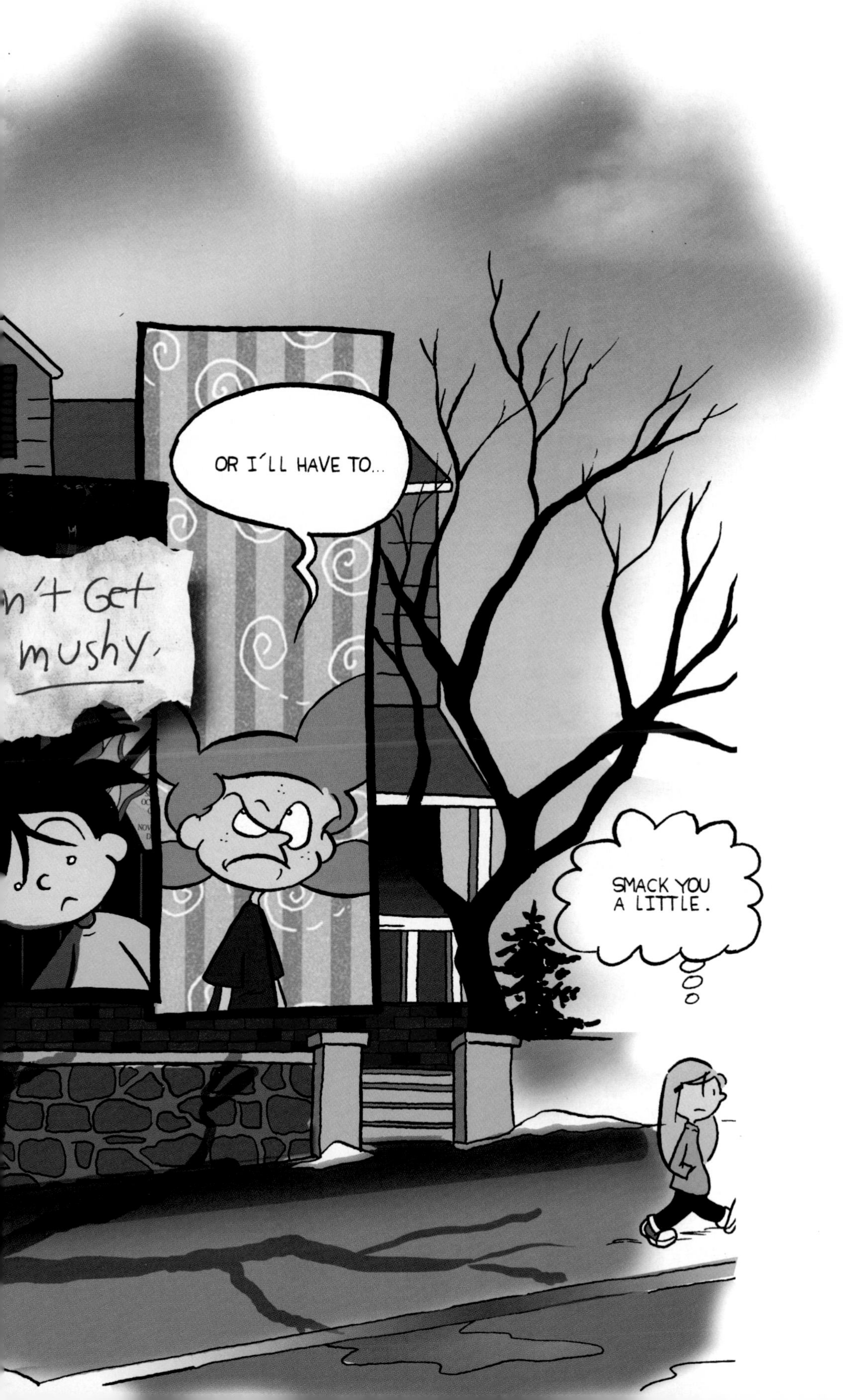
n't Get
mushy.
OR I'LL HAVE TO...
SMACK YOU
A LITTLE.

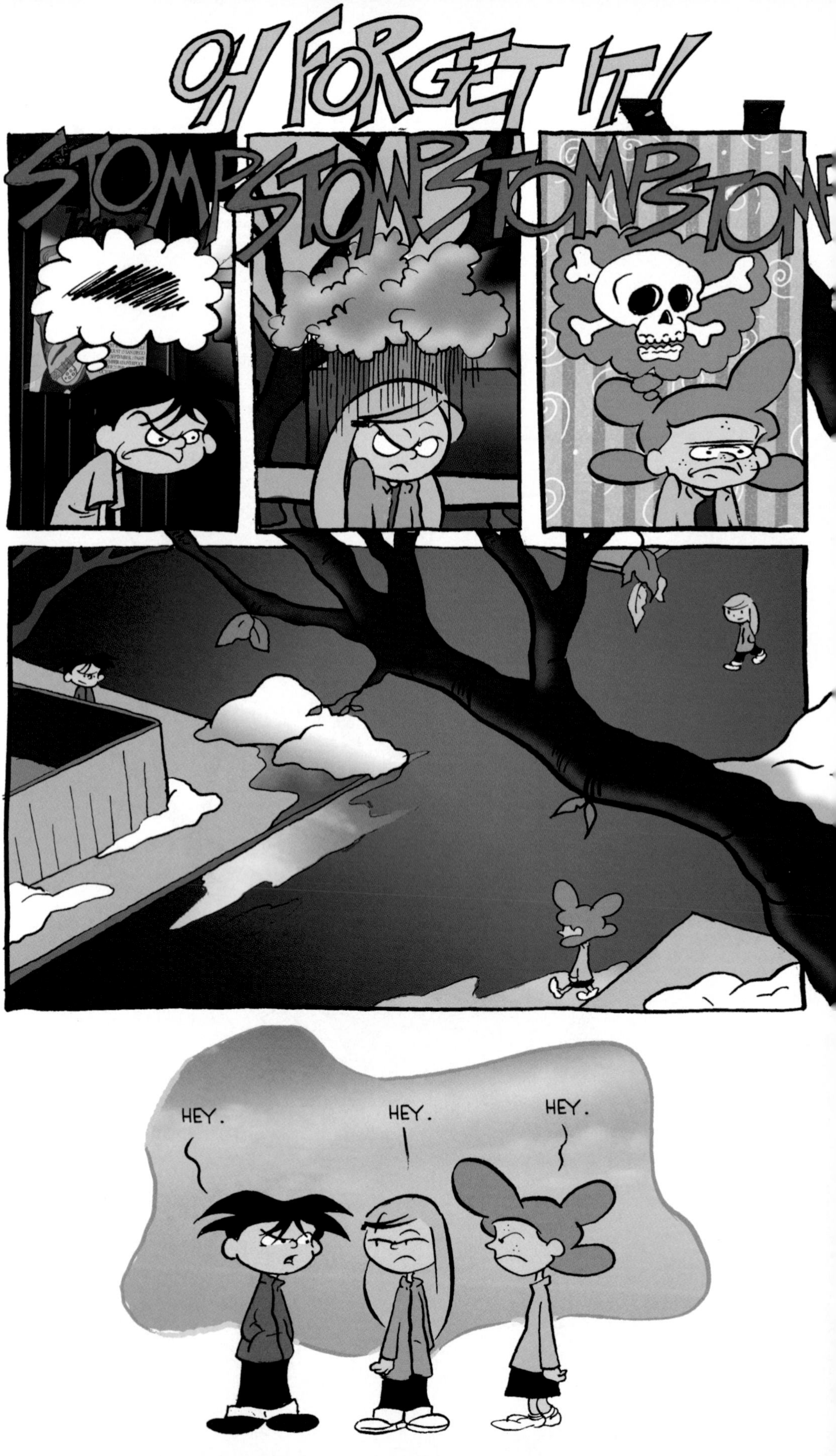
OH FORGET IT!
STOMP
STOMP
STOMP
STOMP
HEY.
HEY.
HEY.

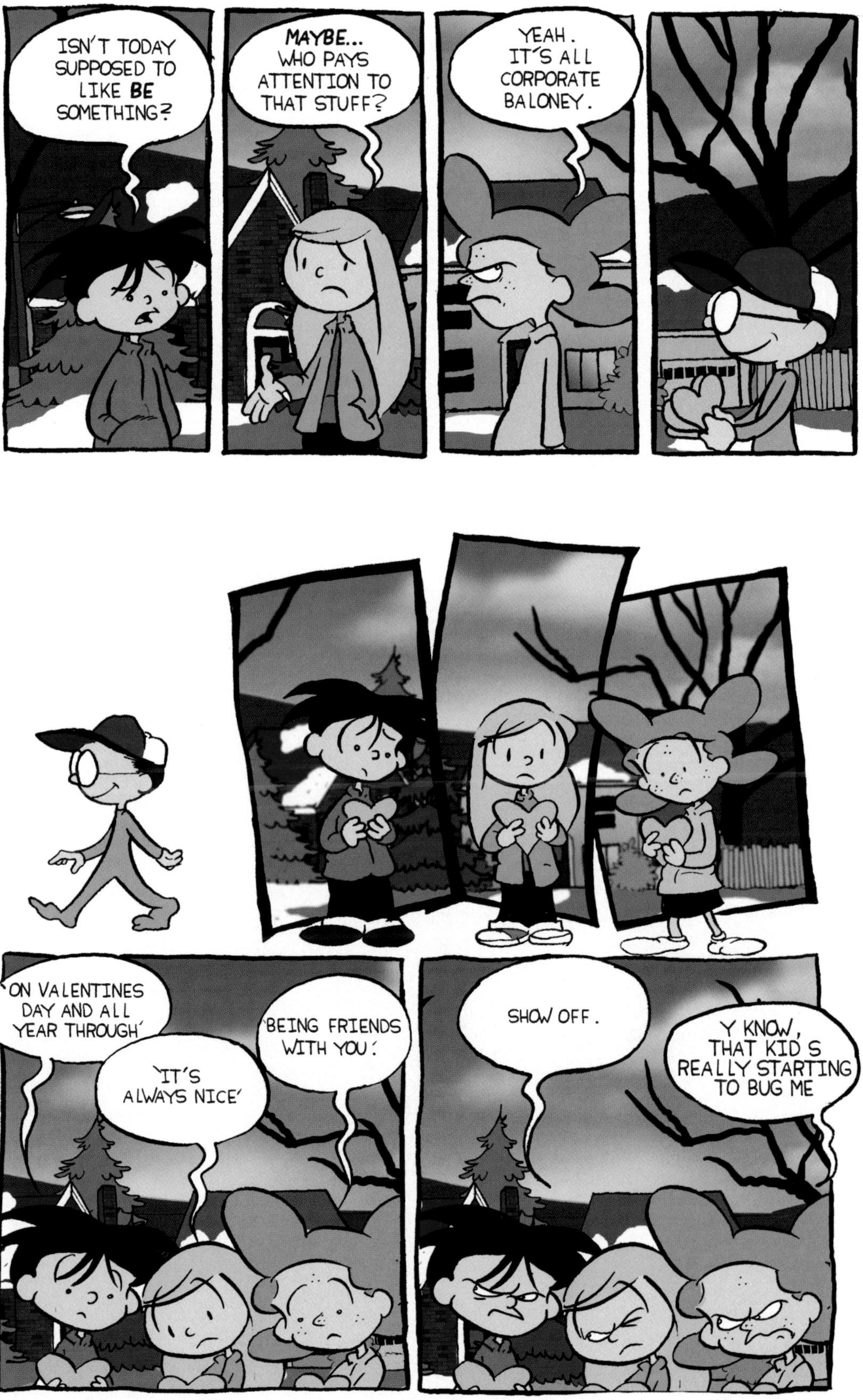
ISN'T TODAY SUPPOSED TO LIKE **BE** SOMETHING?
MAYBE... WHO PAYS ATTENTION TO THAT STUFF?
YEAH. IT'S ALL CORPORATE BALONEY.
'ON VALENTINES DAY AND ALL YEAR THROUGH'
'IT'S ALWAYS NICE'
'BEING FRIENDS WITH YOU.'
SHOW OFF.
Y KNOW, THAT KID S REALLY STARTING TO BUG ME

"I became a superhero, I kissed a ninja, I hung out with a kid in feetie pajamas." - Amelia Louise McBride

Part

TWO

"I'm used to people staring ('cuz of my beauty an' all)."

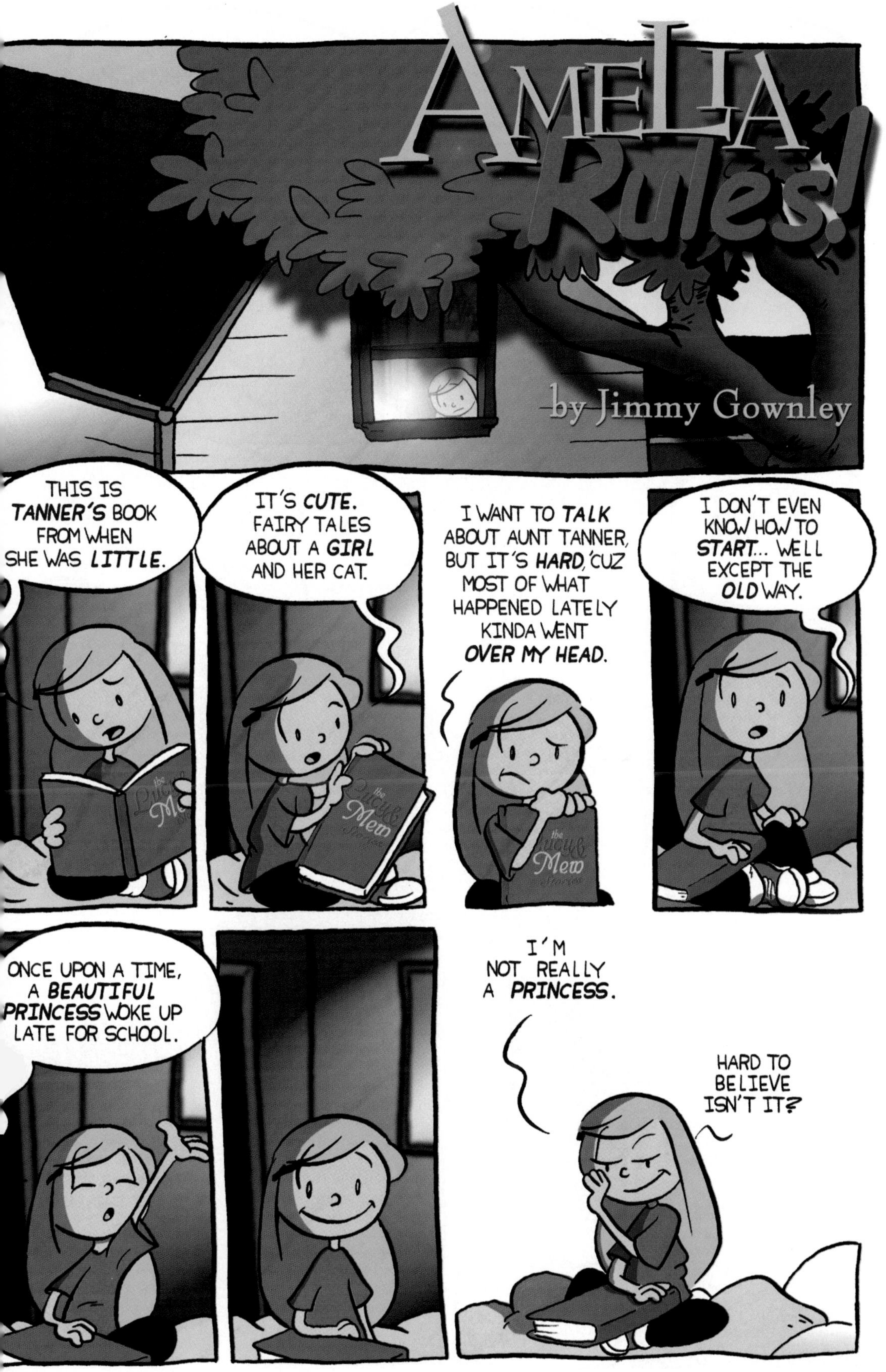
AMELIA Rules!
by Jimmy Gownley
THIS IS TANNER'S BOOK FROM WHEN SHE WAS LITTLE.
IT'S CUTE. FAIRY TALES ABOUT A GIRL AND HER CAT.
I WANT TO TALK ABOUT AUNT TANNER, BUT IT'S HARD, 'CUZ MOST OF WHAT HAPPENED LATELY KINDA WENT OVER MY HEAD.
I DON'T EVEN KNOW HOW TO START... WELL EXCEPT THE OLD WAY.
ONCE UPON A TIME, A BEAUTIFUL PRINCESS WOKE UP LATE FOR SCHOOL.
I'M NOT REALLY A PRINCESS.
HARD TO BELIEVE ISN'T IT?

What Makes You Happy

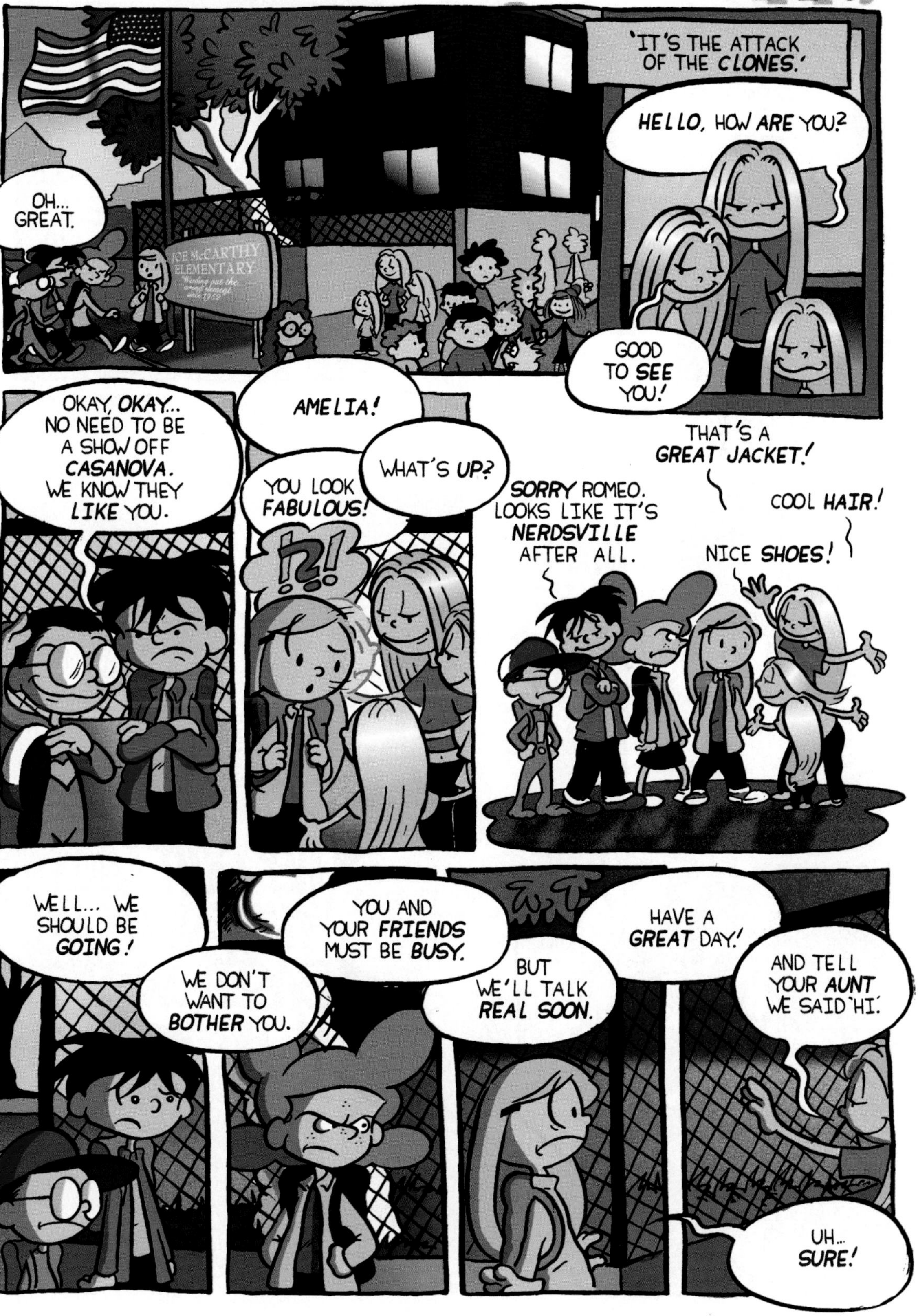
OH... GREAT.
JOE McCARTHY ELEMENTARY
'IT'S THE ATTACK OF THE CLONES.'
HELLO, HOW ARE YOU?
GOOD TO SEE YOU!
OKAY, OKAY... NO NEED TO BE A SHOW OFF CASANOVA. WE KNOW THEY LIKE YOU.
AMELIA!
YOU LOOK FABULOUS!
WHAT'S UP?
?!
SORRY ROMEO. LOOKS LIKE IT'S NERDSVILLE AFTER ALL.
THAT'S A GREAT JACKET!
COOL HAIR!
NICE SHOES!
WELL... WE SHOULD BE GOING!
WE DON'T WANT TO BOTHER YOU.
YOU AND YOUR FRIENDS MUST BE BUSY.
BUT WE'LL TALK REAL SOON.
HAVE A GREAT DAY!
AND TELL YOUR AUNT WE SAID 'HI.'
UH... SURE!

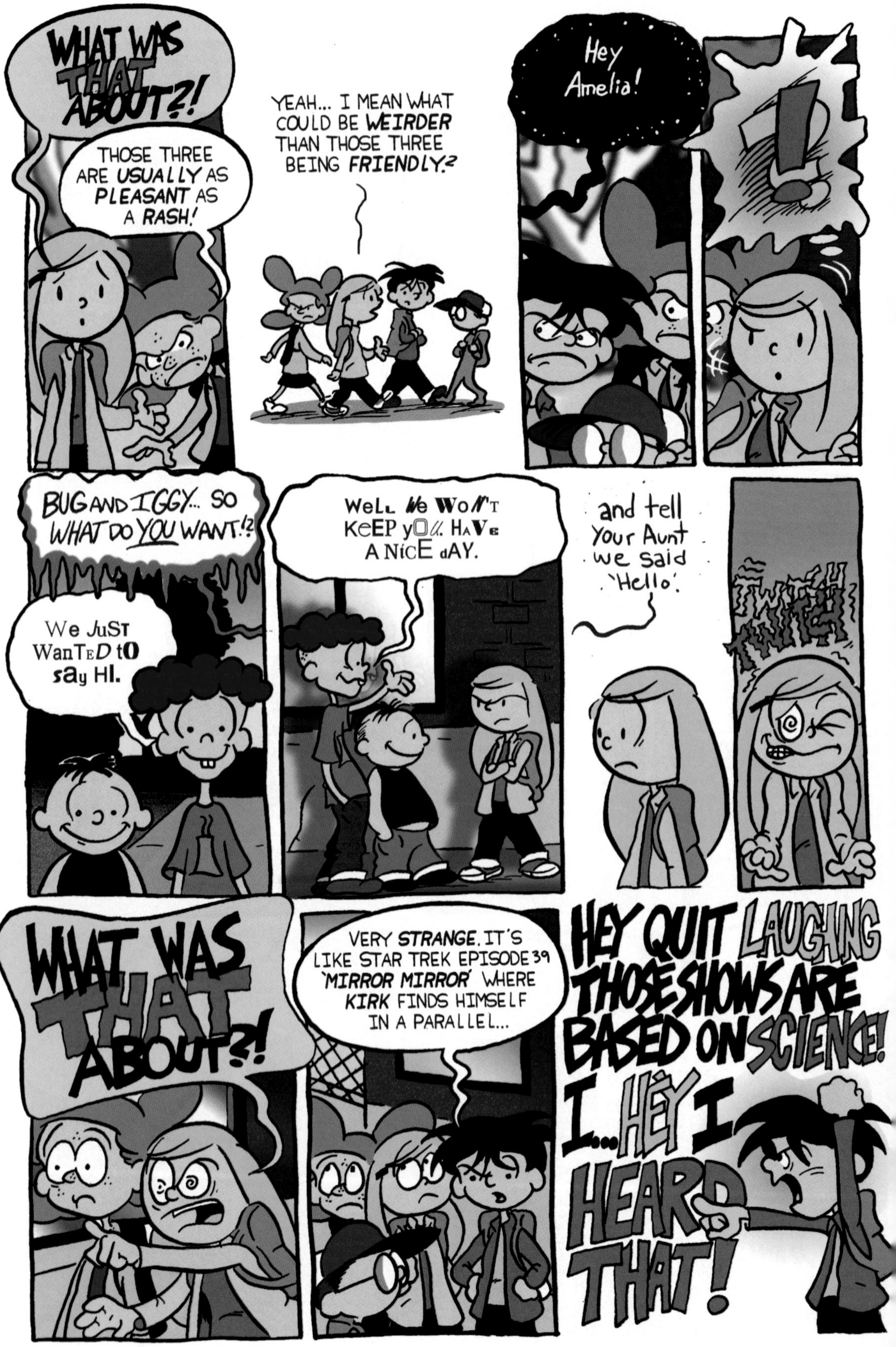

WHAT WAS THAT ABOUT?!
THOSE THREE ARE USUALLY AS PLEASANT AS A RASH!
YEAH... I MEAN WHAT COULD BE WEIRDER THAN THOSE THREE BEING FRIENDLY?
Hey Amelia!
?!
BUG AND IGGY... SO WHAT DO YOU WANT!?
We JuST WanTeD tO say HI.
WeLL We WoN'T KeEP yOU. HaVe A NicE dAY.
and tell Your Aunt we said 'Hello'.
TWITCH TWITCH
WHAT WAS THAT ABOUT?!
VERY STRANGE. IT'S LIKE STAR TREK EPISODE 39 'MIRROR MIRROR' WHERE KIRK FINDS HIMSELF IN A PARALLEL...
HEY QUIT LAUGHING THOSE SHOWS ARE BASED ON SCIENCE! I...HEY I HEARD THAT!

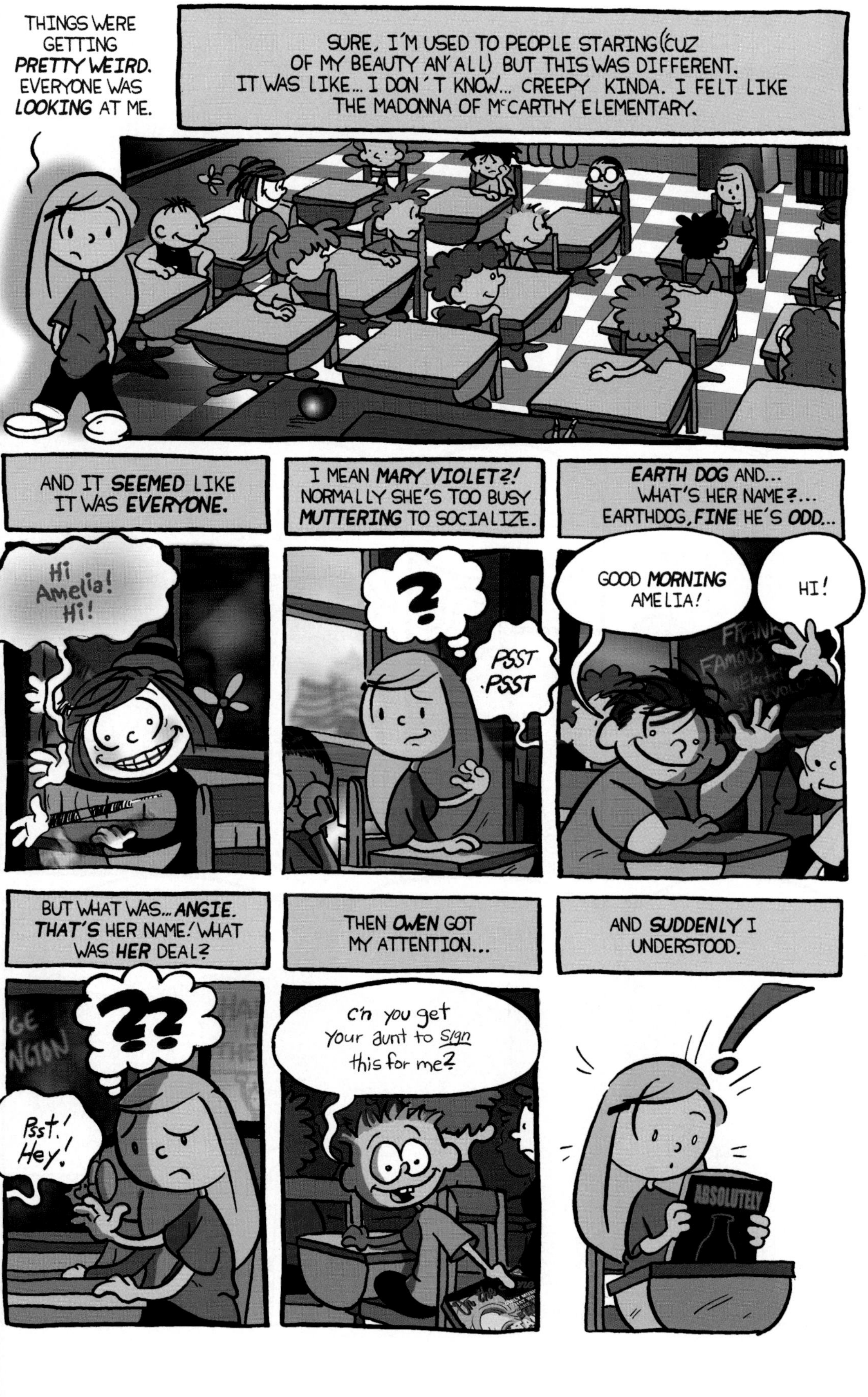
THINGS WERE GETTING PRETTY WEIRD. EVERYONE WAS LOOKING AT ME.
SURE, I'M USED TO PEOPLE STARING ('CUZ OF MY BEAUTY AN' ALL) BUT THIS WAS DIFFERENT. IT WAS LIKE... I DON'T KNOW... CREEPY KINDA. I FELT LIKE THE MADONNA OF McCARTHY ELEMENTARY.
AND IT SEEMED LIKE IT WAS EVERYONE.
Hi Amelia! Hi!
I MEAN MARY VIOLET?! NORMALLY SHE'S TOO BUSY MUTTERING TO SOCIALIZE.
?
PSST PSST
EARTH DOG AND... WHAT'S HER NAME?... EARTHDOG, FINE HE'S ODD...
GOOD MORNING AMELIA!
HI!
BUT WHAT WAS... ANGIE. THAT'S HER NAME! WHAT WAS HER DEAL?
??
Psst! Hey!
THEN OWEN GOT MY ATTENTION...
C'n you get your aunt to sign this for me?
AND SUDDENLY I UNDERSTOOD.
!
ABSOLUTELY

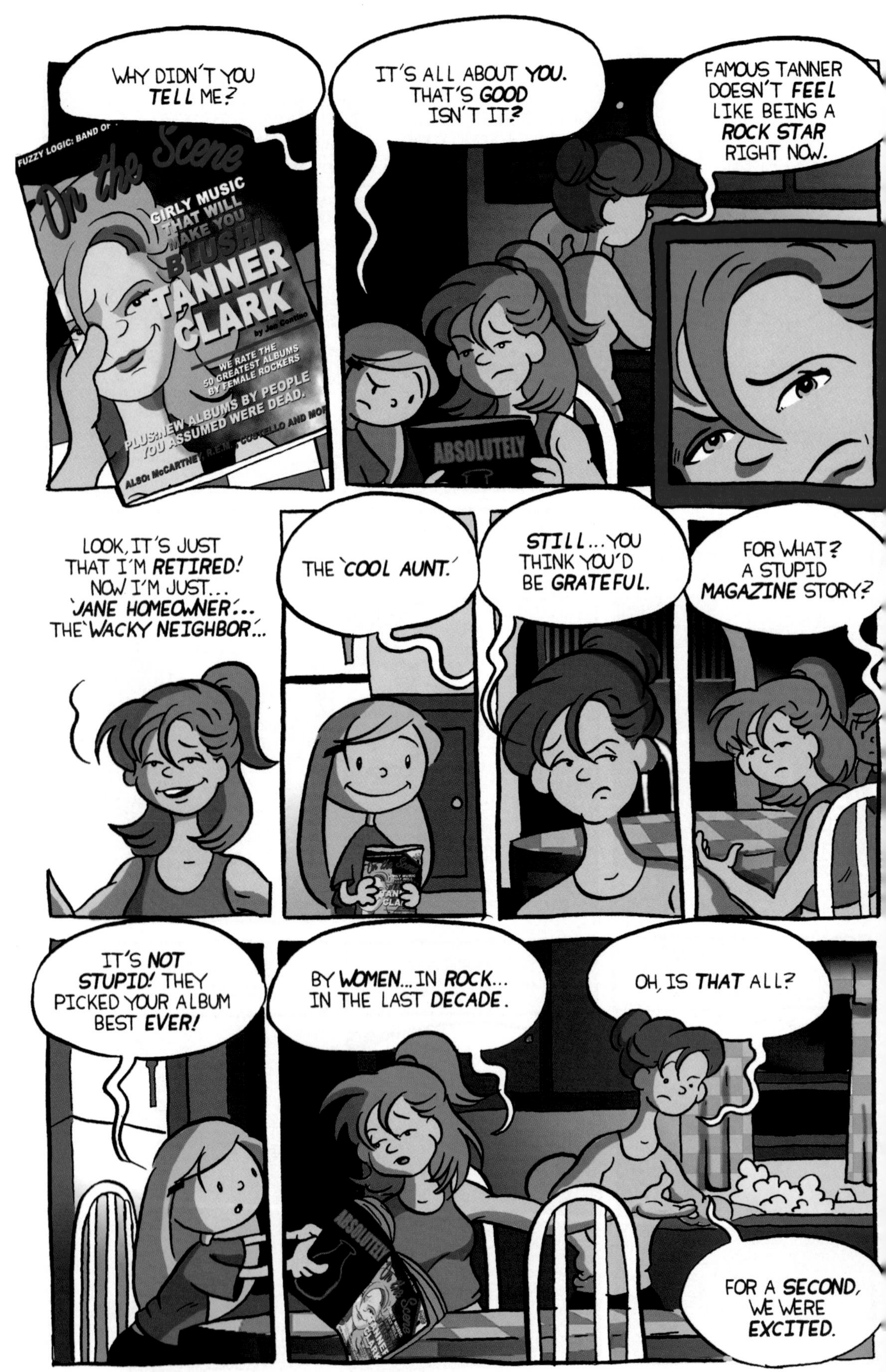

WHY DIDN'T YOU TELL ME?
FUZZY LOGIC: BAND OF
On the Scene
GIRLY MUSIC THAT WILL MAKE YOU BLUSH!
TANNER CLARK
by Jen Contino
WE RATE THE 50 GREATEST ALBUMS BY FEMALE ROCKERS
PLUS: NEW ALBUMS BY PEOPLE YOU ASSUMED WERE DEAD.
ALSO: McCARTNEY, R.E.M., COSTELLO AND MO
IT'S ALL ABOUT YOU. THAT'S GOOD ISN'T IT?
ABSOLUTELY
FAMOUS TANNER DOESN'T FEEL LIKE BEING A ROCK STAR RIGHT NOW.
LOOK, IT'S JUST THAT I'M RETIRED! NOW I'M JUST... 'JANE HOMEOWNER'... THE 'WACKY NEIGHBOR'...
THE 'COOL AUNT.'
STILL... YOU THINK YOU'D BE GRATEFUL.
FOR WHAT? A STUPID MAGAZINE STORY?
IT'S NOT STUPID! THEY PICKED YOUR ALBUM BEST EVER!
BY WOMEN... IN ROCK... IN THE LAST DECADE.
OH, IS THAT ALL?
FOR A SECOND, WE WERE EXCITED.

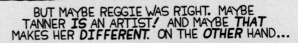

BUT MAYBE REGGIE WAS RIGHT. MAYBE TANNER *IS* AN ARTIST! AND MAYBE *THAT* MAKES HER *DIFFERENT*. ON THE *OTHER* HAND...

NOW *BELIEVE ME*, IT HURTS TO SAY IT...

BALONEY!

YEAH *REGGIE*. I MEAN IF SHE *WAS* AN ARTIST, SHE'D BE WEIRD *ALL* THE TIME!

Y'KNOW SHE'D WEAR *BLACK*, AND LISTEN TO *TECHNO*. AND LIKE... I DON'T KNOW... TALK *FRENCH*!

I HEARD ON TV YOU'RE NOT AN *ARTIST* 'TIL YOU'RE STARVING WITH *LEIF GARRETT*.

OKAY *FINE*. MAYBE SHE'S *NOT* AN ARTIST, BUT THERE'S *SOMETHING* ABOUT HER, AN' I'LL TELL YOU WHAT IT *IS*...

She's a HOTTIE

WHADISAY? WHADISAY?

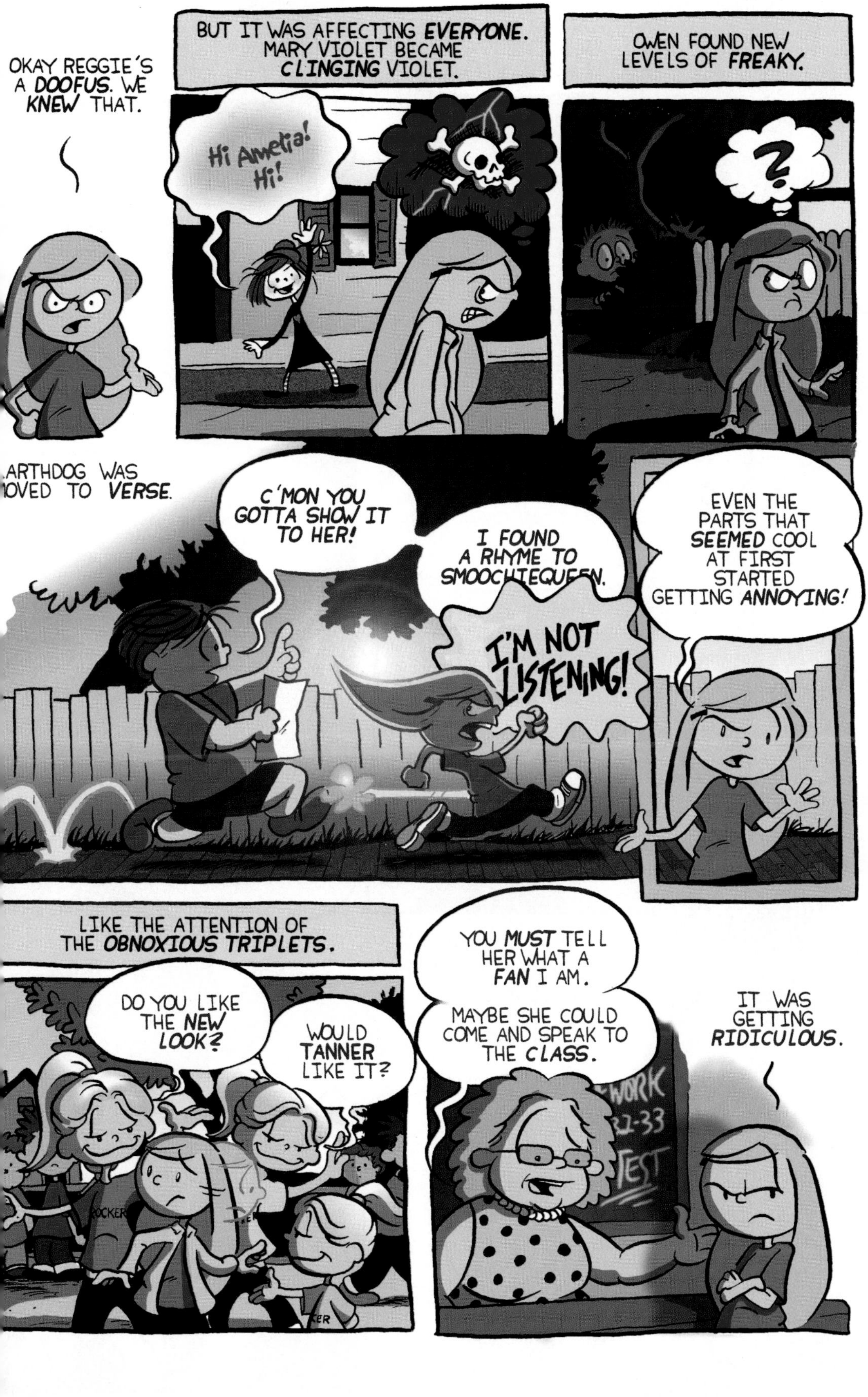
OKAY REGGIE'S A DOOFUS. WE KNEW THAT.
BUT IT WAS AFFECTING EVERYONE. MARY VIOLET BECAME CLINGING VIOLET.
Hi Amelia! Hi!
OWEN FOUND NEW LEVELS OF FREAKY.
?
ARTHDOG WAS IOVED TO VERSE.
C'MON YOU GOTTA SHOW IT TO HER!
I FOUND A RHYME TO SMOOCHIEQUEEN.
I'M NOT LISTENING!
EVEN THE PARTS THAT SEEMED COOL AT FIRST STARTED GETTING ANNOYING!
LIKE THE ATTENTION OF THE OBNOXIOUS TRIPLETS.
DO YOU LIKE THE NEW LOOK?
WOULD TANNER LIKE IT?
YOU MUST TELL HER WHAT A FAN I AM.
MAYBE SHE COULD COME AND SPEAK TO THE CLASS.
IT WAS GETTING RIDICULOUS.

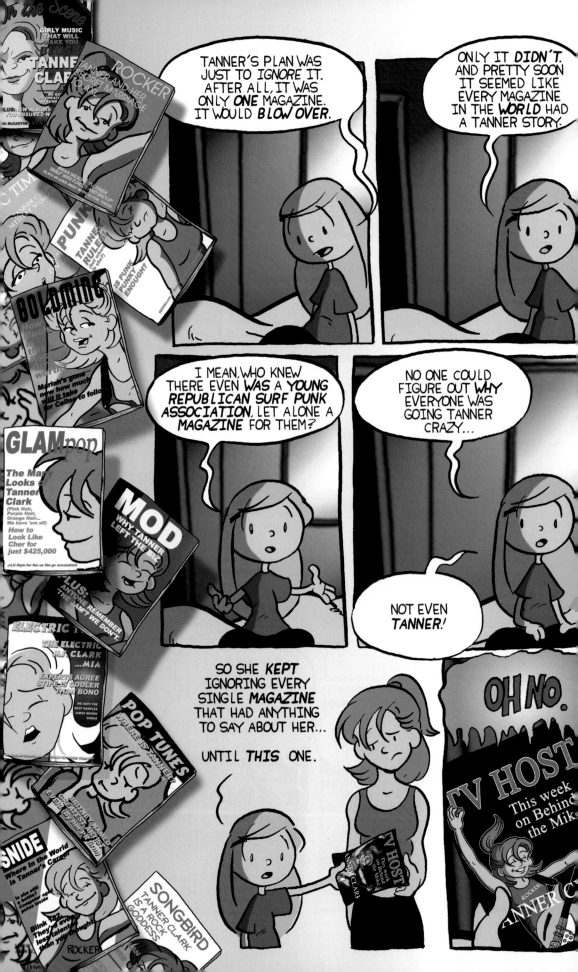

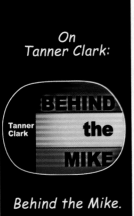

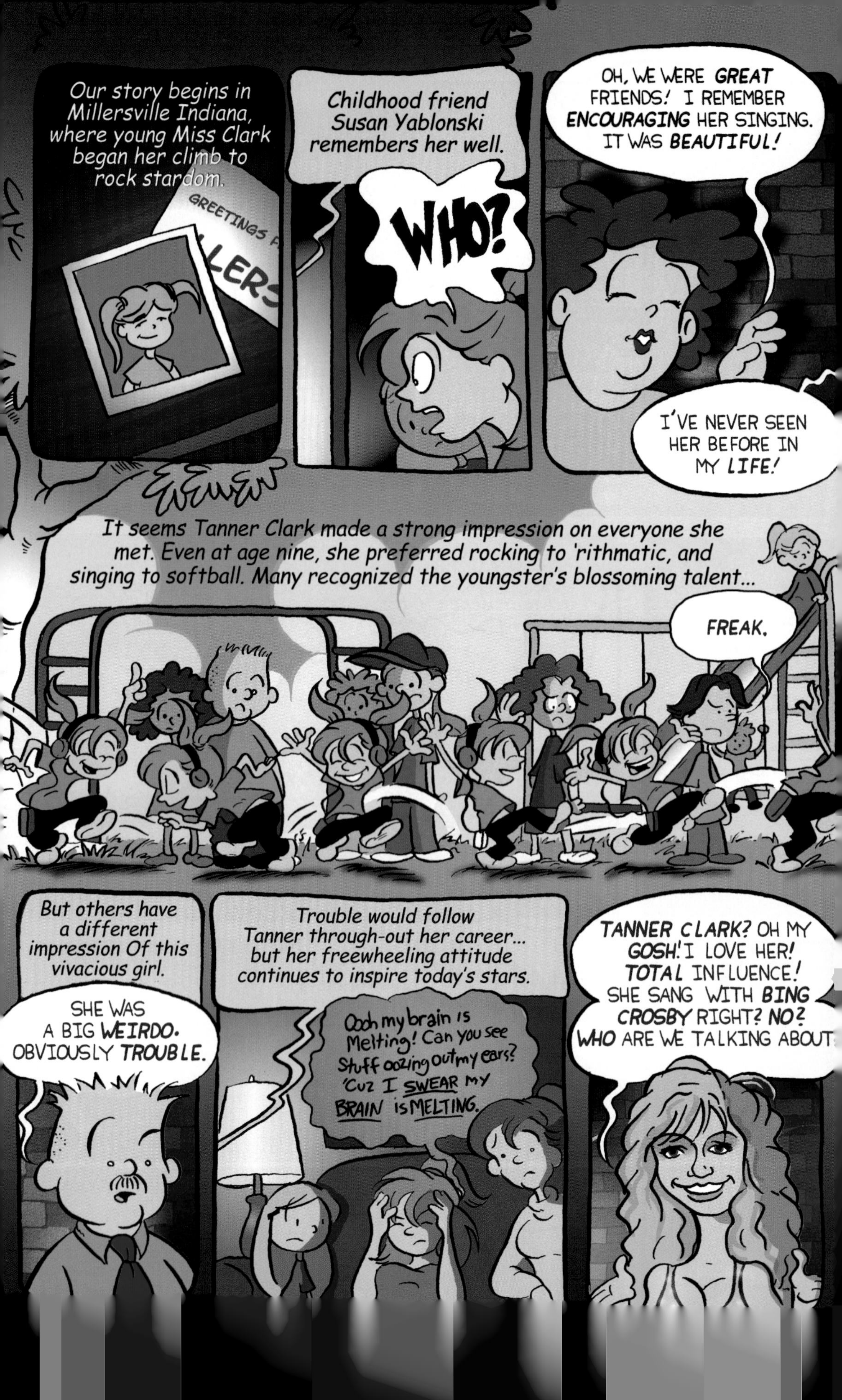

Our story begins in Millersville Indiana, where young Miss Clark began her climb to rock stardom.
GREETINGS F
LLERS
Childhood friend Susan Yablonski remembers her well.
WHO?
OH, WE WERE GREAT FRIENDS! I REMEMBER ENCOURAGING HER SINGING. IT WAS BEAUTIFUL!
I'VE NEVER SEEN HER BEFORE IN MY LIFE!
It seems Tanner Clark made a strong impression on everyone she met. Even at age nine, she preferred rocking to 'rithmatic, and singing to softball. Many recognized the youngster's blossoming talent...
FREAK.
But others have a different impression Of this vivacious girl.
SHE WAS A BIG WEIRDO. OBVIOUSLY TROUBLE.
Trouble would follow Tanner through-out her career... but her freewheeling attitude continues to inspire today's stars.
Oooh my brain is Melting! Can you see stuff oozing out my ears? 'Cuz I SWEAR MY BRAIN is MELTING.
TANNER CLARK? OH MY GOSH! I LOVE HER! TOTAL INFLUENCE! SHE SANG WITH BING CROSBY RIGHT? NO? WHO ARE WE TALKING ABOUT.

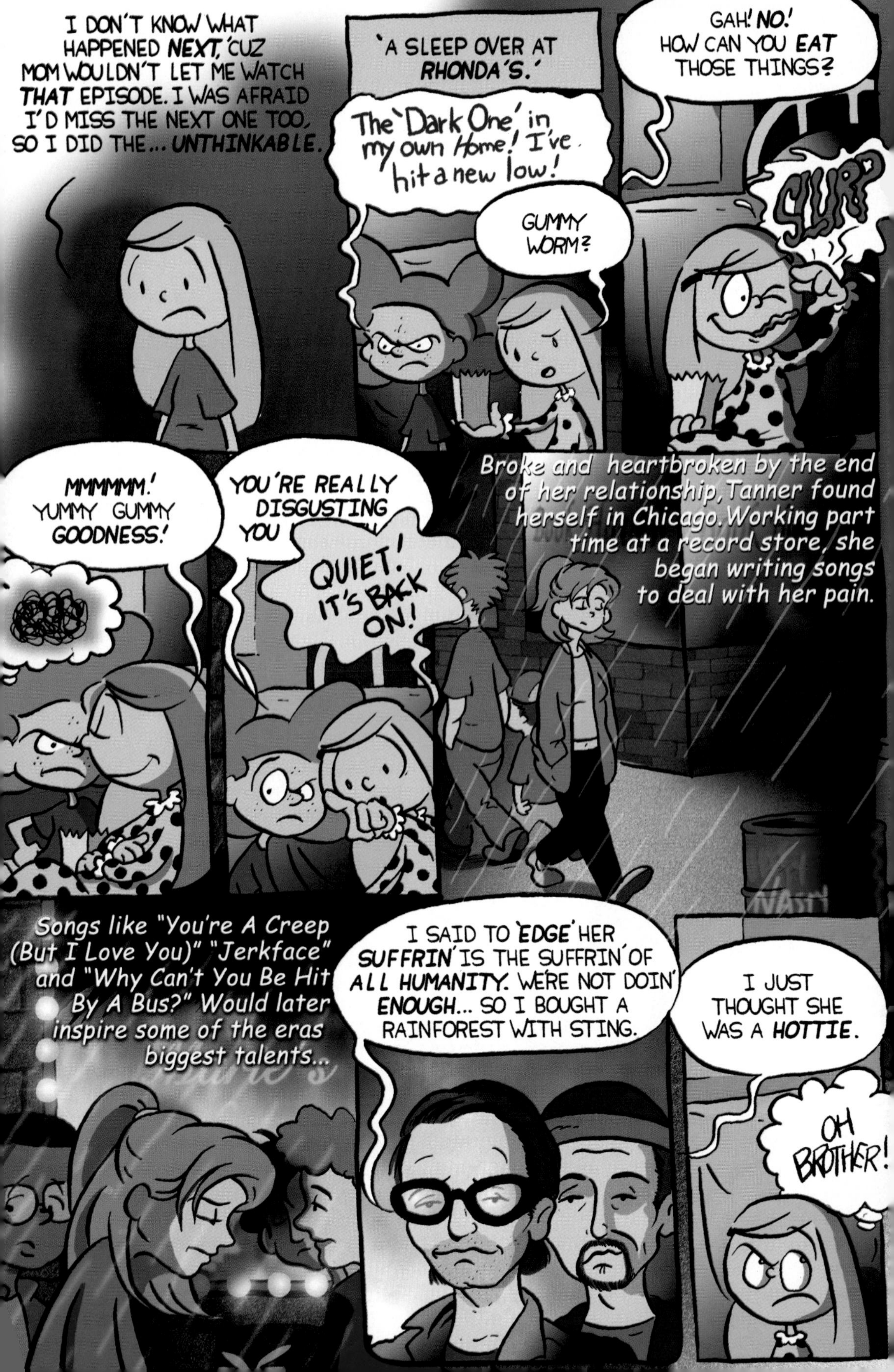

I DON'T KNOW WHAT HAPPENED **NEXT**, 'CUZ MOM WOULDN'T LET ME WATCH **THAT** EPISODE. I WAS AFRAID I'D MISS THE NEXT ONE TOO, SO I DID THE... **UNTHINKABLE**.
'A SLEEP OVER AT **RHONDA'S**.'
The 'Dark One' in my own Home! I've hit a new low!
GUMMY WORM?
GAH! **NO!** HOW CAN YOU **EAT** THOSE THINGS?
SLURP
MMMMMM! YUMMY GUMMY **GOODNESS!**
YOU'RE REALLY DISGUSTING YOU
QUIET! IT'S BACK ON!
Broke and heartbroken by the end of her relationship, Tanner found herself in Chicago. Working part time at a record store, she began writing songs to deal with her pain.
Songs like "You're A Creep (But I Love You)" "Jerkface" and "Why Can't You Be Hit By A Bus?" Would later inspire some of the eras biggest talents...
I SAID TO '**EDGE**' HER **SUFFRIN'** IS THE SUFFRIN' OF **ALL HUMANITY**. WE'RE NOT DOIN' **ENOUGH**... SO I BOUGHT A RAINFOREST WITH STING.
I JUST THOUGHT SHE WAS A **HOTTIE**.
OH BROTHER!

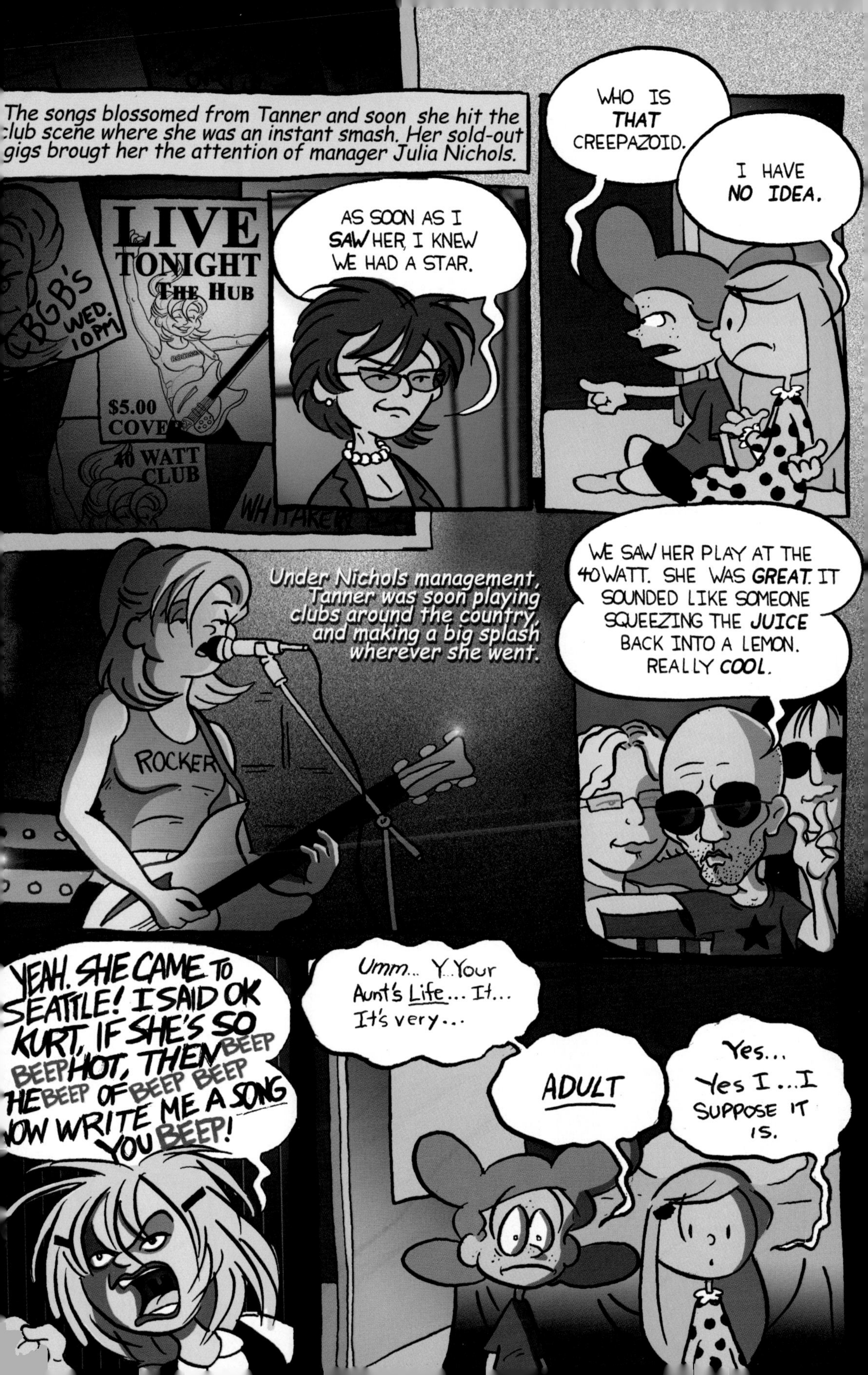
The songs blossomed from Tanner and soon she hit the club scene where she was an instant smash. Her sold-out gigs brougt her the attention of manager Julia Nichols.
LIVE TONIGHT THE HUB
$5.00 COVE
CBGB's WED. 10PM
40 WATT CLUB
AS SOON AS I SAW HER, I KNEW WE HAD A STAR.
WHO IS THAT CREEPAZOID.
I HAVE NO IDEA.
Under Nichols management, Tanner was soon playing clubs around the country, and making a big splash wherever she went.
ROCKER
WE SAW HER PLAY AT THE 40 WATT. SHE WAS GREAT. IT SOUNDED LIKE SOMEONE SQUEEZING THE JUICE BACK INTO A LEMON. REALLY COOL.
YEAH. SHE CAME TO SEATTLE! I SAID OK KURT, IF SHE'S SO BEEP HOT, THEN BEEP HE BEEP OF BEEP BEEP NOW WRITE ME A SONG YOU BEEP!
Umm... Y..Your Aunt's Life... It... It's very...
ADULT
Yes... Yes I...I SUPPOSE IT IS.

I GUESS MOM FIGURED THE LAST EPISODE WOULD BE **TAME**, SO SHE LET ME WATCH IT AT **HOME**. NOT THAT ANY OF US GOT TO **SEE** MUCH ANYWAY.

Nichols was a master of promotion, and Tanner's Debut single "Gaberdeen Prom Queen" was already in the top 20 when her album "Broken Record" hit the shelves. It looked like the beginning of a long pop reign, but then, just days after the release of "Broken Record", Tanner Clark cancelled her tour, stopped further recording, and vanished from the music scene entirely.
NIRVANA PEARL JAM SMASHING PUMPKINS
Rolling Stone
BROKEN RECORD
IT WAS A REAL SHOCK. I DIDN'T SEE IT COMING. NO ONE KNOWS WHY SHE DID WHAT SHE DID, BUT I HOPE TO WORK WITH HER AGAIN.
YOU DO TOO KNOW WHY, YOU... YOU... YOU... NERDYBUTTBRAINFACE!
<SIGH> YA KNOW, I COULD USE BETTER WORDS IF YOU WEREN'T HERE.
SORRY.
Even though her time in the spotlight was brief, her influence was strong, and her peers remember her fondly.
THE LAST TIME I SAW HER, SHE SAID, 'ALANIS IN YOUR NEXT VIDEO YOU SHOULD BE NAKED.' I REALIZE NOW SHE WAS KIDDING.
Oh of COURSE I was kidding you DUMB... OOOOOH!
CLICK
I WENT UP TO BED, AND LAYED THERE FOR A WHILE LISTENING TO TANNER USE WORDS LESS CREATIVE THAN 'NERDYBUTTBRAINFACE.'

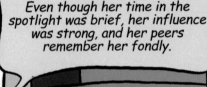

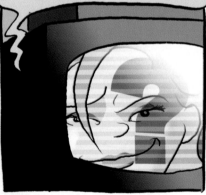

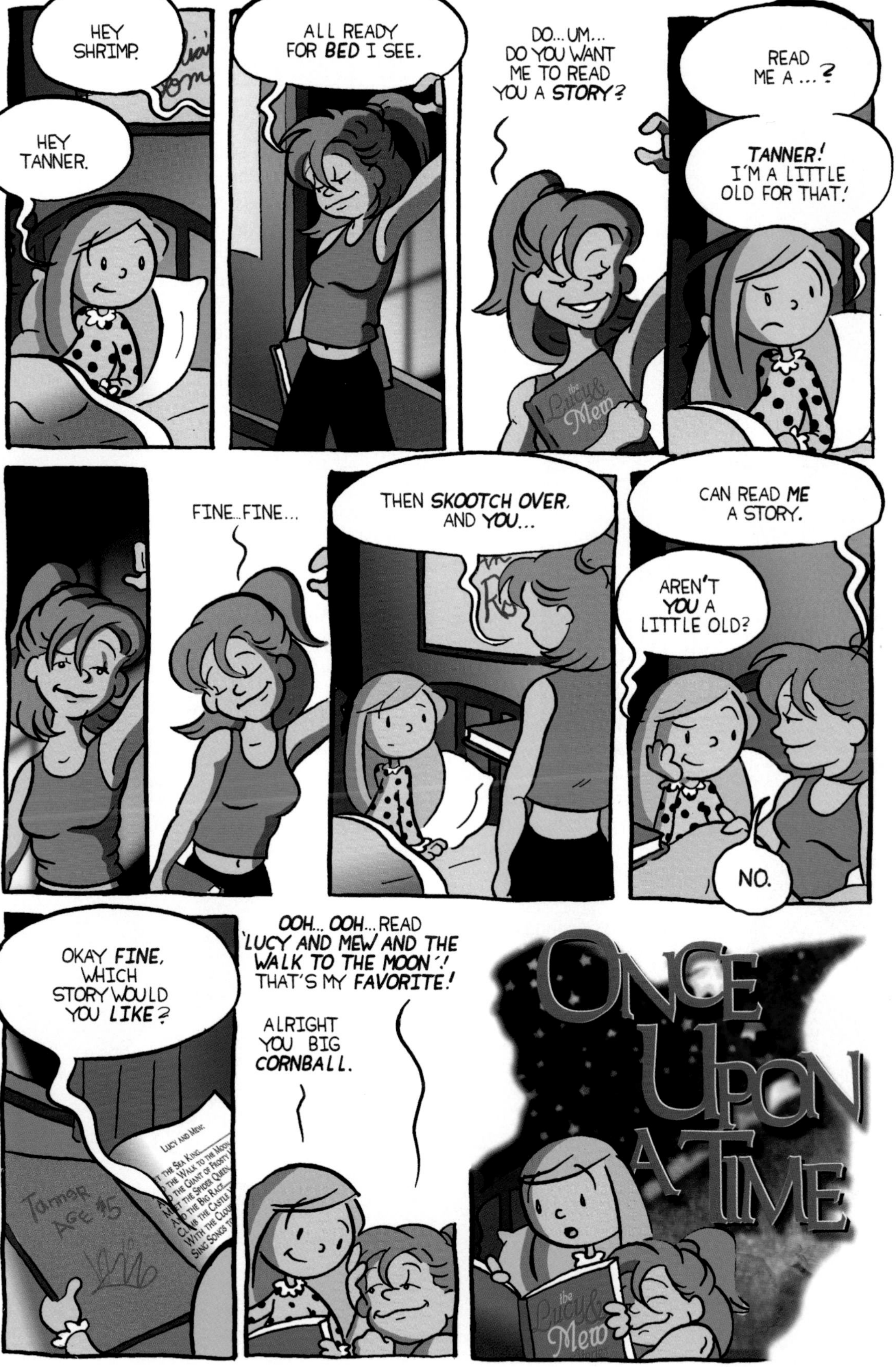
HEY SHRIMP.
HEY TANNER.
ALL READY FOR BED I SEE.
DO...UM... DO YOU WANT ME TO READ YOU A STORY?
READ ME A ...?
TANNER! I'M A LITTLE OLD FOR THAT!
FINE...FINE...
THEN SKOOTCH OVER, AND YOU...
CAN READ ME A STORY.
AREN'T YOU A LITTLE OLD?
NO.
OKAY FINE, WHICH STORY WOULD YOU LIKE?
OOH... OOH... READ 'LUCY AND MEW AND THE WALK TO THE MOON'! THAT'S MY FAVORITE!
ALRIGHT YOU BIG CORNBALL.
ONCE UPON A TIME

The Walk to the Moon

By Beth Ellen Welch

Once upon a time there was a poor young girl named Lucy, who lived with a cat named Mew. Lucy and Mew lived in a very small house in a very small village in an enormous country which probably never existed, but which seemed quite nice. Lucy had no parents, and so she relied on Mew to care for her. This was not a problem, for Mew was a talented cat and earned more than many of the men in the village, and even as much as a few of the more prominent sheep. In exchange for her keep, Lucy kept the house tidy, the food and water dishes full, and the litter box clean. But Lucy was bored.

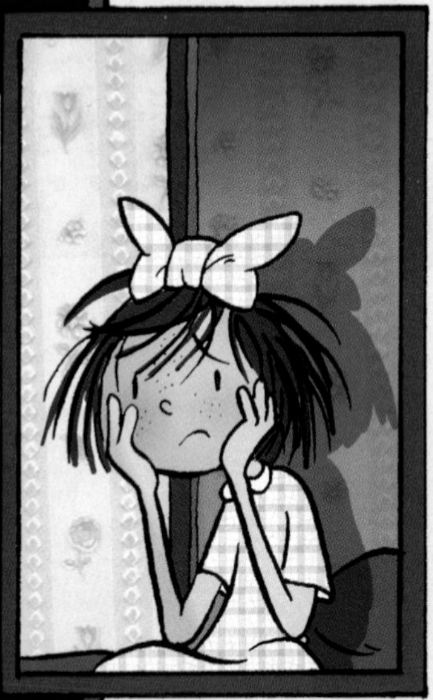

"There's nothing ever to do in this village," she complained to Mew. "I've heard other girls speak of villages with many dwellings under one roof, staircases that carry you magically from floor to floor, merchants with goods from far away lands. Shops of all kinds of selling fragrances, literature, garments, and equipment for sport. A common area where people may sample morsels and delicacies from all the world over. And outside yet another dining hall, set under glorious, illuminated golden arches."

"My business dealings have taken me to such villages," said Mew. "The people seem no happier there than they do any place else on earth."

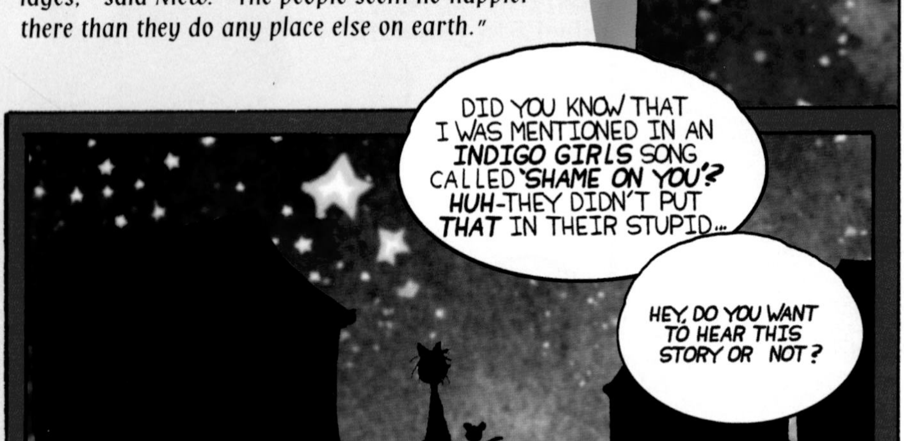
DID YOU KNOW THAT I WAS MENTIONED IN AN **INDIGO GIRLS** SONG CALLED **'SHAME ON YOU'?** **HUH**-THEY DIDN'T PUT **THAT** IN THEIR STUPID...
HEY, DO YOU WANT TO HEAR THIS STORY OR NOT?

It was then that Lucy
had a brilliant idea.

"But what about off the earth?" she cried.
"What about the village on the moon!" Mew
had to admit that he had never heard of such villages, but still he was intrigued. "I imagine a cat with
my skills in accounting could make as good a living on the
moon as in this village," he said. And so Lucy and Mew
decided to walk to the moon.

The plan was simple. Wait until the next rainbow appeared, walk to the
top, and then jump the remaining distance to the moon. "A brilliant plan,"
said Mew. "It's a wonder no one had thought of it before."

The two travelers took nothing with them save Lucy's umbrella, and a large
roll of cash. Everything they needed, they reasoned, they would get in the
wondrous moon village.

The trip was longer than they expected and Mew was very cross at Lucy for
not having thought to bring even a small can of tuna. Lucy's legs
got tired, but she sustained herself by thinking of the won-
ders the moon villages were sure to contain.

Finally, the top of the rainbow was reached.
The leap was taken, and Lucy and Mew
landed on the moon. They were so
happy to have arrived that they
danced as only an orphan girl and
her benefactor cat can dance.

Unfortunately, after celebrating,
they realized there was not a
village in sight. "I'm sure
they're here," said Lucy. "We
just need to explore a bit."

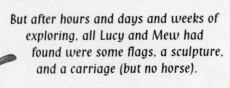

But after hours and days and weeks of
exploring, all Lucy and Mew had
found were some flags, a sculpture,
and a carriage (but no horse).

"This is terrible!" cried Lucy. "We're
completely alone!"

"We're never alone if we have each other,"
said Mew.

"Oh shut up," said Lucy.

With nothing to do but sit on the rim of a crater
and stare at the Earth, Lucy and Mew both
became melancholy.

"I miss having a home to clean and dishes to fill
and well...maybe not the litterbox," said Lucy.

I'm just glad that cheese thing turned out to be
true," said Mew. "Otherwise we would have
starved.

Lucy decided that enough was enough and grab-
bing Mew with one hand and her umbrella with
the other, she leapt off the edge of the moon.

Lucy opened her umbrella and used it to slow
their fall, so they drift-
ed down to earth in
just a little under
four days.

They landed back in
the square of the very
village they had left so
long ago, and It
seemed as if it had not changed at all.

"You know," Lucy said. "Before we left, I wanted
nothing more than to live the rest of my life on the
moon, but now that we're back, I can't imagine
why we ever left."

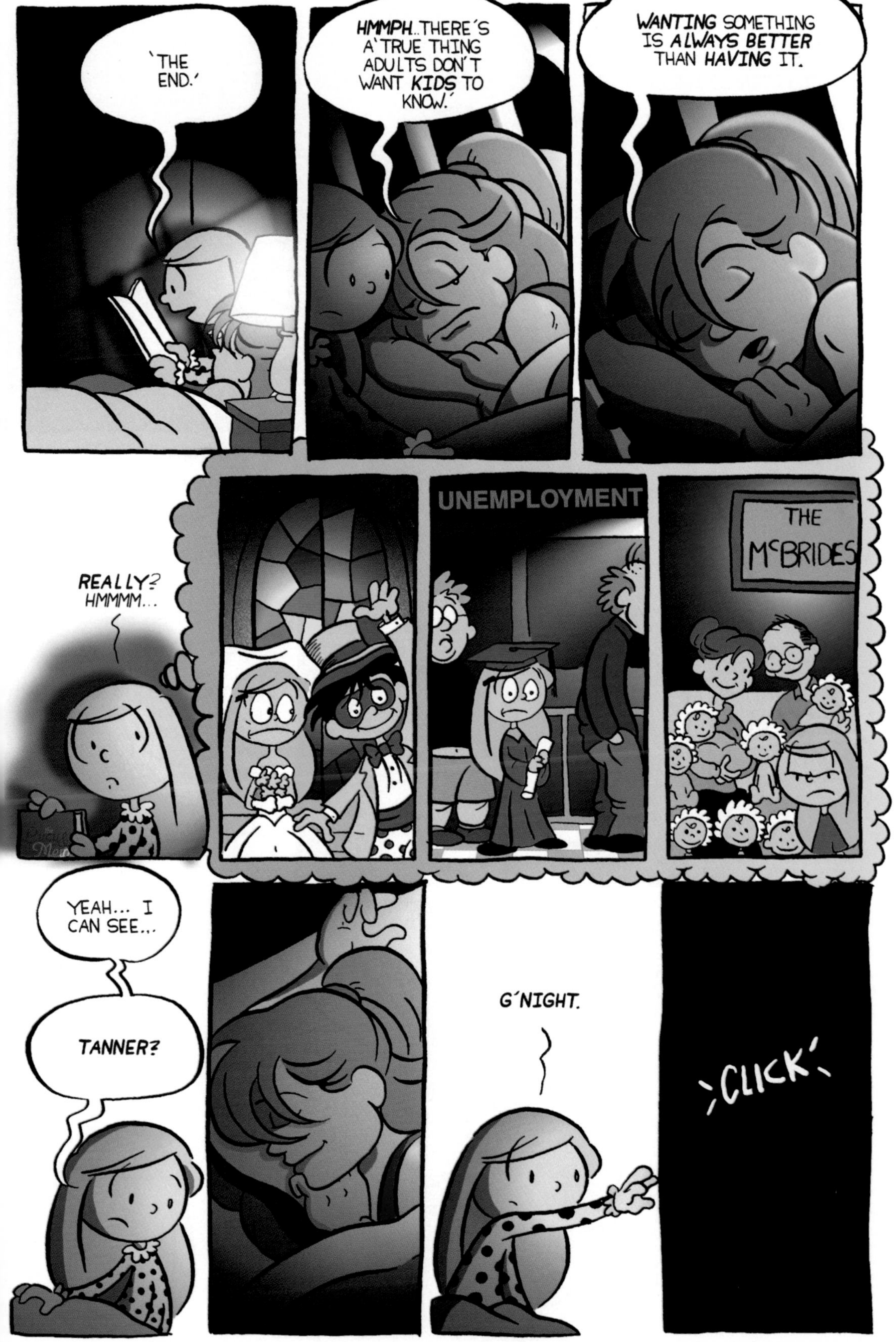

'THE END.'
HMMPH.. THERE'S A 'TRUE THING ADULTS DON'T WANT KIDS TO KNOW.'
WANTING SOMETHING IS ALWAYS BETTER THAN HAVING IT.
REALLY? HMMMM...
UNEMPLOYMENT
THE McBRIDES
YEAH... I CAN SEE...
TANNER?
G'NIGHT.
CLICK

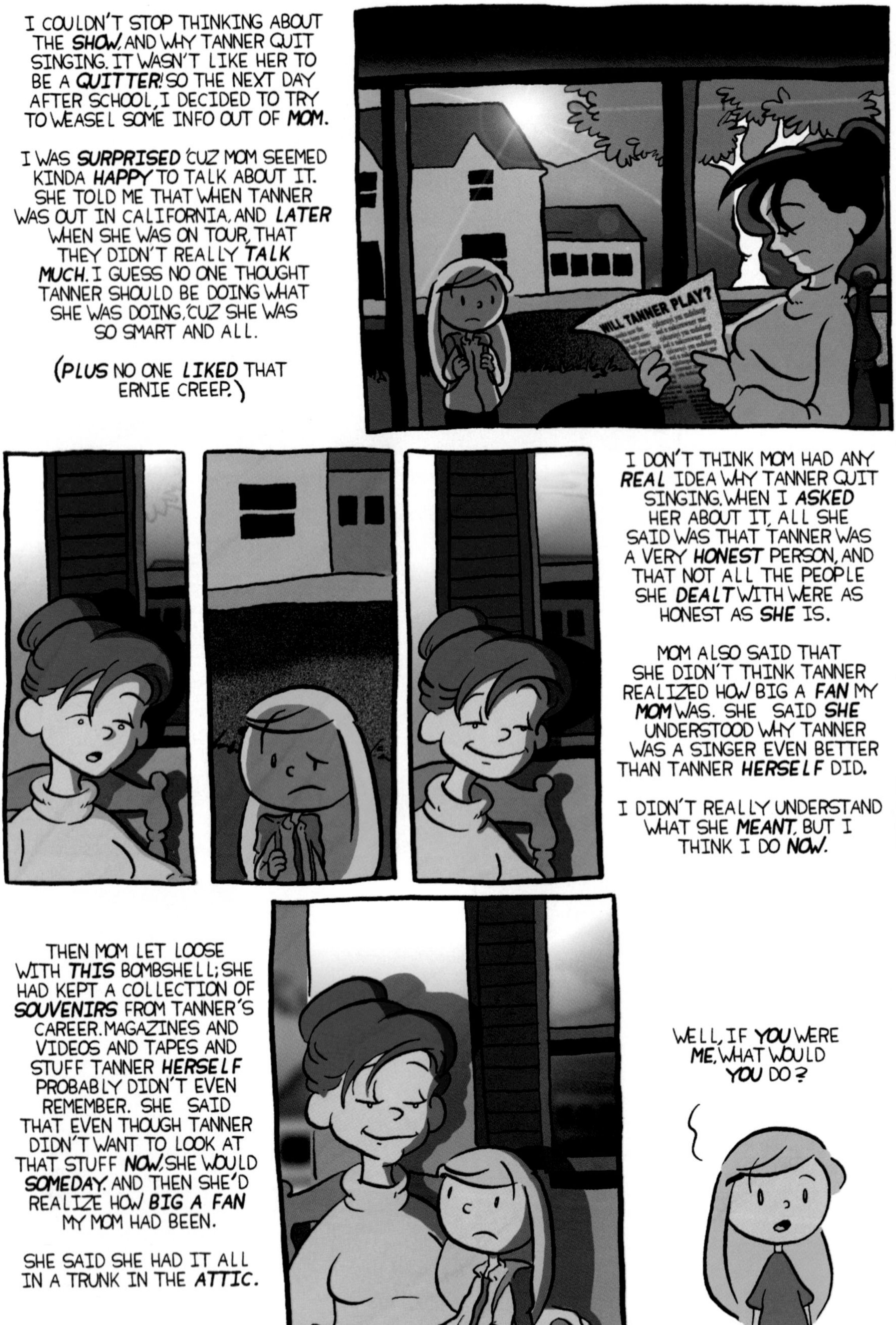
I COULDN'T STOP THINKING ABOUT THE **SHOW**, AND WHY TANNER QUIT SINGING. IT WASN'T LIKE HER TO BE A **QUITTER**! SO THE NEXT DAY AFTER SCHOOL, I DECIDED TO TRY TO WEASEL SOME INFO OUT OF **MOM**.
I WAS **SURPRISED** 'CUZ MOM SEEMED KINDA **HAPPY** TO TALK ABOUT IT. SHE TOLD ME THAT WHEN TANNER WAS OUT IN CALIFORNIA, AND **LATER** WHEN SHE WAS ON TOUR, THAT THEY DIDN'T REALLY **TALK MUCH**. I GUESS NO ONE THOUGHT TANNER SHOULD BE DOING WHAT SHE WAS DOING, 'CUZ SHE WAS SO SMART AND ALL.
(**PLUS** NO ONE **LIKED** THAT ERNIE CREEP.)
WILL TANNER PLAY?
I DON'T THINK MOM HAD ANY **REAL** IDEA WHY TANNER QUIT SINGING. WHEN I **ASKED** HER ABOUT IT, ALL SHE SAID WAS THAT TANNER WAS A VERY **HONEST** PERSON, AND THAT NOT ALL THE PEOPLE SHE **DEALT** WITH WERE AS HONEST AS **SHE** IS.
MOM ALSO SAID THAT SHE DIDN'T THINK TANNER REALIZED HOW BIG A **FAN** MY **MOM** WAS. SHE SAID **SHE** UNDERSTOOD WHY TANNER WAS A SINGER EVEN BETTER THAN TANNER **HERSELF** DID.
I DIDN'T REALLY UNDERSTAND WHAT SHE **MEANT**, BUT I THINK I DO **NOW**.
THEN MOM LET LOOSE WITH **THIS** BOMBSHELL; SHE HAD KEPT A COLLECTION OF **SOUVENIRS** FROM TANNER'S CAREER. MAGAZINES AND VIDEOS AND TAPES AND STUFF TANNER **HERSELF** PROBABLY DIDN'T EVEN REMEMBER. SHE SAID THAT EVEN THOUGH TANNER DIDN'T WANT TO LOOK AT THAT STUFF **NOW**, SHE WOULD **SOMEDAY**. AND THEN SHE'D REALIZE HOW **BIG A FAN** MY MOM HAD BEEN.
SHE SAID SHE HAD IT ALL IN A TRUNK IN THE **ATTIC**.
WELL, IF **YOU** WERE **ME**, WHAT WOULD **YOU** DO?

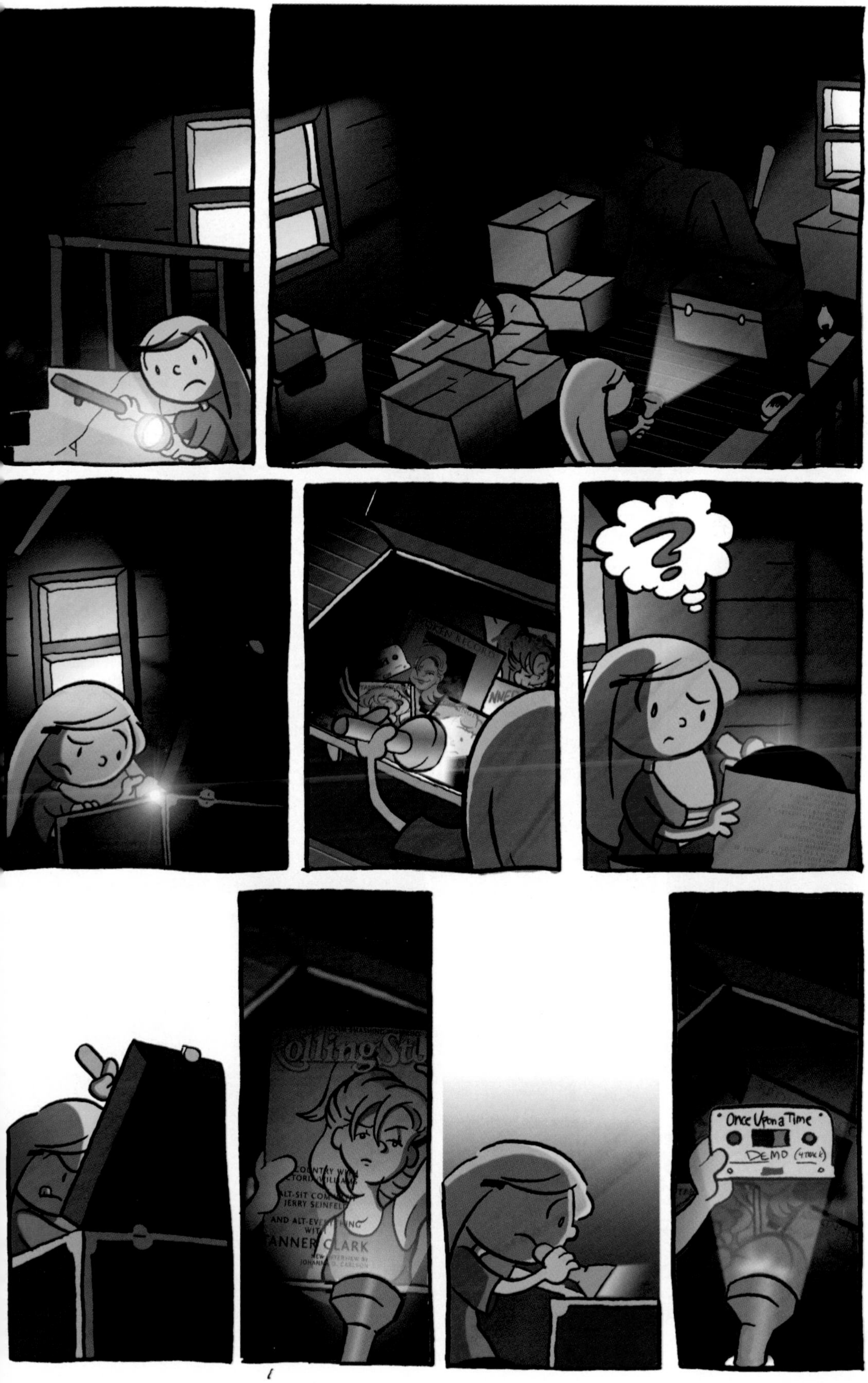

Once Upon a Time
DEMO (4 track)

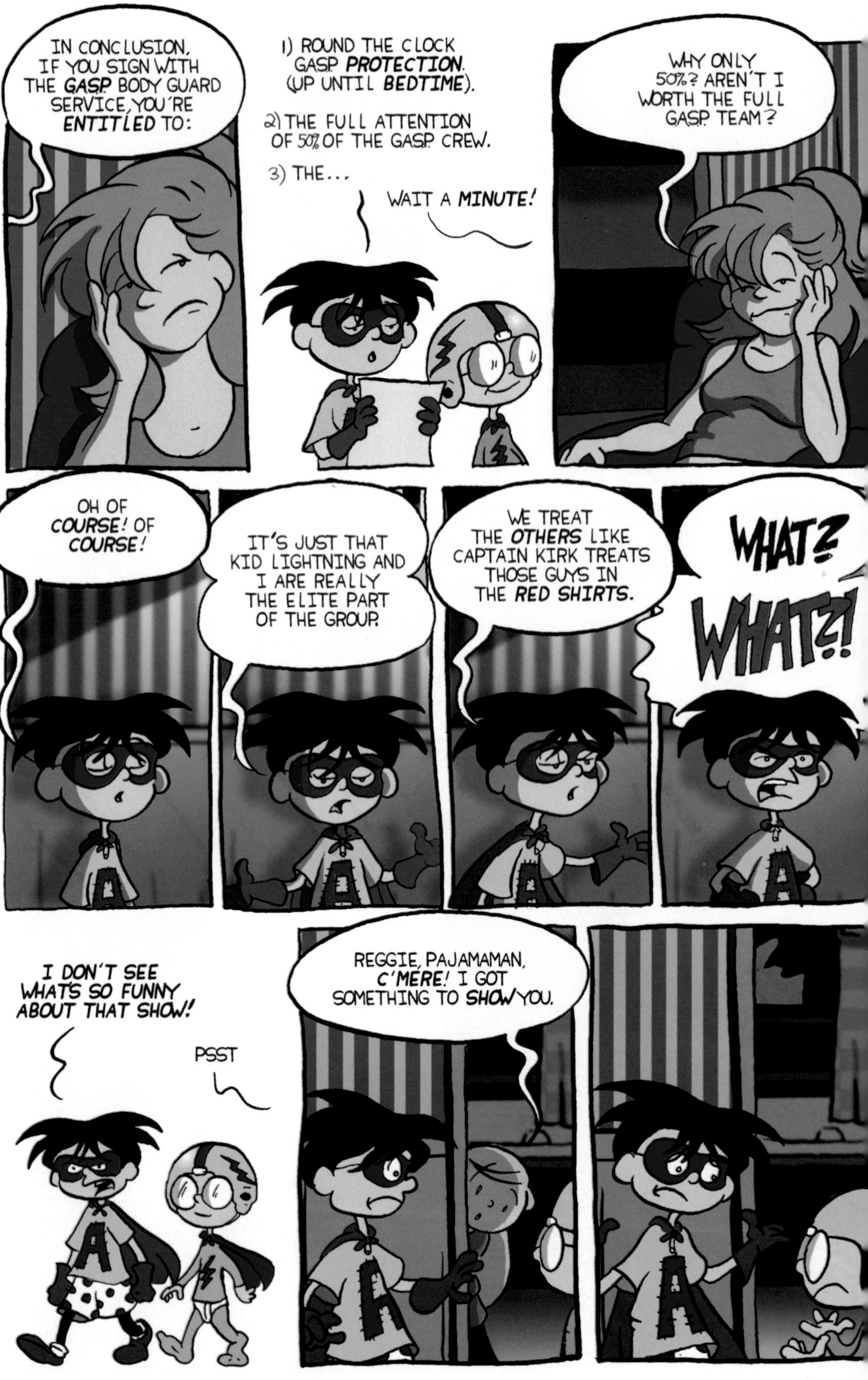
IN CONCLUSION, IF YOU SIGN WITH THE **GASP** BODY GUARD SERVICE, YOU'RE **ENTITLED** TO:
1) ROUND THE CLOCK GASP **PROTECTION**. (UP UNTIL **BEDTIME**).
2) THE FULL ATTENTION OF 50% OF THE GASP CREW.
3) THE...
WAIT A **MINUTE!**
WHY ONLY 50%? AREN'T I WORTH THE FULL GASP TEAM?
OH OF *COURSE!* OF *COURSE!*
IT'S JUST THAT KID LIGHTNING AND I ARE REALLY THE ELITE PART OF THE GROUP.
WE TREAT THE **OTHERS** LIKE CAPTAIN KIRK TREATS THOSE GUYS IN THE **RED SHIRTS**.
WHAT?
WHAT?!
I DON'T SEE WHAT'S SO FUNNY ABOUT THAT SHOW!
PSST
REGGIE, PAJAMAMAN, **C'MERE!** I GOT SOMETHING TO **SHOW** YOU.

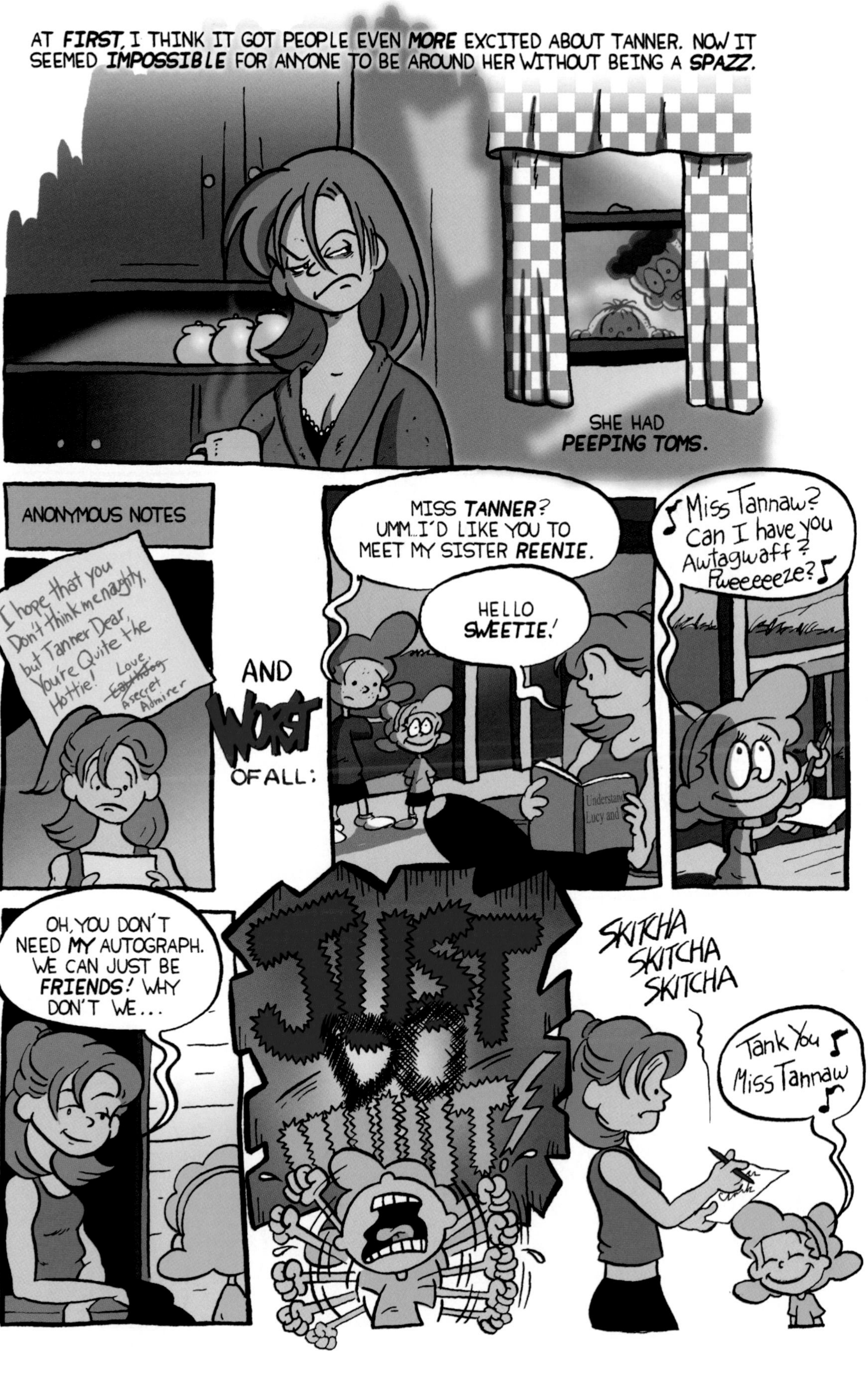
AT **FIRST**, I THINK IT GOT PEOPLE EVEN **MORE** EXCITED ABOUT TANNER. NOW IT SEEMED **IMPOSSIBLE** FOR ANYONE TO BE AROUND HER WITHOUT BEING A **SPAZZ**.
SHE HAD **PEEPING TOMS**.
ANONYMOUS NOTES
I hope that you Don't think me naughty, but Tanner Dear, You're Quite the Hottie! Love, A secret Admirer
AND WORST OF ALL:
MISS **TANNER**? UMM...I'D LIKE YOU TO MEET MY SISTER **REENIE**.
HELLO **SWEETIE**!
Understand Lucy and
Miss Tannaw? Can I have you Awtagwaff? Pweeeeeze?
OH, YOU DON'T NEED **MY** AUTOGRAPH. WE CAN JUST BE **FRIENDS**! WHY DON'T WE...
JUST DO IT!
SKITCHA SKITCHA SKITCHA
Tank You Miss Tannaw

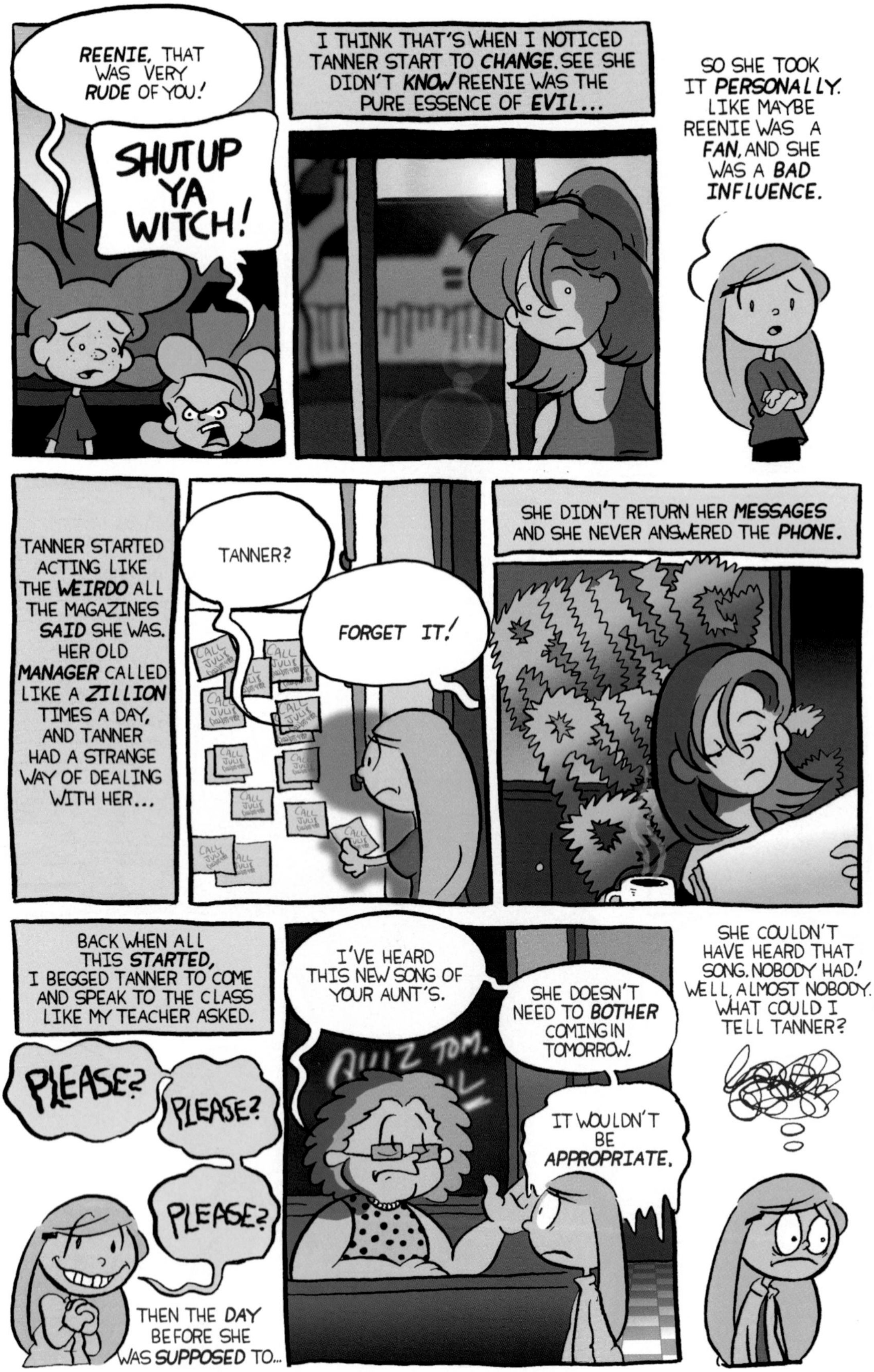
REENIE, THAT WAS VERY RUDE OF YOU!
SHUT UP YA WITCH!
I THINK THAT'S WHEN I NOTICED TANNER START TO CHANGE. SEE SHE DIDN'T KNOW REENIE WAS THE PURE ESSENCE OF EVIL...
SO SHE TOOK IT PERSONALLY. LIKE MAYBE REENIE WAS A FAN, AND SHE WAS A BAD INFLUENCE.
TANNER STARTED ACTING LIKE THE WEIRDO ALL THE MAGAZINES SAID SHE WAS. HER OLD MANAGER CALLED LIKE A ZILLION TIMES A DAY, AND TANNER HAD A STRANGE WAY OF DEALING WITH HER...
TANNER?
FORGET IT!
SHE DIDN'T RETURN HER MESSAGES AND SHE NEVER ANSWERED THE PHONE.
BACK WHEN ALL THIS STARTED, I BEGGED TANNER TO COME AND SPEAK TO THE CLASS LIKE MY TEACHER ASKED.
PLEASE?
PLEASE?
PLEASE?
THEN THE DAY BEFORE SHE WAS SUPPOSED TO...
I'VE HEARD THIS NEW SONG OF YOUR AUNT'S.
SHE DOESN'T NEED TO BOTHER COMING IN TOMORROW.
IT WOULDN'T BE APPROPRIATE.
SHE COULDN'T HAVE HEARD THAT SONG. NOBODY HAD! WELL, ALMOST NOBODY. WHAT COULD I TELL TANNER?

I DECIDED THE ONLY THING I COULD DO, WAS TELL HER THE *TRUTH* ABOUT HOW I WENT THROUGH MOM'S *STUFF*, AND FOUND THE *TAPE*, AND LET PEOPLE *LISTEN* TO IT.

BUT SHE WASN'T UPSET! SHE JUST KEPT YELLING, 'YOU FOUND THE *SONG*!' 'YOU FOUND THE *SONG*!'

THEN SHE RAN TO MY MOM, AND STARTED *BABBLING*, AND *HUGGING* HER, AND THANKING HER FOR *SAVING* IT.

AND THEN SHE AGREED TO DO ONE LAST *SHOW*.

THEN THE *WEIRDEST THING* HAPPENED.

TANNER PICKED UP THE *PHONE*, AND CALLED HER OLD *MANAGER*.

I FIGURED I WAS PROBABLY *STILL* GONNA BE IN TROUBLE FOR *SNOOPING*, SO I DIDN'T EVEN ASK TO *GO*.

SO I WAS REALLY *SURPRISED* WHEN MOM SAID SHE WANTED TO *TAKE* ME.

TONIGHT: TANNER CLARK

SEEING TANNER'S NAME ON THE *SIGN* WAS *SUPER* COOL.

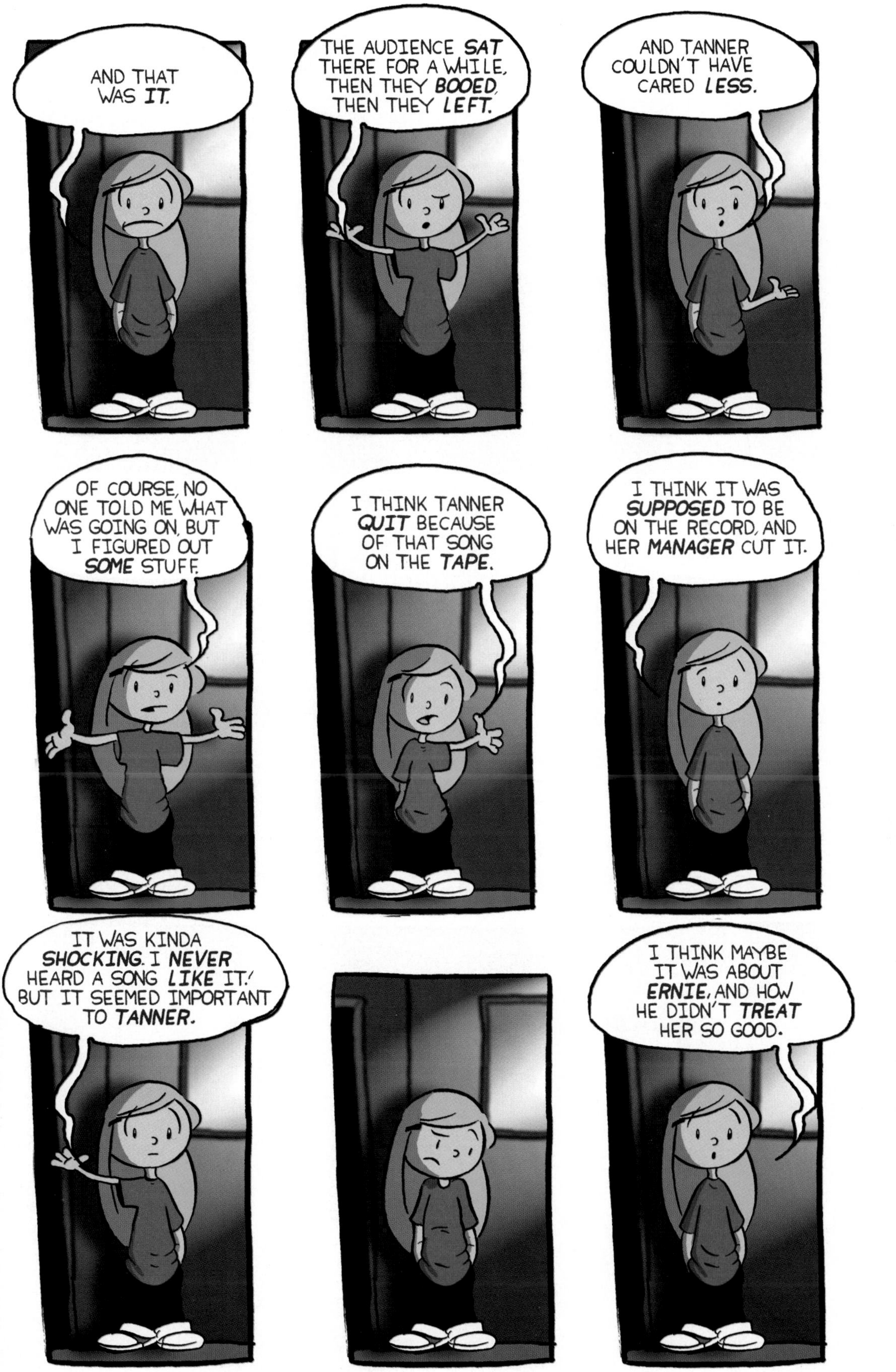
AND THAT WAS IT.
THE AUDIENCE SAT THERE FOR A WHILE, THEN THEY BOOED, THEN THEY LEFT.
AND TANNER COULDN'T HAVE CARED LESS.
OF COURSE, NO ONE TOLD ME WHAT WAS GOING ON, BUT I FIGURED OUT SOME STUFF.
I THINK TANNER QUIT BECAUSE OF THAT SONG ON THE TAPE.
I THINK IT WAS SUPPOSED TO BE ON THE RECORD, AND HER MANAGER CUT IT.
IT WAS KINDA SHOCKING. I NEVER HEARD A SONG LIKE IT! BUT IT SEEMED IMPORTANT TO TANNER.
I THINK MAYBE IT WAS ABOUT ERNIE, AND HOW HE DIDN'T TREAT HER SO GOOD.

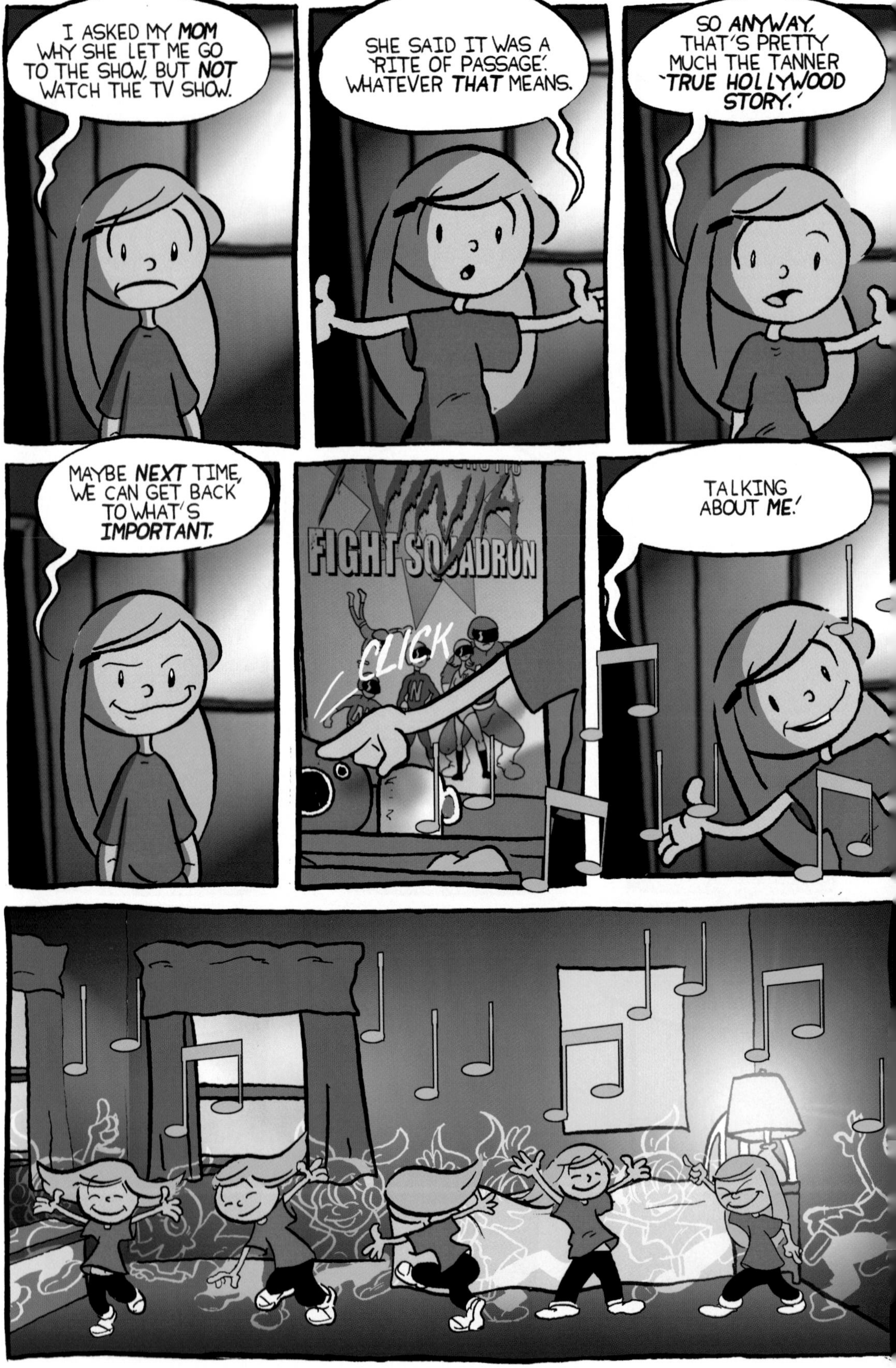

I ASKED MY **MOM** WHY SHE LET ME GO TO THE SHOW, BUT **NOT** WATCH THE TV SHOW.
SHE SAID IT WAS A 'RITE OF PASSAGE.' WHATEVER **THAT** MEANS.
SO **ANYWAY**, THAT'S PRETTY MUCH THE TANNER '**TRUE HOLLYWOOD STORY**.'
MAYBE **NEXT** TIME, WE CAN GET BACK TO WHAT'S **IMPORTANT**.
FIGHT SQUADRON
CLICK
TALKING ABOUT **ME**!

Part

THREE

"Deh awa bunka woonatwiks."

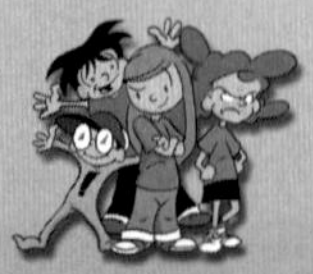

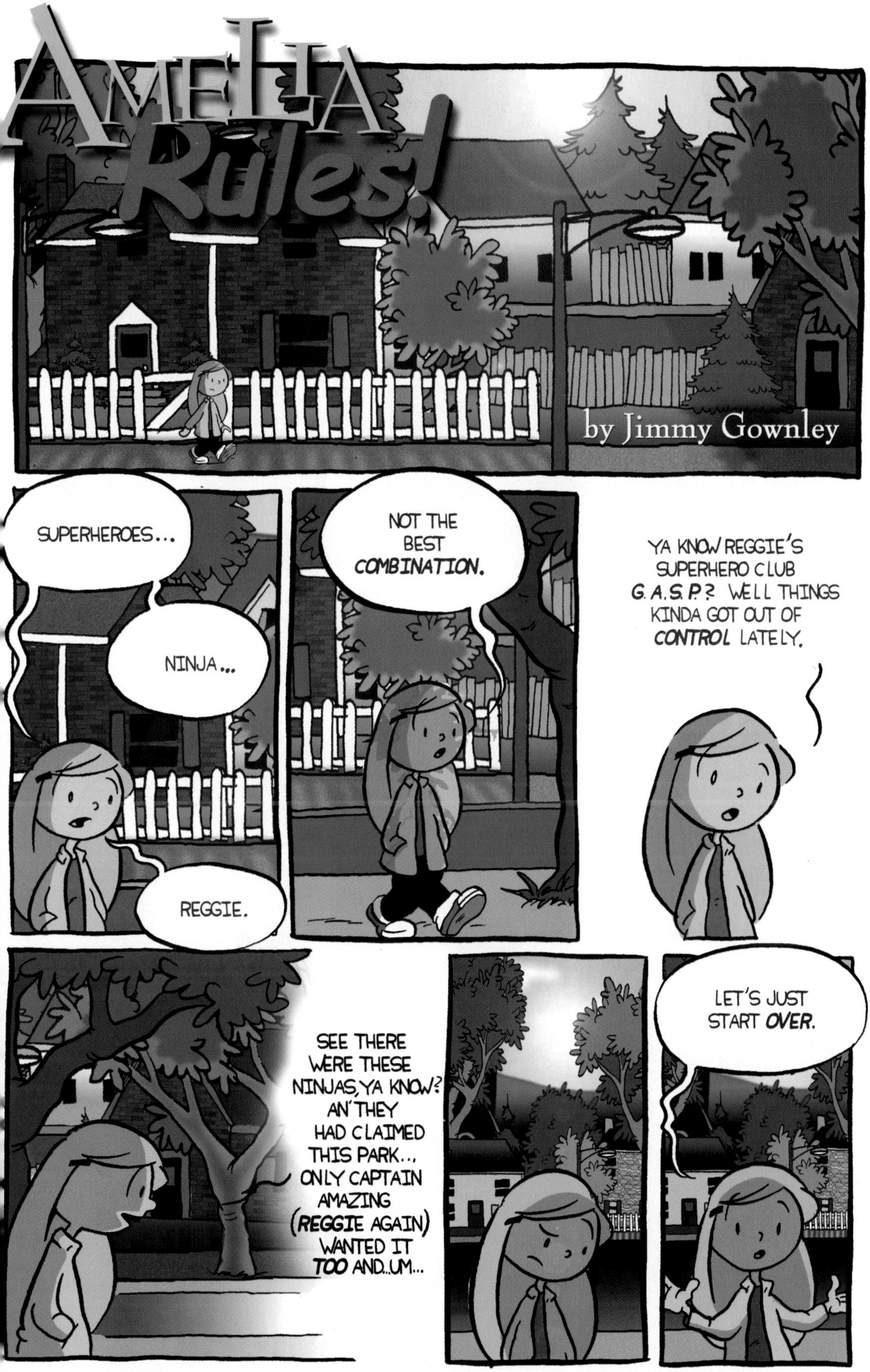

AMELIA Rules!
by Jimmy Gownley
SUPERHEROES...
NINJA...
REGGIE.
NOT THE BEST COMBINATION.
YA KNOW REGGIE'S SUPERHERO CLUB G.A.S.P.? WELL THINGS KINDA GOT OUT OF CONTROL LATELY.
SEE THERE WERE THESE NINJAS, YA KNOW? AN' THEY HAD CLAIMED THIS PARK... ONLY CAPTAIN AMAZING (REGGIE AGAIN) WANTED IT TOO AND...UM...
LET'S JUST START OVER.

LIFE DURING WARTIME

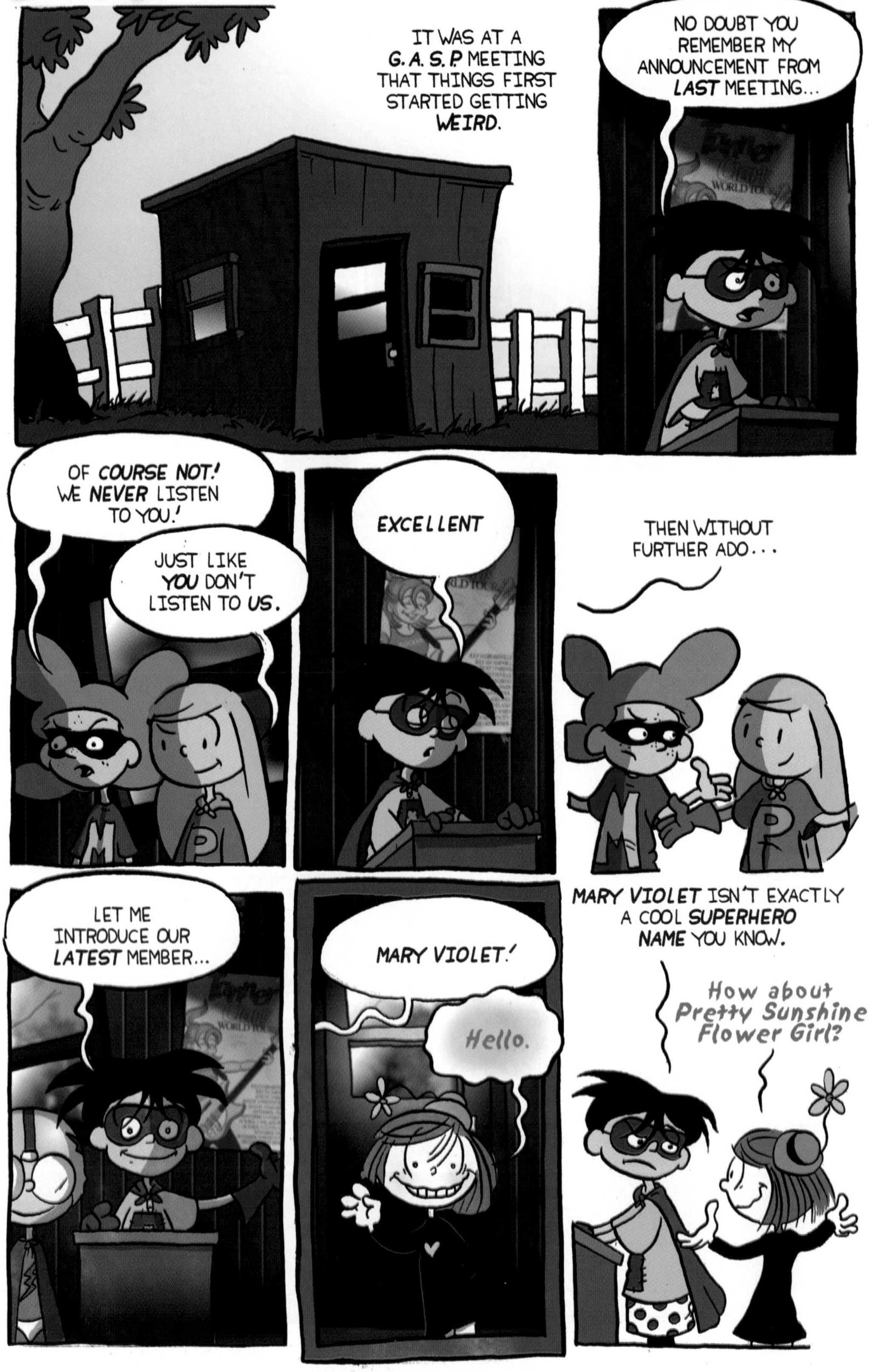

IT WAS AT A G. A. S. P. MEETING THAT THINGS FIRST STARTED GETTING WEIRD.
NO DOUBT YOU REMEMBER MY ANNOUNCEMENT FROM LAST MEETING...
OF COURSE NOT! WE NEVER LISTEN TO YOU!
JUST LIKE YOU DON'T LISTEN TO US.
EXCELLENT
THEN WITHOUT FURTHER ADO...
LET ME INTRODUCE OUR LATEST MEMBER...
MARY VIOLET!
Hello.
MARY VIOLET ISN'T EXACTLY A COOL SUPERHERO NAME YOU KNOW.
How about Pretty Sunshine Flower Girl?

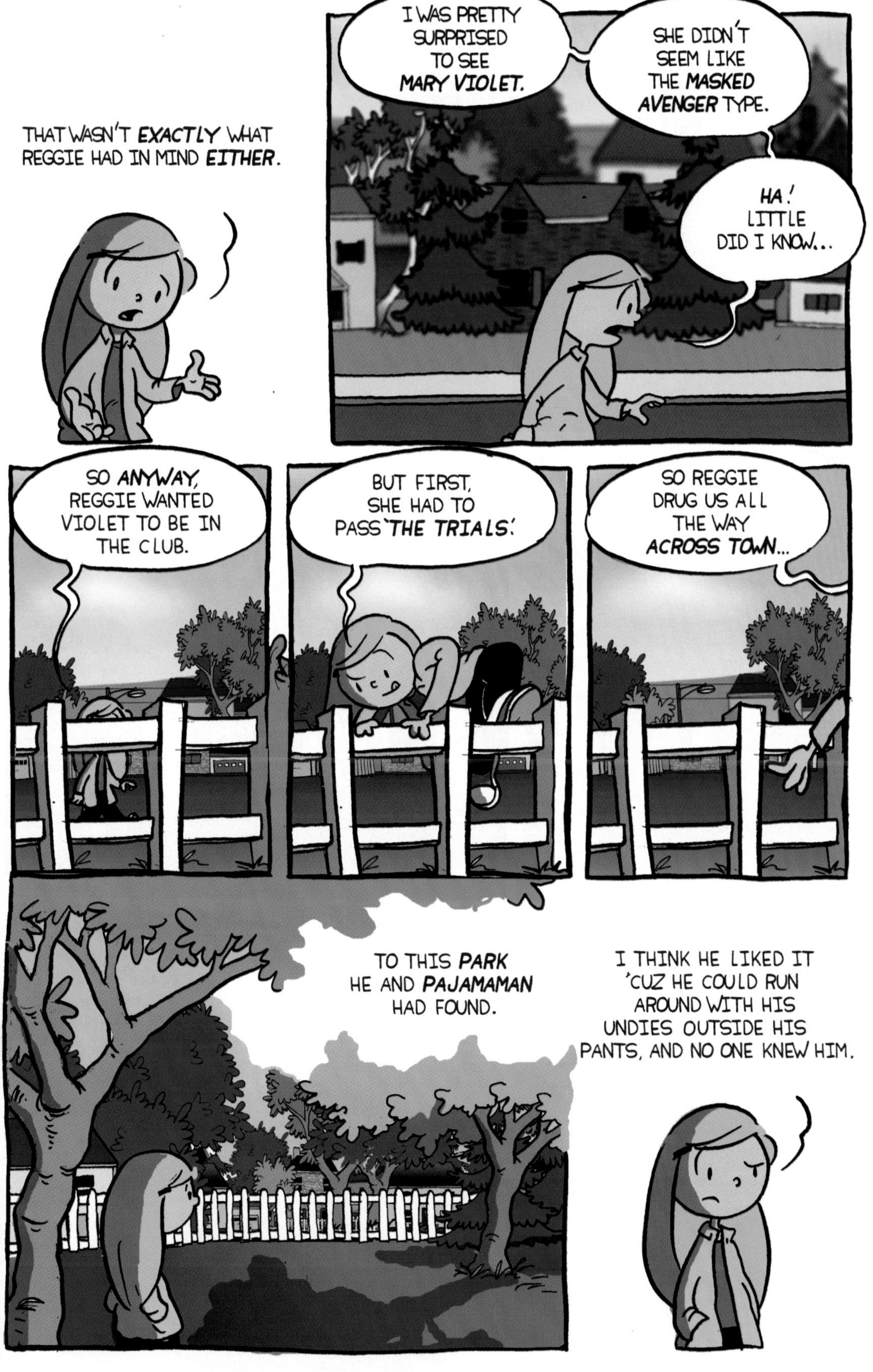

THAT WASN'T EXACTLY WHAT REGGIE HAD IN MIND EITHER.
I WAS PRETTY SURPRISED TO SEE MARY VIOLET.
SHE DIDN'T SEEM LIKE THE MASKED AVENGER TYPE.
HA! LITTLE DID I KNOW...
SO ANYWAY, REGGIE WANTED VIOLET TO BE IN THE CLUB.
BUT FIRST, SHE HAD TO PASS "THE TRIALS."
SO REGGIE DRUG US ALL THE WAY ACROSS TOWN...
TO THIS PARK HE AND PAJAMAMAN HAD FOUND.
I THINK HE LIKED IT 'CUZ HE COULD RUN AROUND WITH HIS UNDIES OUTSIDE HIS PANTS, AND NO ONE KNEW HIM.

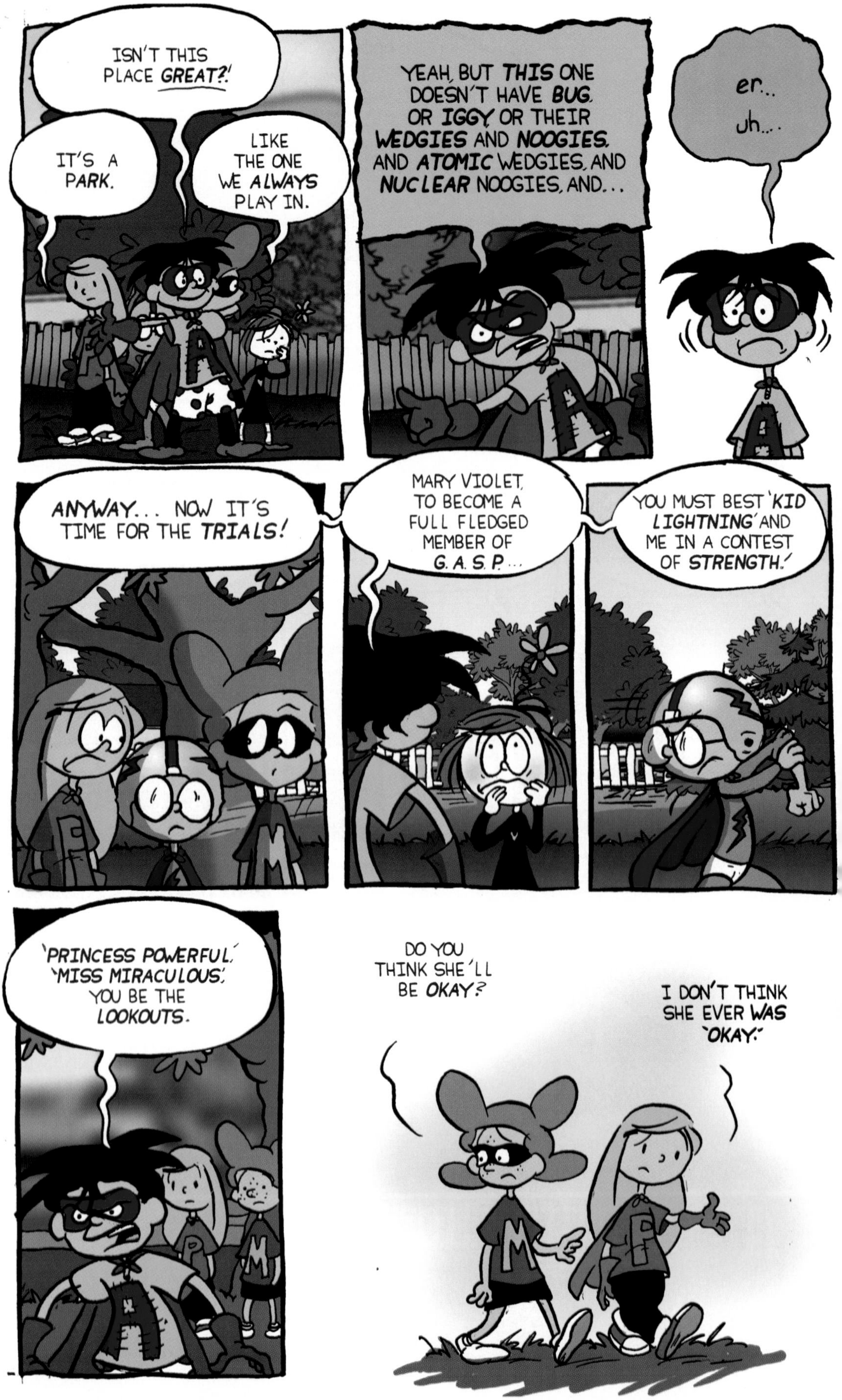
ISN'T THIS PLACE GREAT?!
IT'S A PARK.
LIKE THE ONE WE ALWAYS PLAY IN.
YEAH, BUT THIS ONE DOESN'T HAVE BUG, OR IGGY, OR THEIR WEDGIES AND NOOGIES. AND ATOMIC WEDGIES, AND NUCLEAR NOOGIES, AND...
er... uh...
ANYWAY... NOW IT'S TIME FOR THE TRIALS!
MARY VIOLET, TO BECOME A FULL FLEDGED MEMBER OF G.A.S.P....
YOU MUST BEST 'KID LIGHTNING' AND ME IN A CONTEST OF STRENGTH!
'PRINCESS POWERFUL,' 'MISS MIRACULOUS,' YOU BE THE LOOKOUTS.
DO YOU THINK SHE'LL BE OKAY?
I DON'T THINK SHE EVER WAS 'OKAY.'

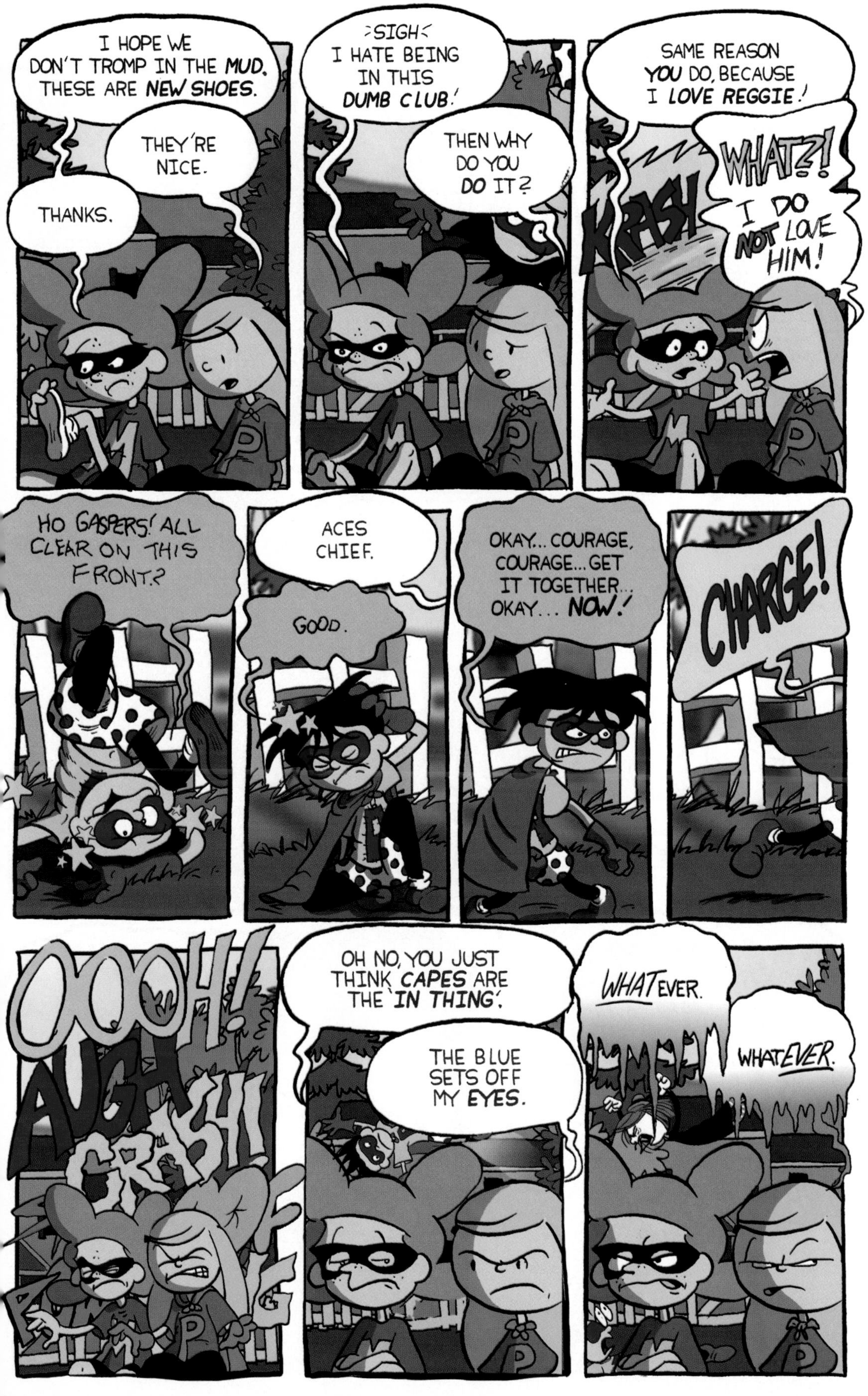

I HOPE WE DON'T TROMP IN THE MUD. THESE ARE NEW SHOES.
THEY'RE NICE.
THANKS.
>SIGH< I HATE BEING IN THIS DUMB CLUB!
THEN WHY DO YOU DO IT?
SAME REASON YOU DO, BECAUSE I LOVE REGGIE!
KRASH
WHAT?! I DO NOT LOVE HIM!
HO GASPERS! ALL CLEAR ON THIS FRONT?
ACES CHIEF.
GOOD.
OKAY... COURAGE, COURAGE... GET IT TOGETHER... OKAY... NOW!
CHARGE!
OOOH!
AUGH
CRASH!
OH NO, YOU JUST THINK CAPES ARE THE 'IN THING'.
THE BLUE SETS OFF MY EYES.
WHATEVER.
WHATEVER.

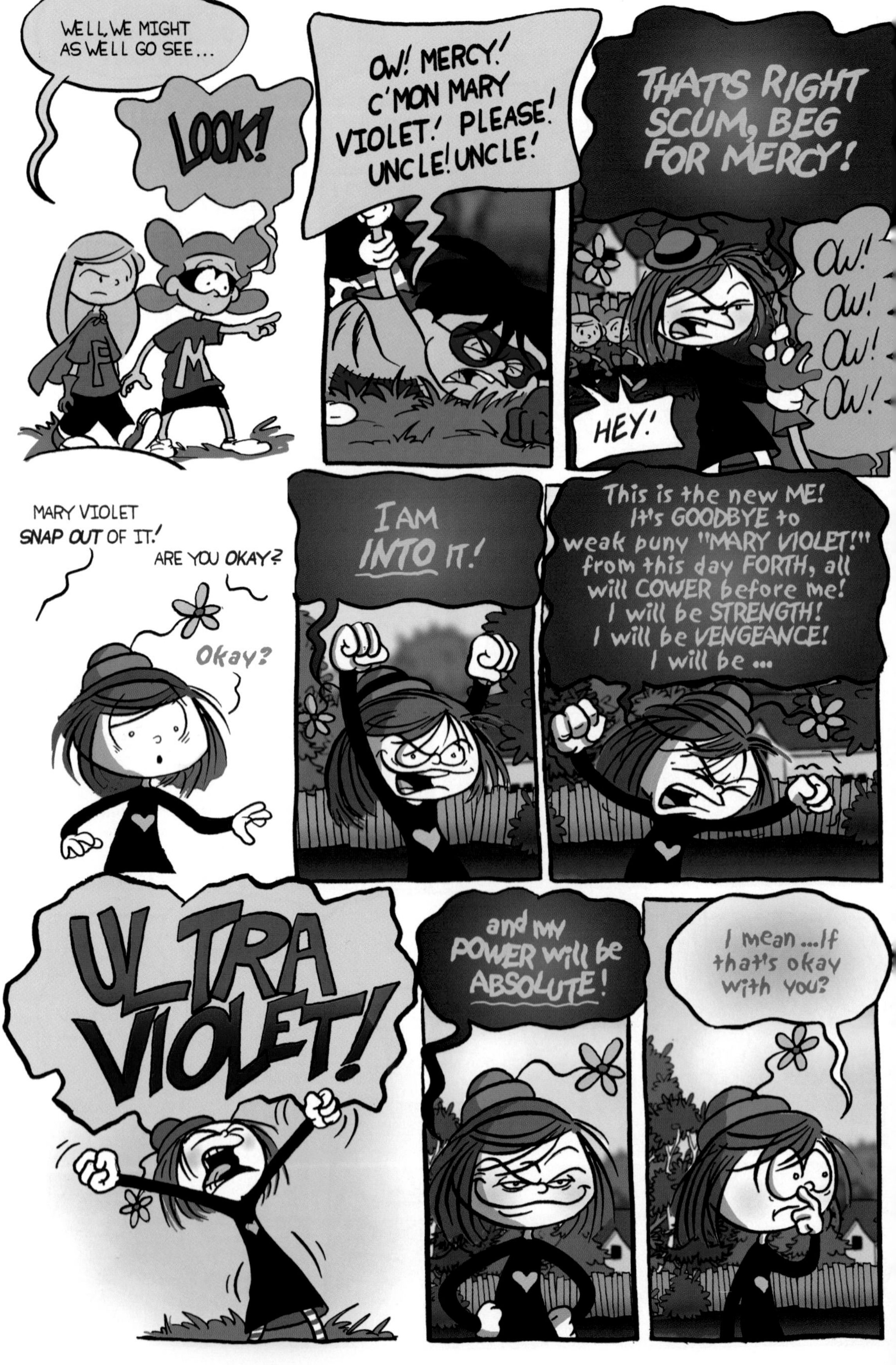

WELL, WE MIGHT AS WELL GO SEE...
LOOK!
OW! MERCY! C'MON MARY VIOLET! PLEASE! UNCLE! UNCLE!
THAT'S RIGHT SCUM, BEG FOR MERCY!
Ow! Ow! Ow! Ow!
HEY!
MARY VIOLET SNAP OUT OF IT!
ARE YOU OKAY?
Okay?
I AM INTO IT!
This is the new ME! It's GOODBYE to weak puny "MARY VIOLET!" from this day FORTH, all will COWER before me! I will be STRENGTH! I will be VENGEANCE! I will be ...
ULTRA VIOLET!
and my POWER will be ABSOLUTE!
I mean ...If that's okay with you?

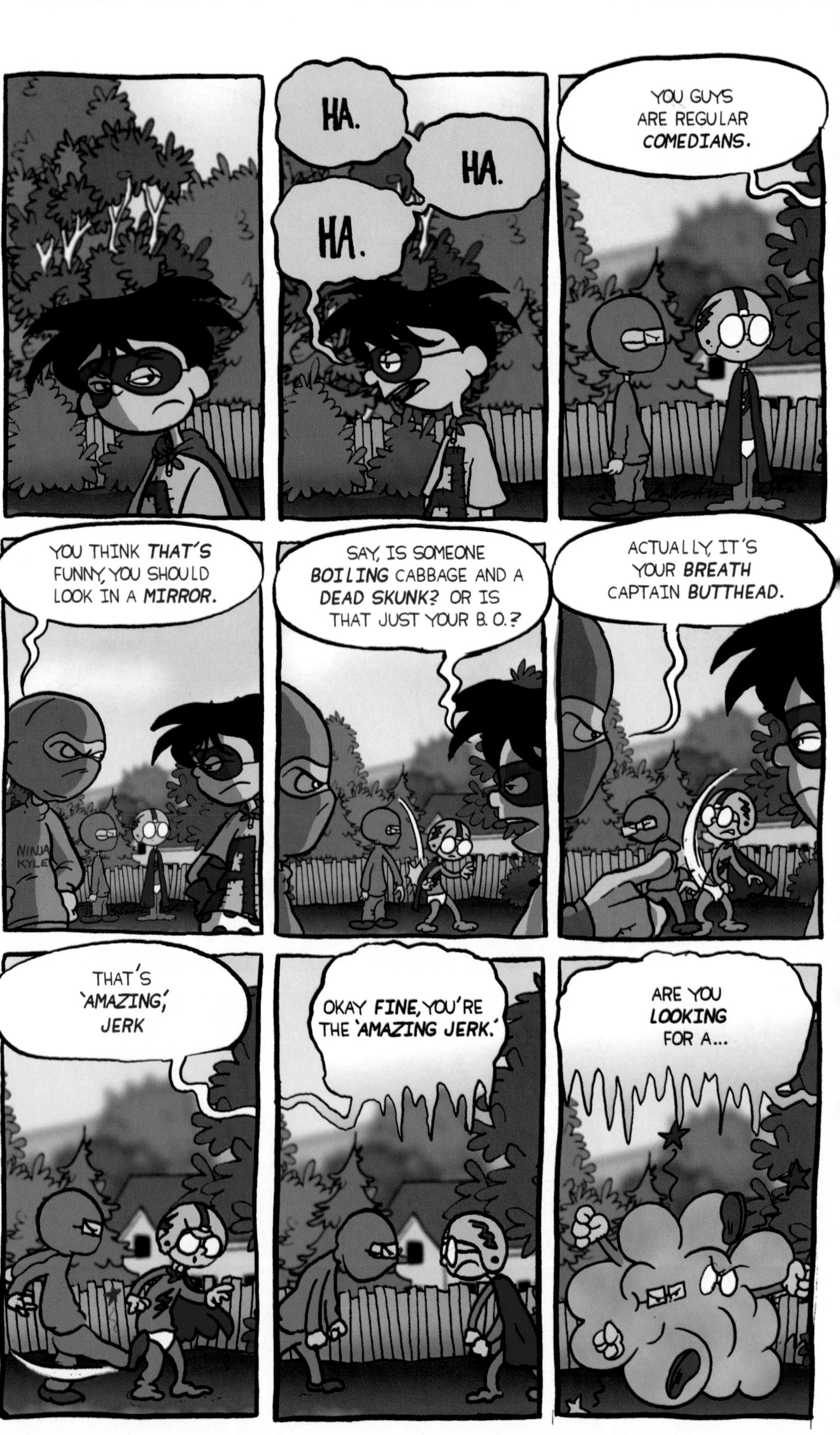
HA.
HA.
HA.
YOU GUYS ARE REGULAR **COMEDIANS**.
YOU THINK **THAT'S** FUNNY, YOU SHOULD LOOK IN A **MIRROR**.
NINJA KYLE
SAY, IS SOMEONE **BOILING** CABBAGE AND A **DEAD SKUNK?** OR IS THAT JUST YOUR B. O.?
ACTUALLY, IT'S YOUR **BREATH** CAPTAIN **BUTTHEAD**.
THAT'S **'AMAZING,'** **JERK**
OKAY **FINE**, YOU'RE THE **'AMAZING JERK.'**
ARE YOU **LOOKING** FOR A...

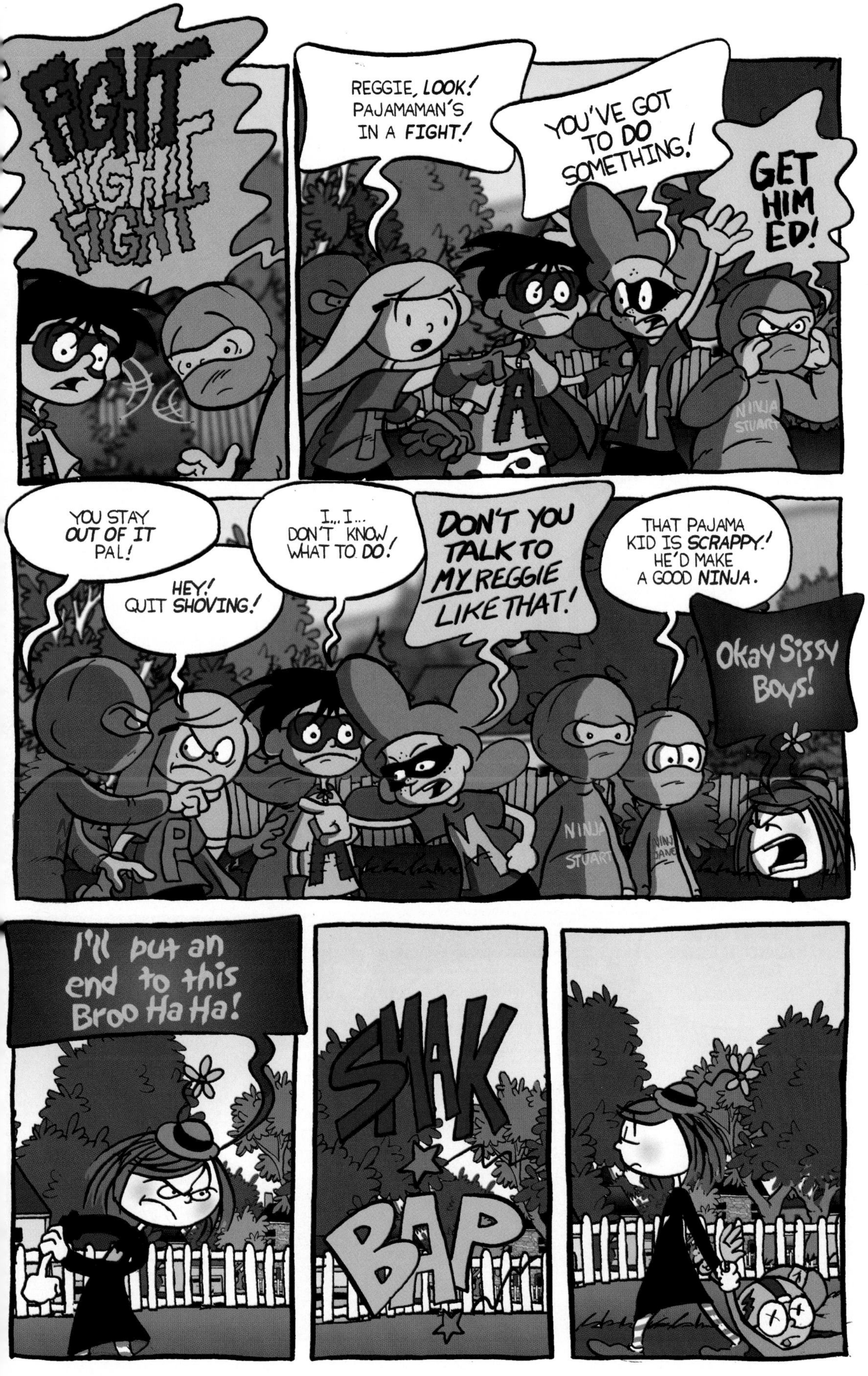
FIGHT FIGHT FIGHT
REGGIE, LOOK! PAJAMAMAN'S IN A FIGHT!
YOU'VE GOT TO DO SOMETHING!
GET HIM ED!
YOU STAY OUT OF IT PAL!
HEY! QUIT SHOVING!
I... I... DON'T KNOW WHAT TO DO!
DON'T YOU TALK TO MY REGGIE LIKE THAT!
THAT PAJAMA KID IS SCRAPPY! HE'D MAKE A GOOD NINJA.
Okay Sissy Boys!
I'll put an end to this Broo Ha Ha!
SMAK
BAP

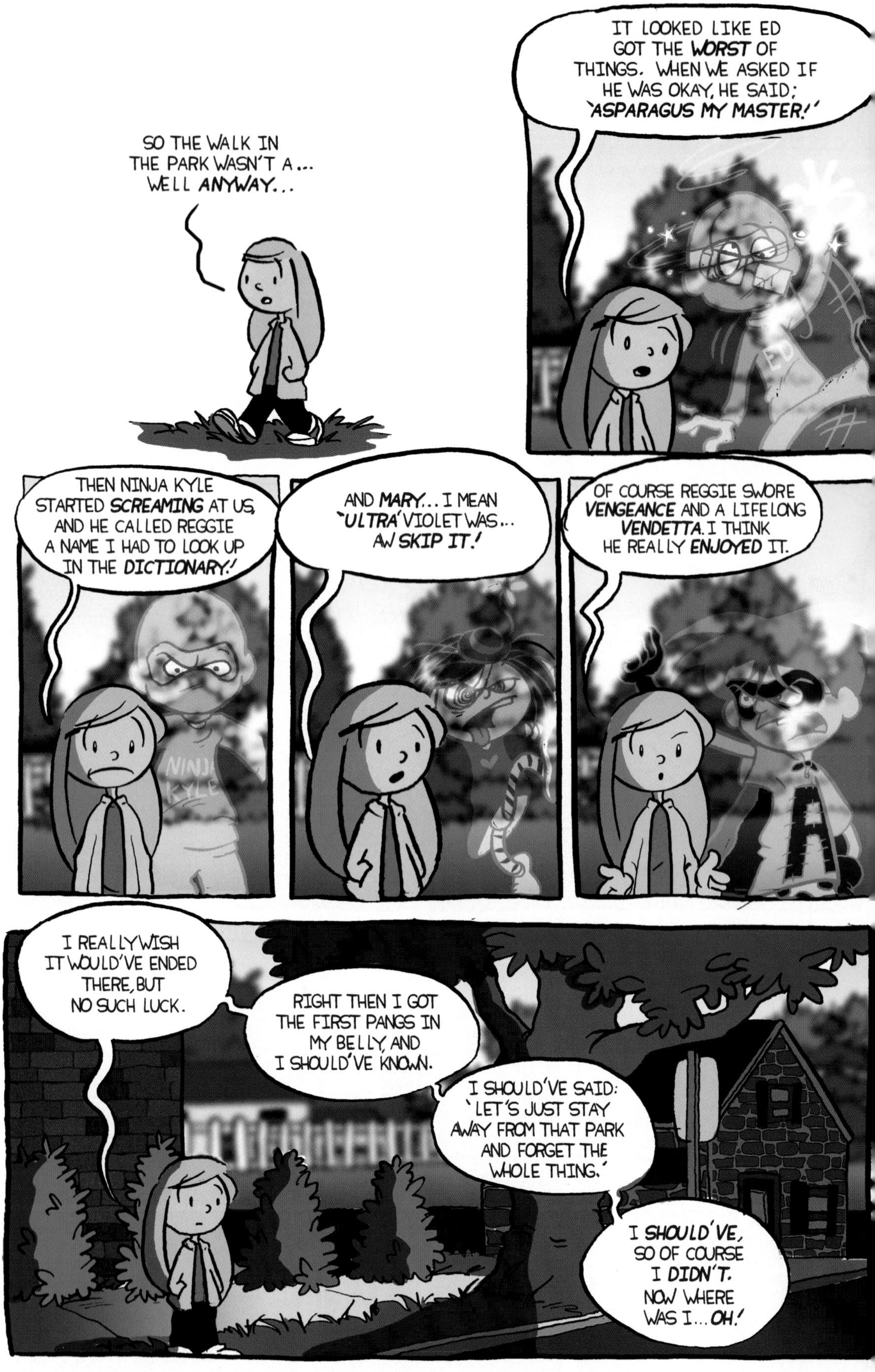
SO THE WALK IN THE PARK WASN'T A... WELL ANYWAY...
IT LOOKED LIKE ED GOT THE WORST OF THINGS. WHEN WE ASKED IF HE WAS OKAY, HE SAID: 'ASPARAGUS MY MASTER!'
ED
THEN NINJA KYLE STARTED SCREAMING AT US, AND HE CALLED REGGIE A NAME I HAD TO LOOK UP IN THE DICTIONARY!
NINJA KYLE
AND MARY... I MEAN 'ULTRA' VIOLET WAS... AW SKIP IT!
OF COURSE REGGIE SWORE VENGEANCE AND A LIFELONG VENDETTA. I THINK HE REALLY ENJOYED IT.
I REALLY WISH IT WOULD'VE ENDED THERE, BUT NO SUCH LUCK.
RIGHT THEN I GOT THE FIRST PANGS IN MY BELLY, AND I SHOULD'VE KNOWN.
I SHOULD'VE SAID: 'LET'S JUST STAY AWAY FROM THAT PARK AND FORGET THE WHOLE THING.'
I SHOULD'VE, SO OF COURSE I DIDN'T. NOW WHERE WAS I... OH!

SO REGGIE WAS OFFICIALLY *OBSESSED,* PAJAMAMAN JUST SEEMED... I DON'T KNOW... LIKE *PAJAMAMAN.* AND OF COURSE *RHONDA* JUST DID WHATEVER REGGIE *SAID...* BUT WORST OF ALL...

MARY VIOLET WAS BECOMING *SCARY* VIOLET.

AND I DON'T KNOW... I WAS NEVER *THAT* INTO THE WHOLE *SUPERHERO* THING.

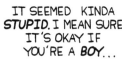

IT SEEMED KINDA *STUPID.* I MEAN SURE, IT'S OKAY IF YOU'RE A *BOY*...

CUZ Y'KNOW, BOYS ARE *STUPID.*

BUT IT WAS SUDDENLY *ALL* WE EVER DID.

THIS DUMB *CLUB* WAS BECOMING A *JOB.*

AND REGGIE IS A *LOUSY* BOSS.

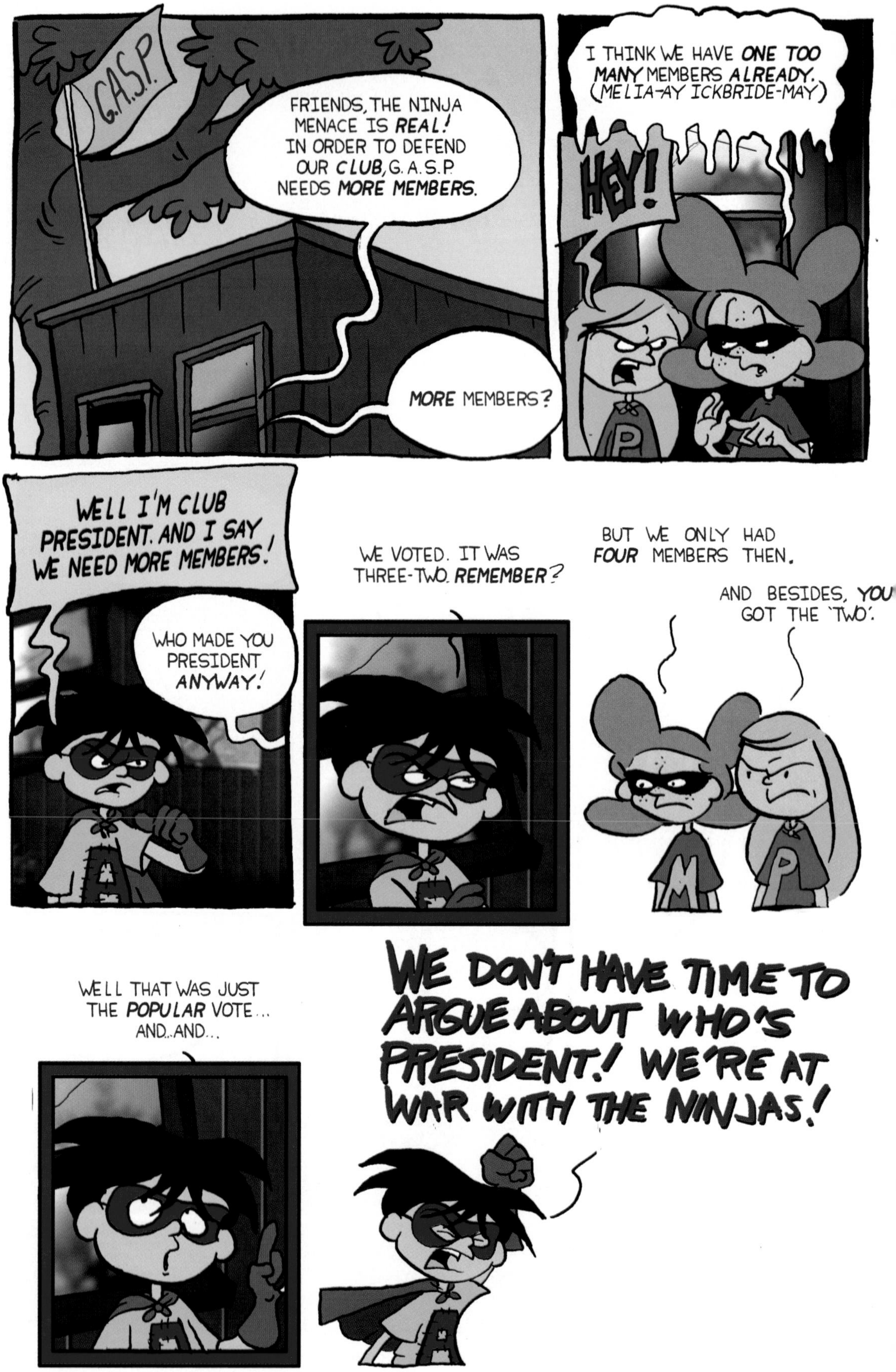

G.A.S.P.
FRIENDS, THE NINJA MENACE IS REAL! IN ORDER TO DEFEND OUR CLUB, G.A.S.P. NEEDS MORE MEMBERS.
MORE MEMBERS?
I THINK WE HAVE ONE TOO MANY MEMBERS ALREADY. (MELIA-AY ICKBRIDE-MAY)
HEY!
WELL I'M CLUB PRESIDENT. AND I SAY WE NEED MORE MEMBERS!
WHO MADE YOU PRESIDENT ANYWAY!
WE VOTED. IT WAS THREE-TWO. REMEMBER?
BUT WE ONLY HAD FOUR MEMBERS THEN.
AND BESIDES, YOU GOT THE 'TWO'.
WELL THAT WAS JUST THE POPULAR VOTE... AND..AND...
WE DON'T HAVE TIME TO ARGUE ABOUT WHO'S PRESIDENT! WE'RE AT WAR WITH THE NINJAS!

SO THAT ENDED *THAT* DEBATE, AND REGGIE GOT STARTED ON HIS *ANTI-NINJA* CAMPAIGN.

I DREW THE *POSTERS*, AND I THINK THEY CAME OUT PRETTY *COOL*.

I MEAN Y'KNOW, FOR *ANTI-NINJA POSTERS* THAT IS.

FIGHT THE NINJA menace! JOIN G.A.S.P. today!

BUT BY OUR NEXT MEETING, THE RESULTS WERE PRETTY *LAME*.

THIS IS IT?

Hey Man, How's it Goin?

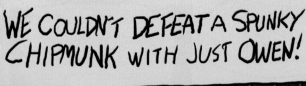

WE COULDN'T DEFEAT A SPUNKY CHIPMUNK WITH JUST OWEN!

May I give him 'The Trials?'

ULTRA VIOLET PLEASE DON'T BREAK OUR *ONLY RECRUIT.*

Spunky Chipmunk? What kinda Club *IS* this?

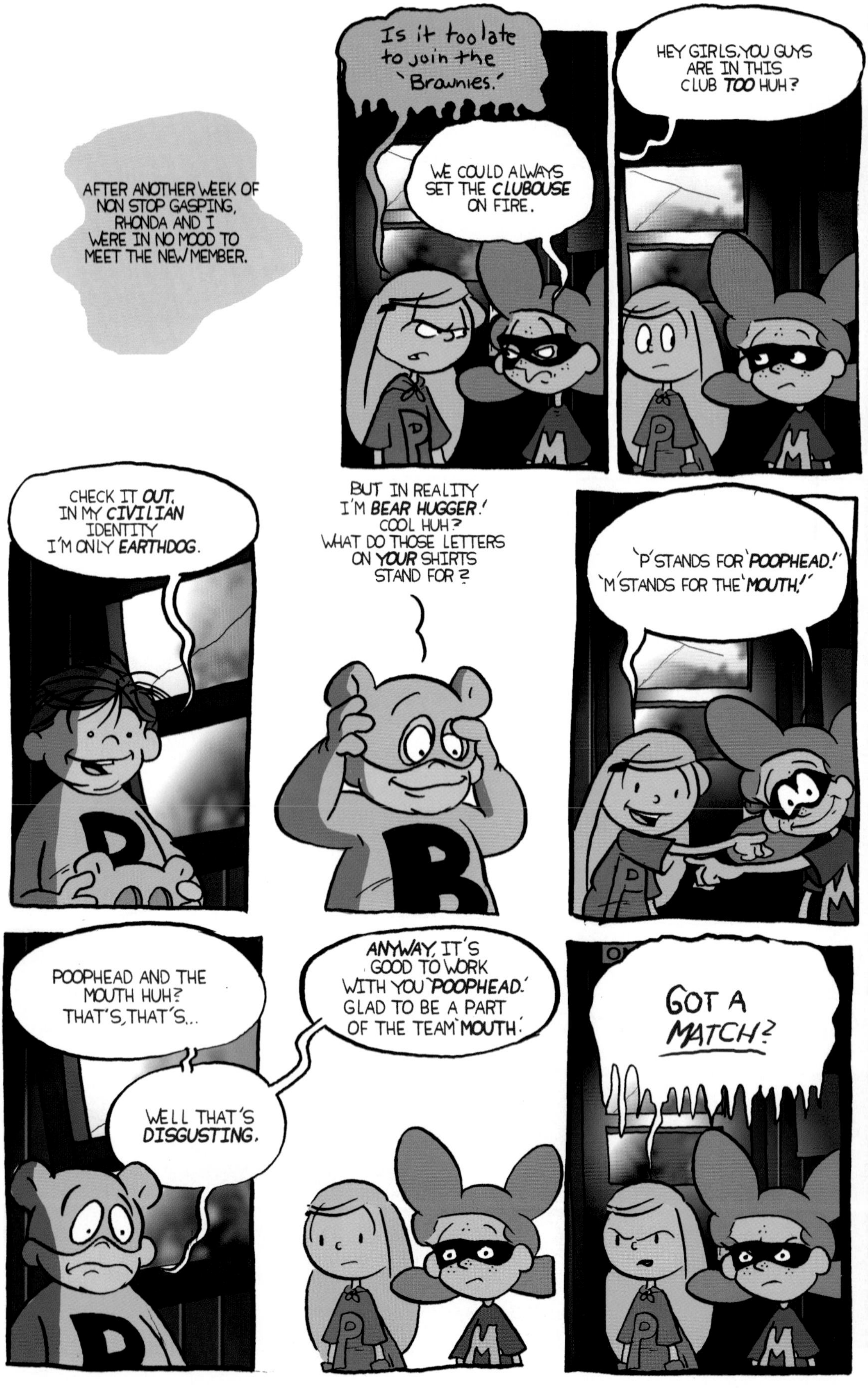

AFTER ANOTHER WEEK OF NON STOP GASPING, RHONDA AND I WERE IN NO MOOD TO MEET THE NEW MEMBER.
Is it too late to join the 'Brownies.'
WE COULD ALWAYS SET THE CLUBOUSE ON FIRE.
HEY GIRLS, YOU GUYS ARE IN THIS CLUB TOO HUH?
CHECK IT OUT. IN MY CIVILIAN IDENTITY I'M ONLY EARTHDOG.
BUT IN REALITY I'M BEAR HUGGER.' COOL HUH? WHAT DO THOSE LETTERS ON YOUR SHIRTS STAND FOR?
'P' STANDS FOR 'POOPHEAD.' 'M' STANDS FOR THE 'MOUTH.'
POOPHEAD AND THE MOUTH HUH? THAT'S, THAT'S...
WELL THAT'S DISGUSTING.
ANYWAY, IT'S GOOD TO WORK WITH YOU 'POOPHEAD.' GLAD TO BE A PART OF THE TEAM 'MOUTH.'
GOT A MATCH?

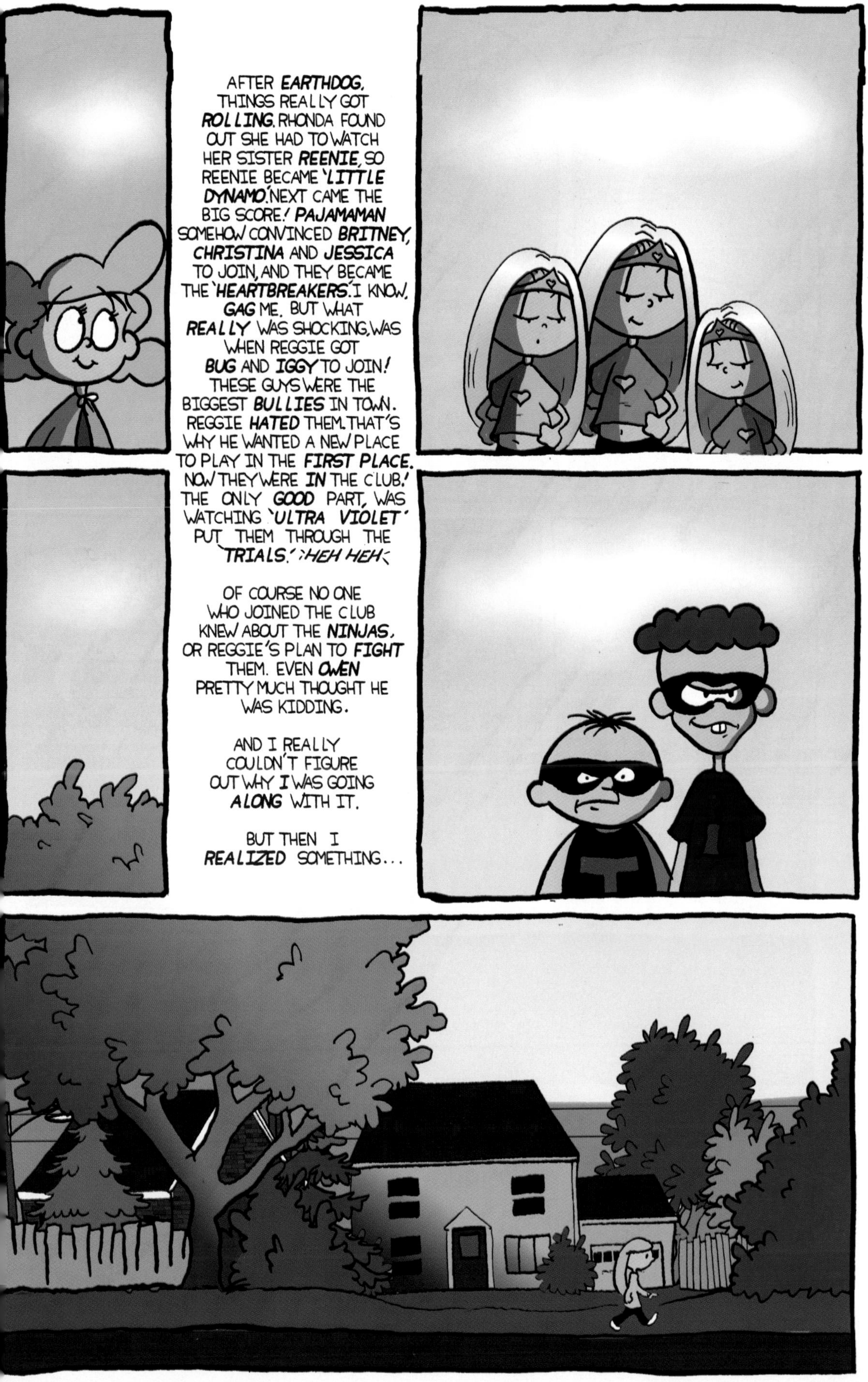
AFTER EARTHDOG, THINGS REALLY GOT ROLLING. RHONDA FOUND OUT SHE HAD TO WATCH HER SISTER REENIE, SO REENIE BECAME 'LITTLE DYNAMO.' NEXT CAME THE BIG SCORE! PAJAMAMAN SOMEHOW CONVINCED BRITNEY, CHRISTINA AND JESSICA TO JOIN, AND THEY BECAME THE 'HEARTBREAKERS.' I KNOW, GAG ME. BUT WHAT REALLY WAS SHOCKING, WAS WHEN REGGIE GOT BUG AND IGGY TO JOIN! THESE GUYS WERE THE BIGGEST BULLIES IN TOWN. REGGIE HATED THEM. THAT'S WHY HE WANTED A NEW PLACE TO PLAY IN THE FIRST PLACE. NOW THEY WERE IN THE CLUB! THE ONLY GOOD PART, WAS WATCHING 'ULTRA VIOLET' PUT THEM THROUGH THE 'TRIALS.' HEH HEH
OF COURSE NO ONE WHO JOINED THE CLUB KNEW ABOUT THE NINJAS, OR REGGIE'S PLAN TO FIGHT THEM. EVEN OWEN PRETTY MUCH THOUGHT HE WAS KIDDING.
AND I REALLY COULDN'T FIGURE OUT WHY I WAS GOING ALONG WITH IT.
BUT THEN I REALIZED SOMETHING...

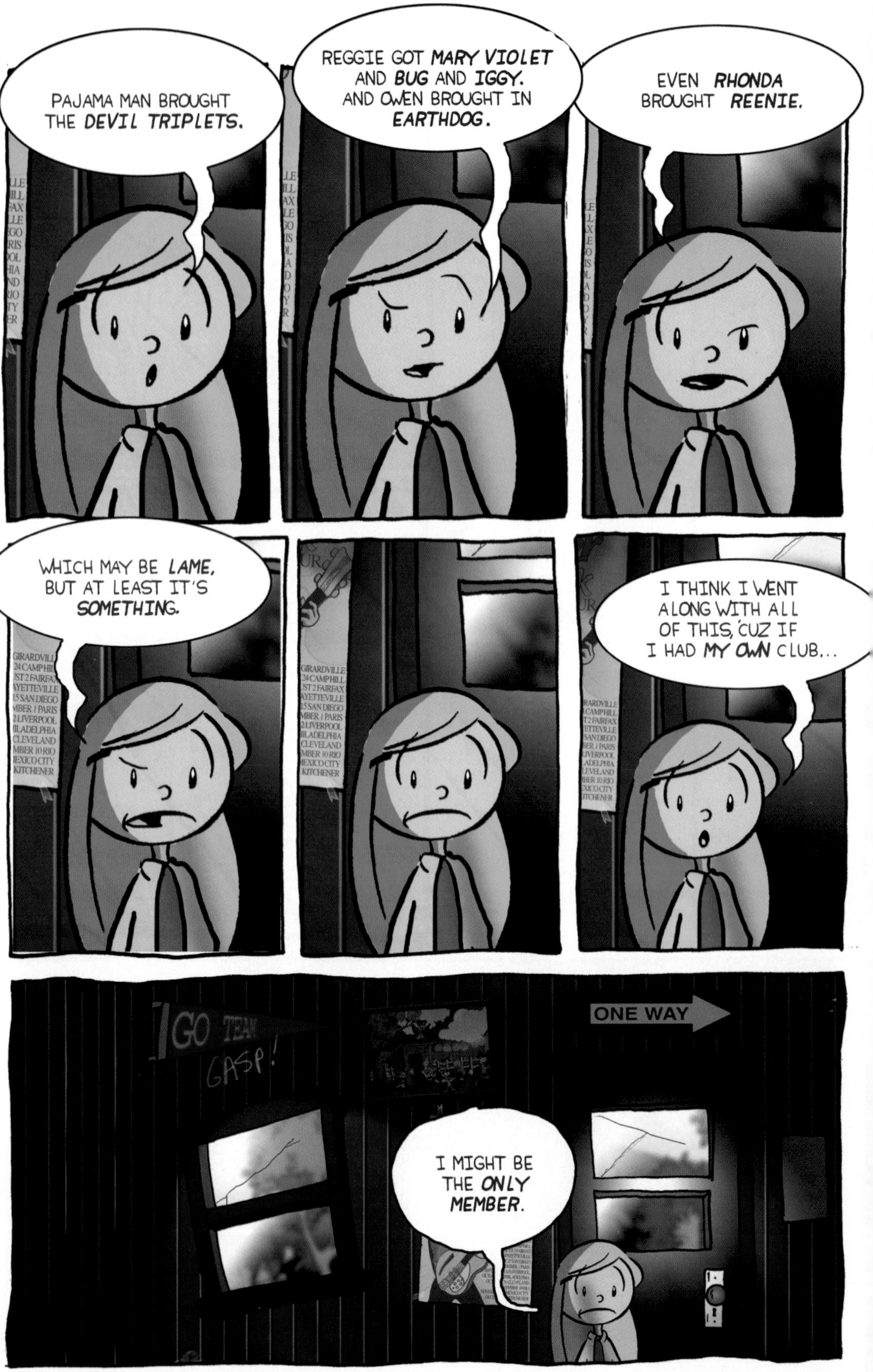

PAJAMA MAN BROUGHT THE DEVIL TRIPLETS.
REGGIE GOT MARY VIOLET AND BUG AND IGGY. AND OWEN BROUGHT IN EARTHDOG.
EVEN RHONDA BROUGHT REENIE.
WHICH MAY BE LAME, BUT AT LEAST IT'S SOMETHING.
I THINK I WENT ALONG WITH ALL OF THIS, 'CUZ IF I HAD MY OWN CLUB...
GO TEAM
GASP!
ONE WAY
I MIGHT BE THE ONLY MEMBER.

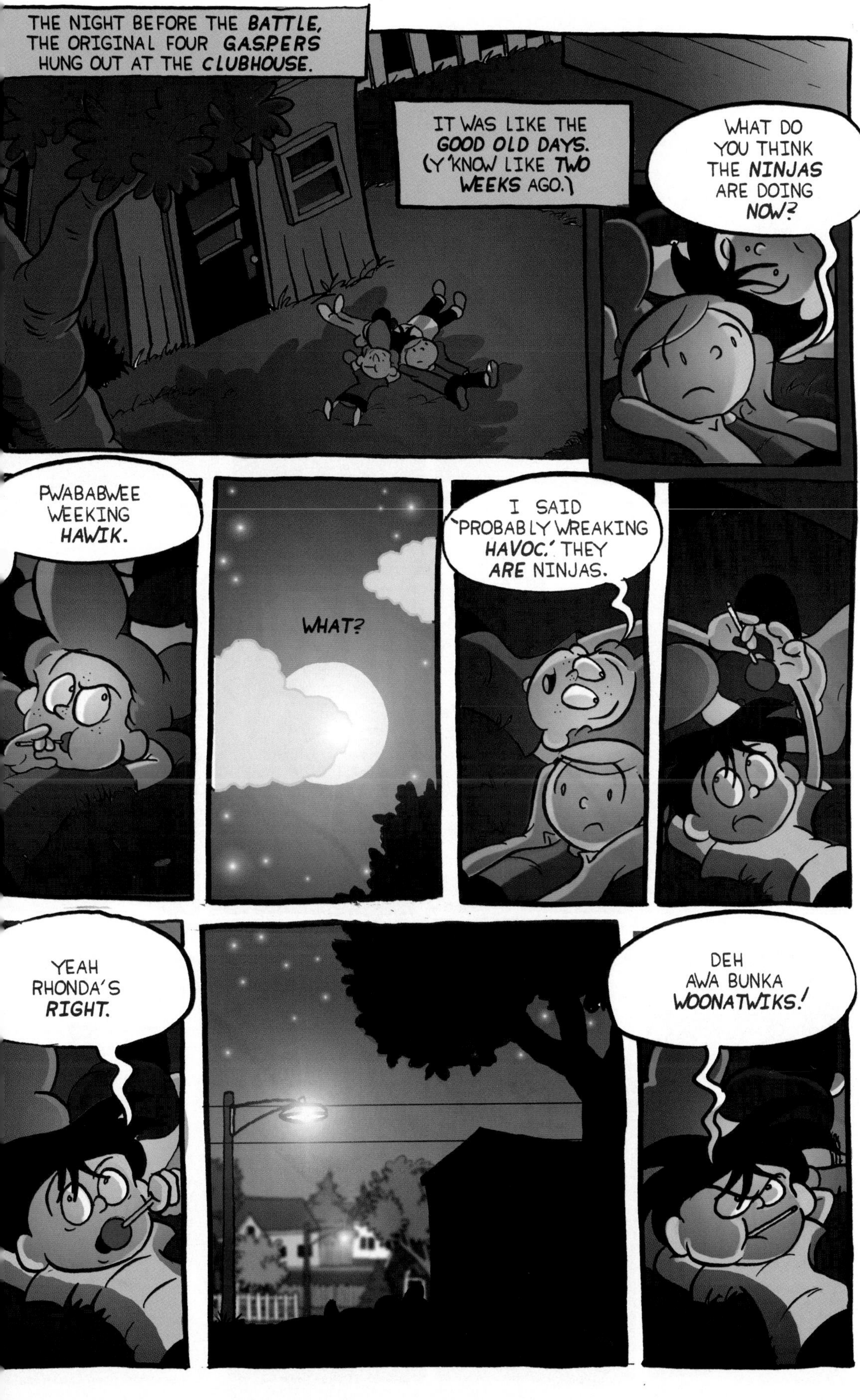
THE NIGHT BEFORE THE BATTLE, THE ORIGINAL FOUR GASPERS HUNG OUT AT THE CLUBHOUSE.
IT WAS LIKE THE GOOD OLD DAYS. (Y'KNOW LIKE TWO WEEKS AGO.)
WHAT DO YOU THINK THE NINJAS ARE DOING NOW?
PWABABWEE WEEKING HAWIK.
WHAT?
I SAID 'PROBABLY WREAKING HAVOC.' THEY ARE NINJAS.
YEAH RHONDA'S RIGHT.
DEH AWA BUNKA WOONATWIKS!

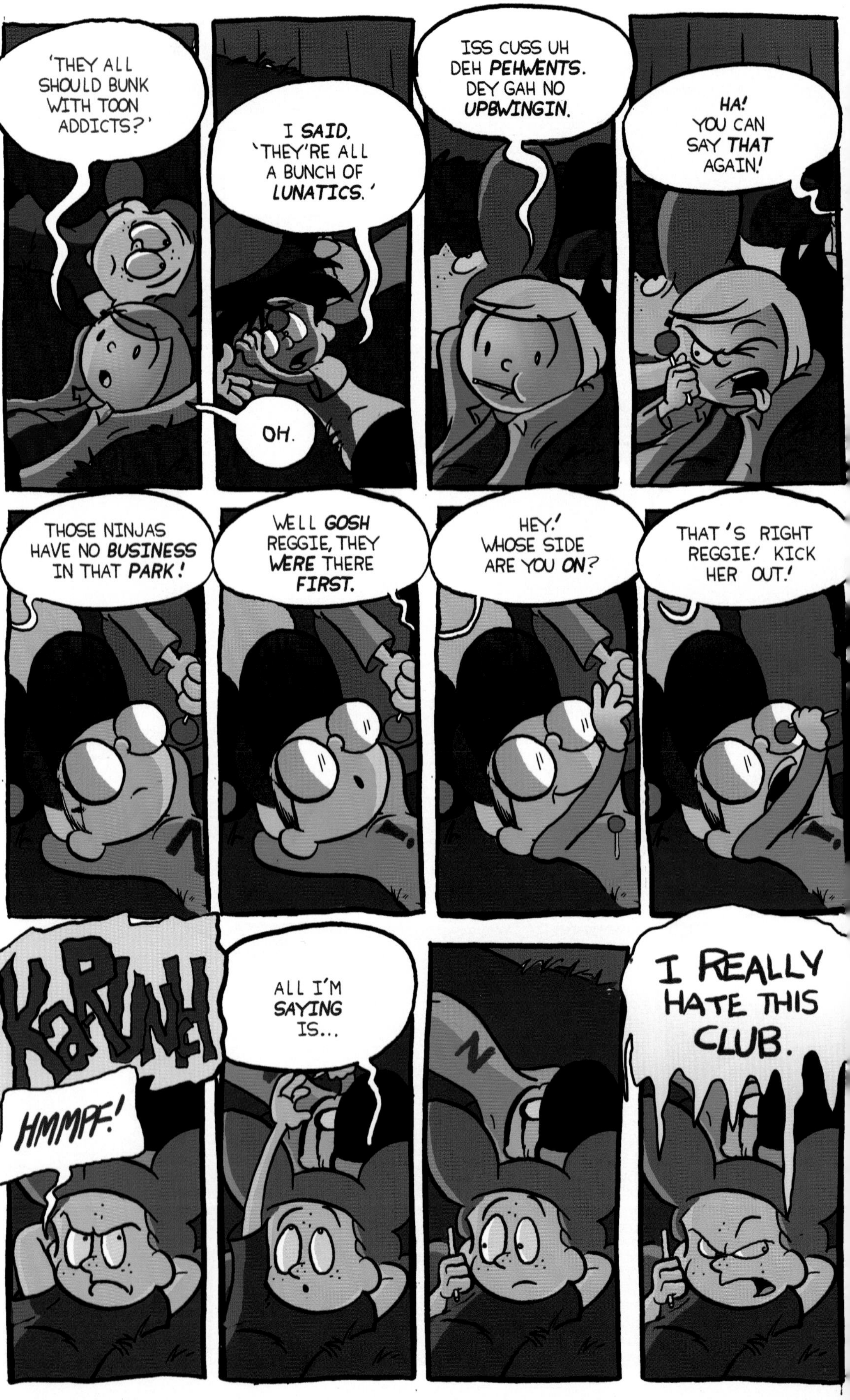

'THEY ALL SHOULD BUNK WITH TOON ADDICTS?'
I SAID, 'THEY'RE ALL A BUNCH OF LUNATICS.'
OH.
ISS CUSS UH DEH PEHWENTS. DEY GAH NO UPBWINGIN.
HA! YOU CAN SAY THAT AGAIN!
THOSE NINJAS HAVE NO BUSINESS IN THAT PARK!
WELL GOSH REGGIE, THEY WERE THERE FIRST.
HEY! WHOSE SIDE ARE YOU ON?
THAT'S RIGHT REGGIE! KICK HER OUT!
KaRUNCH
HMMPF!
ALL I'M SAYING IS...
I REALLY HATE THIS CLUB.

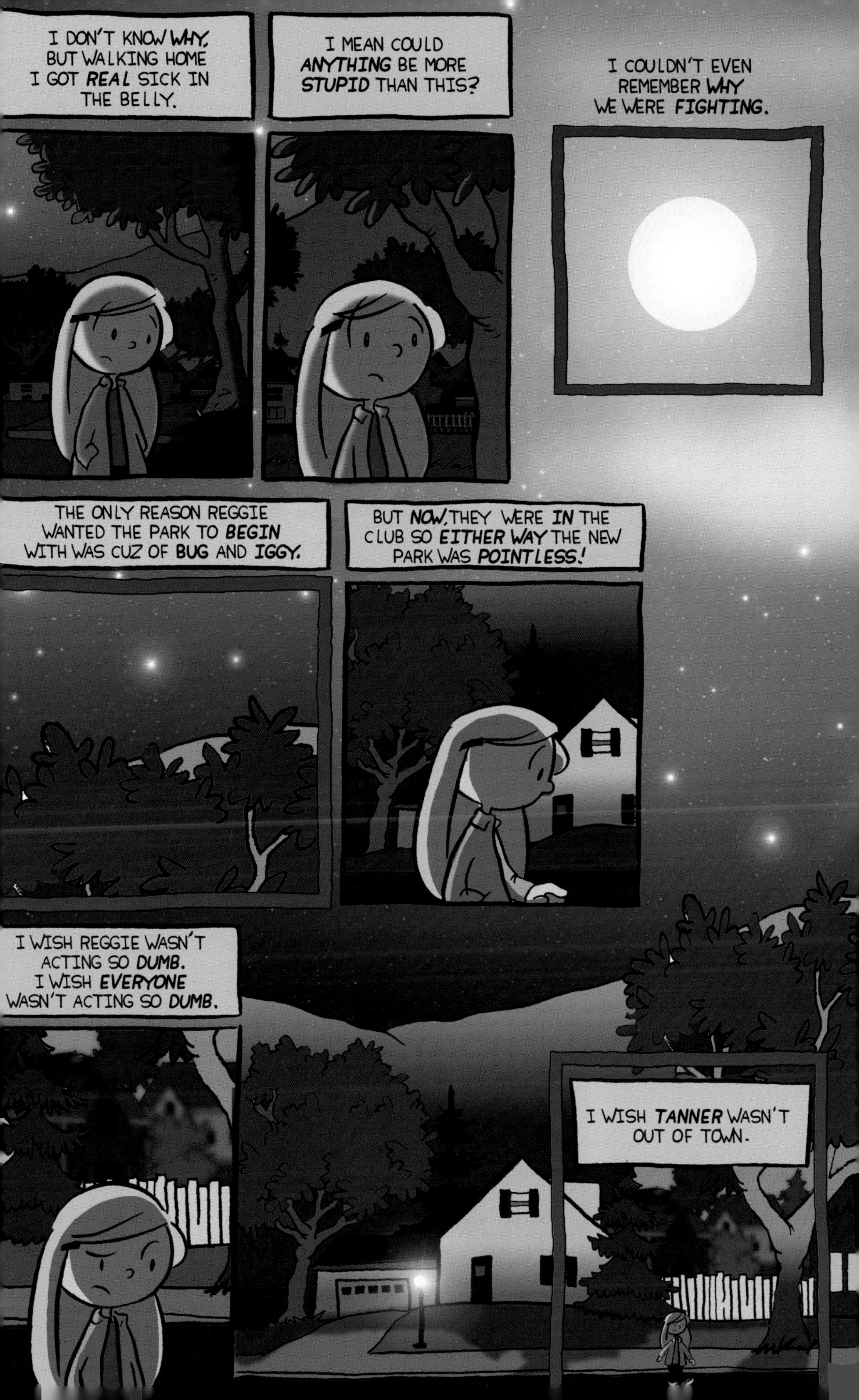

I DON'T KNOW WHY, BUT WALKING HOME I GOT REAL SICK IN THE BELLY.
I MEAN COULD ANYTHING BE MORE STUPID THAN THIS?
I COULDN'T EVEN REMEMBER WHY WE WERE FIGHTING.
THE ONLY REASON REGGIE WANTED THE PARK TO BEGIN WITH WAS CUZ OF BUG AND IGGY.
BUT NOW, THEY WERE IN THE CLUB SO EITHER WAY THE NEW PARK WAS POINTLESS!
I WISH REGGIE WASN'T ACTING SO DUMB. I WISH EVERYONE WASN'T ACTING SO DUMB.
I WISH TANNER WASN'T OUT OF TOWN.

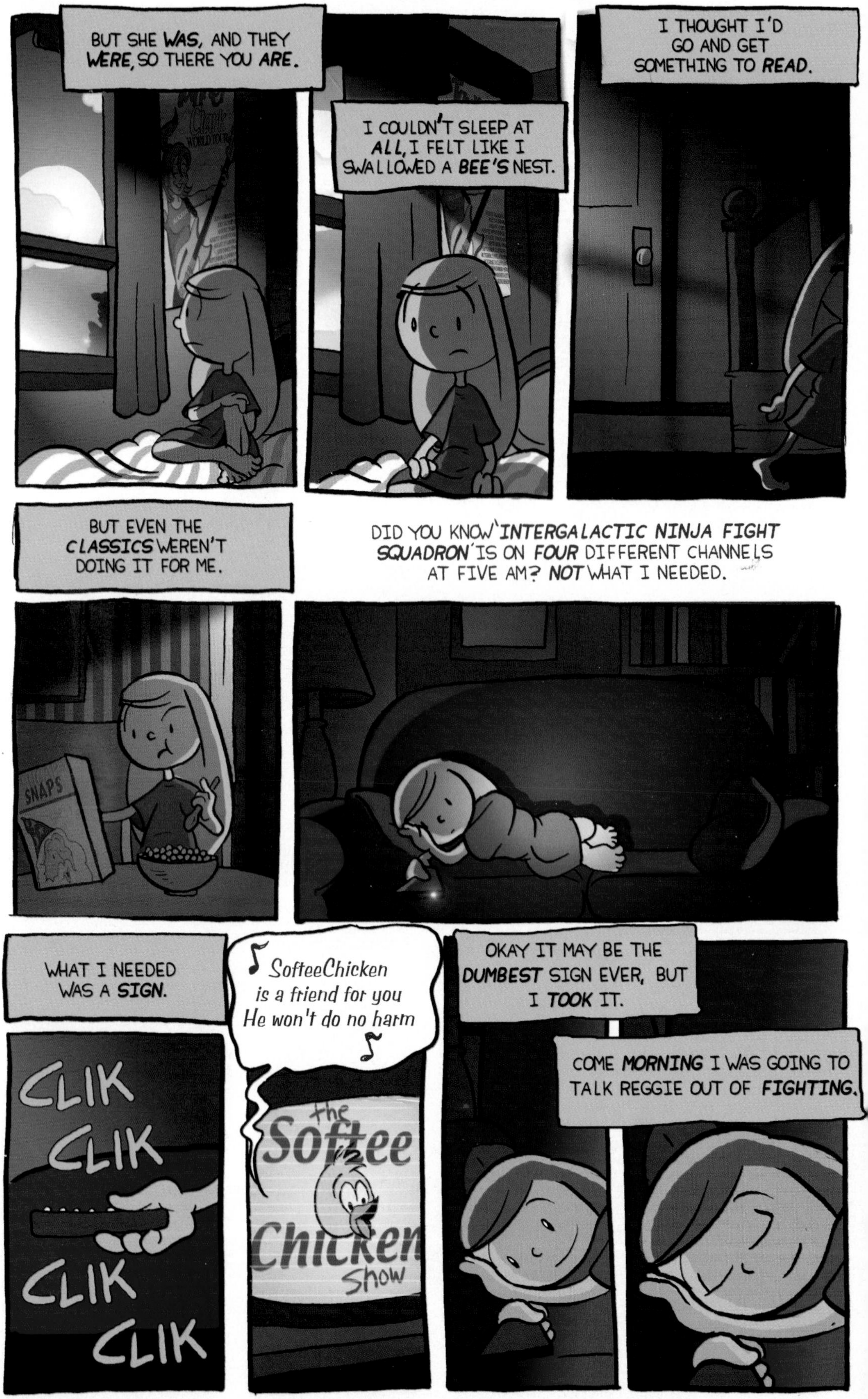
BUT SHE WAS, AND THEY WERE, SO THERE YOU ARE.
I COULDN'T SLEEP AT ALL, I FELT LIKE I SWALLOWED A BEE'S NEST.
I THOUGHT I'D GO AND GET SOMETHING TO READ.
BUT EVEN THE CLASSICS WEREN'T DOING IT FOR ME.
SNAPS
DID YOU KNOW 'INTERGALACTIC NINJA FIGHT SQUADRON' IS ON FOUR DIFFERENT CHANNELS AT FIVE AM? NOT WHAT I NEEDED.
WHAT I NEEDED WAS A SIGN.
CLIK CLIK CLIK CLIK
SofteeChicken is a friend for you He won't do no harm
the Softee Chicken Show
OKAY IT MAY BE THE DUMBEST SIGN EVER, BUT I TOOK IT.
COME MORNING I WAS GOING TO TALK REGGIE OUT OF FIGHTING.

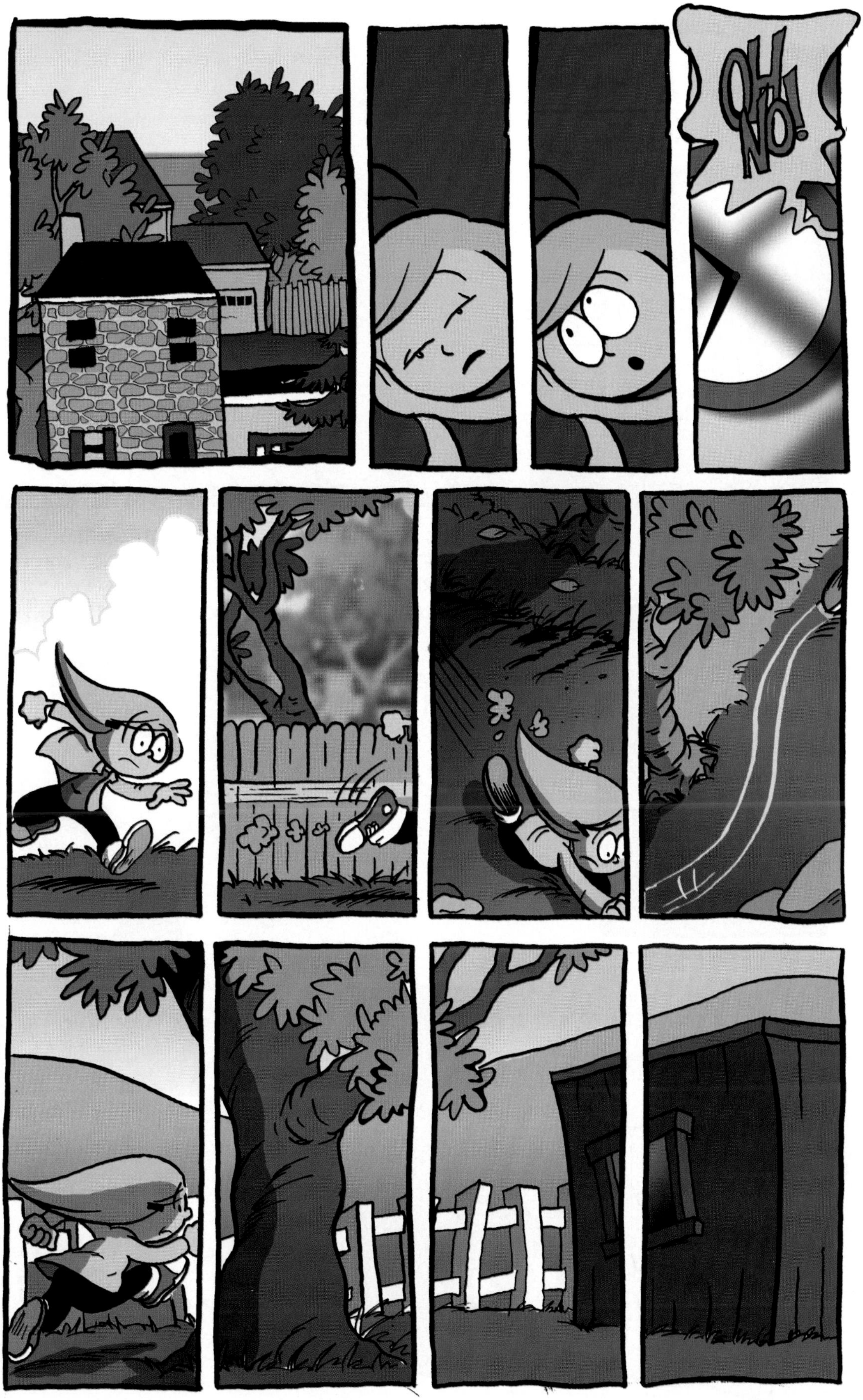
OH NO!

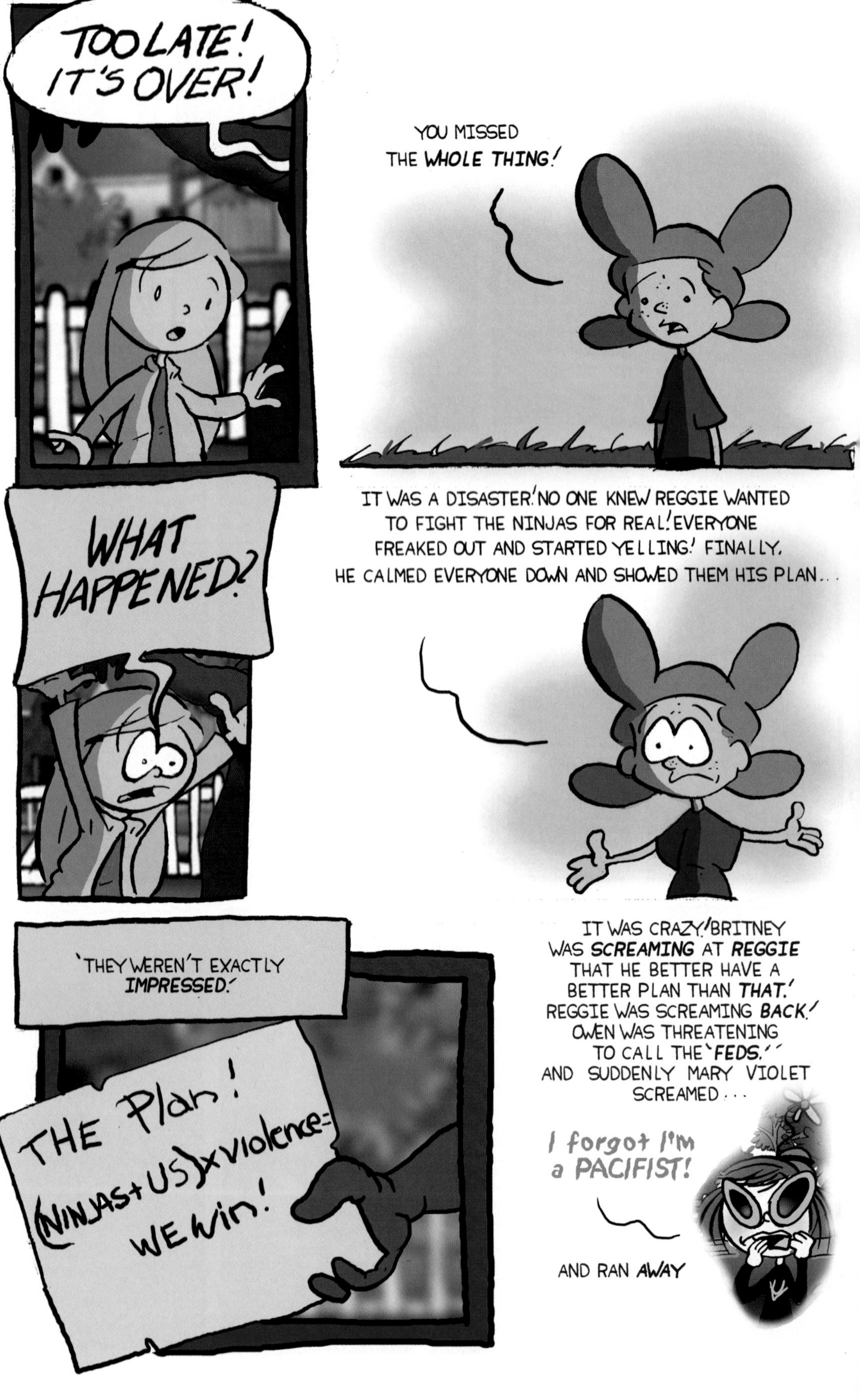
TOO LATE! IT'S OVER!
YOU MISSED THE WHOLE THING!
WHAT HAPPENED?
IT WAS A DISASTER! NO ONE KNEW REGGIE WANTED TO FIGHT THE NINJAS FOR REAL! EVERYONE FREAKED OUT AND STARTED YELLING! FINALLY, HE CALMED EVERYONE DOWN AND SHOWED THEM HIS PLAN...
'THEY WEREN'T EXACTLY IMPRESSED.'
THE Plan!
(NINJAS+US)x violence= WE win!
IT WAS CRAZY! BRITNEY WAS SCREAMING AT REGGIE THAT HE BETTER HAVE A BETTER PLAN THAN THAT.' REGGIE WAS SCREAMING BACK! OWEN WAS THREATENING TO CALL THE 'FEDS.' AND SUDDENLY MARY VIOLET SCREAMED...
I forgot I'm a PACIFIST!
AND RAN AWAY

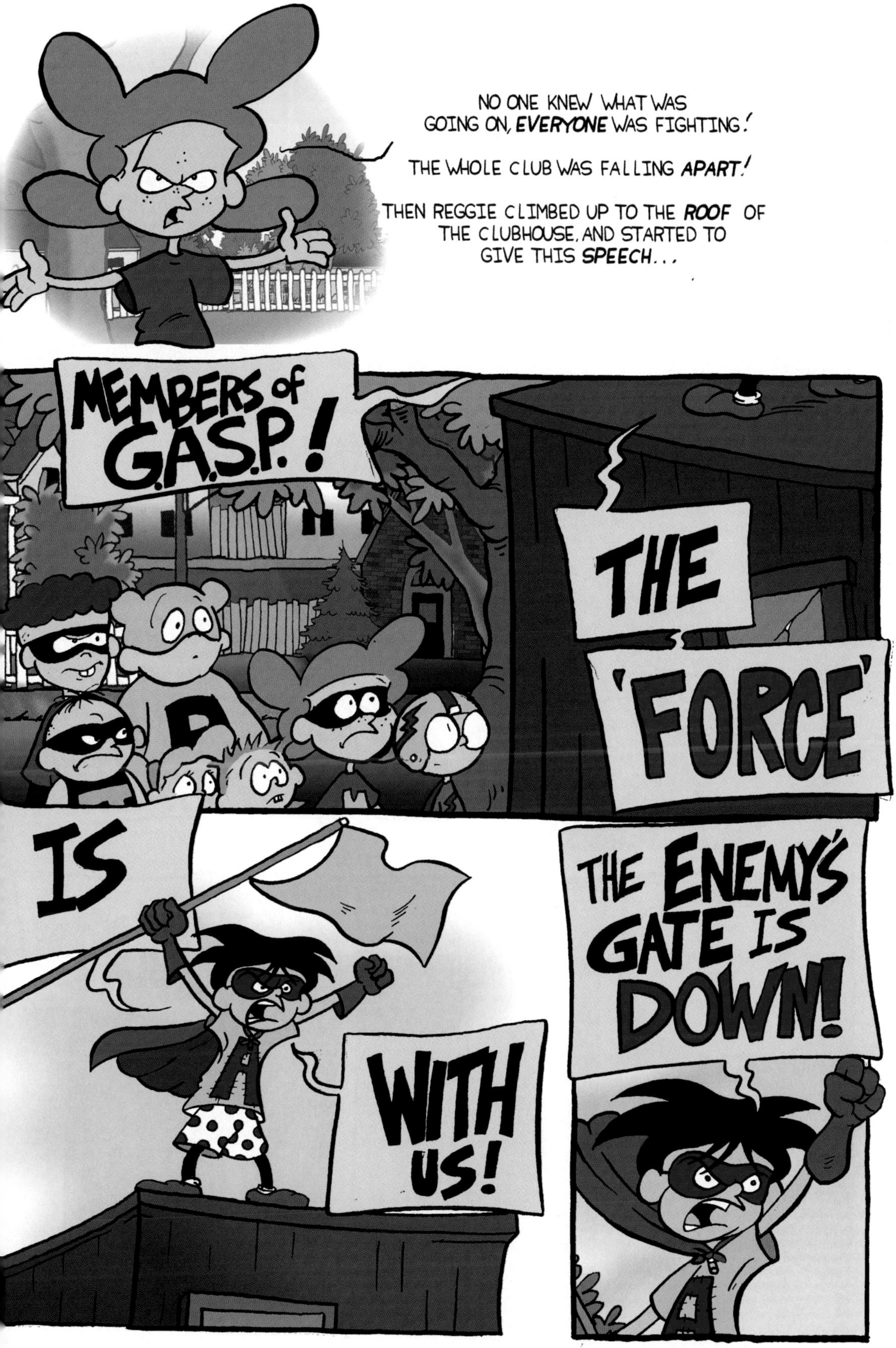
NO ONE KNEW WHAT WAS GOING ON, EVERYONE WAS FIGHTING!
THE WHOLE CLUB WAS FALLING APART!
THEN REGGIE CLIMBED UP TO THE ROOF OF THE CLUBHOUSE, AND STARTED TO GIVE THIS SPEECH...
MEMBERS of G.A.S.P.!
THE
'FORCE'
IS
WITH US!
THE ENEMY'S GATE IS DOWN!

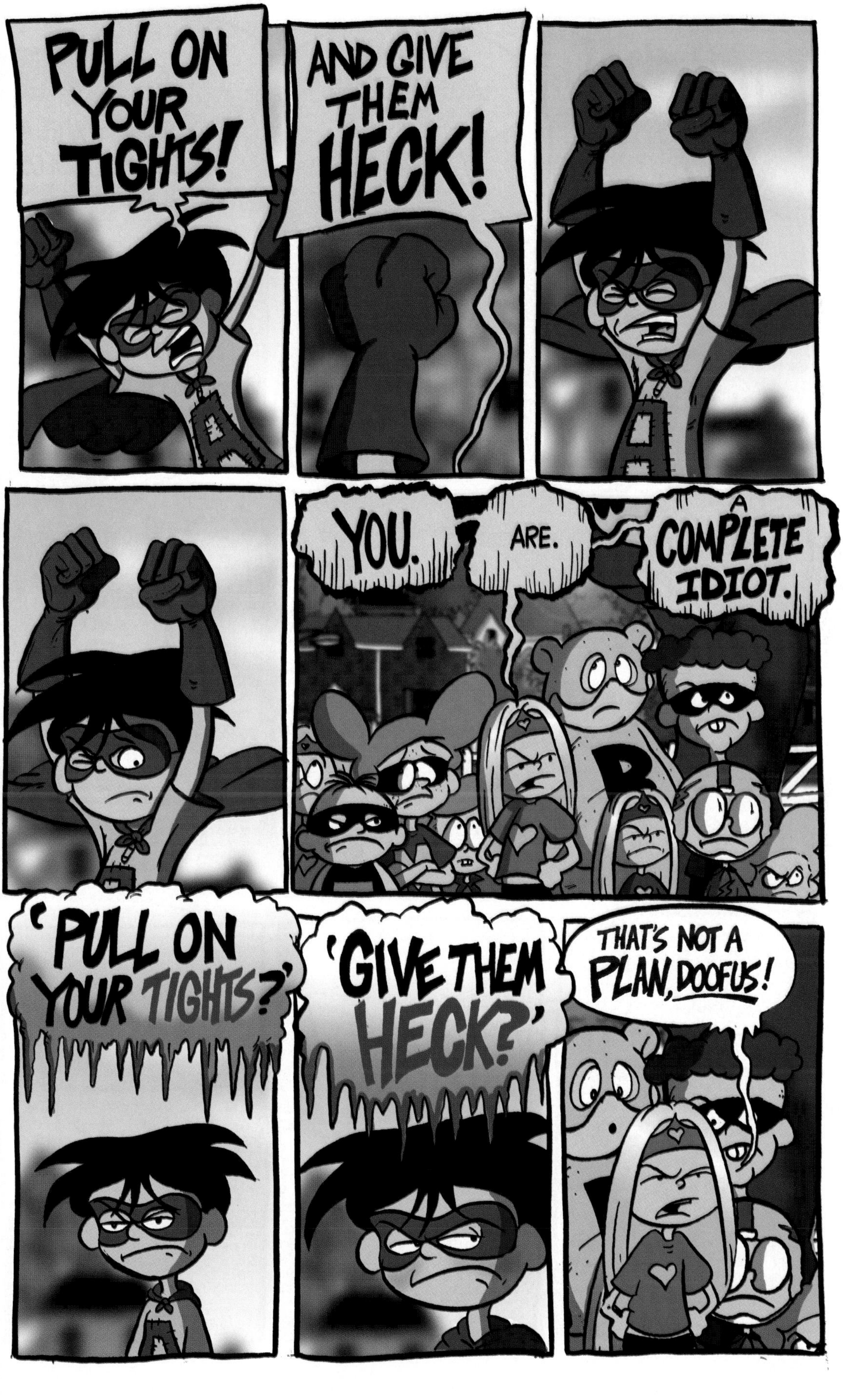
PULL ON YOUR TIGHTS!
AND GIVE THEM HECK!
YOU.
ARE.
A COMPLETE IDIOT.
'PULL ON YOUR TIGHTS?'
'GIVE THEM HECK?'
THAT'S NOT A PLAN, DOOFUS!

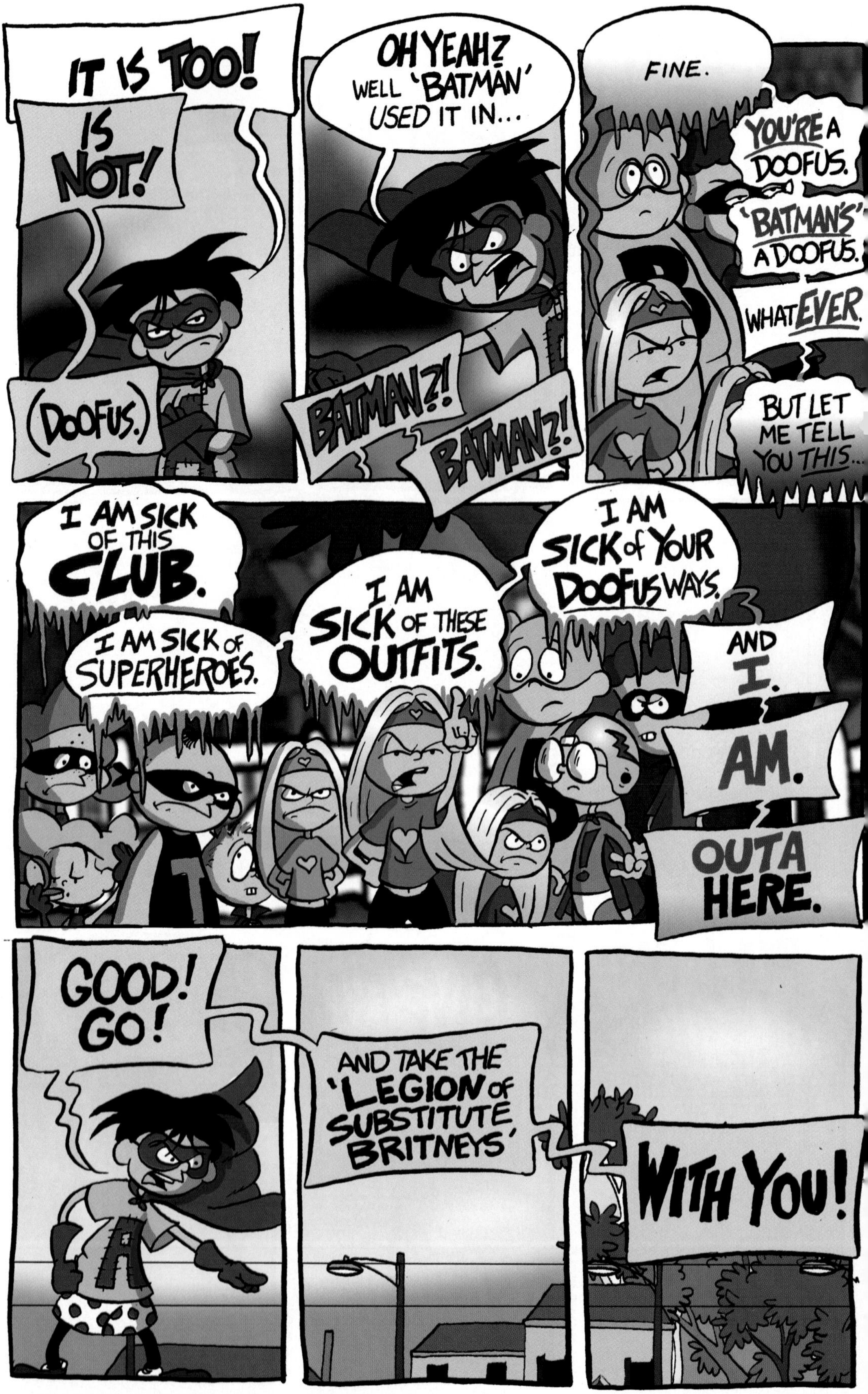
IT IS TOO!
IS NOT!
(DOOFUS.)
OH YEAH? WELL 'BATMAN' USED IT IN...
BATMAN?!
BATMAN?!
FINE.
YOU'RE A DOOFUS.
'BATMAN'S' A DOOFUS.
WHATEVER.
BUT LET ME TELL YOU THIS...
I AM SICK OF THIS CLUB.
I AM SICK OF SUPERHEROES.
I AM SICK OF THESE OUTFITS.
I AM SICK of YOUR DOOFUS WAYS.
AND I.
AM.
OUTA HERE.
GOOD! GO!
AND TAKE THE 'LEGION of SUBSTITUTE BRITNEYS'
WITH YOU!

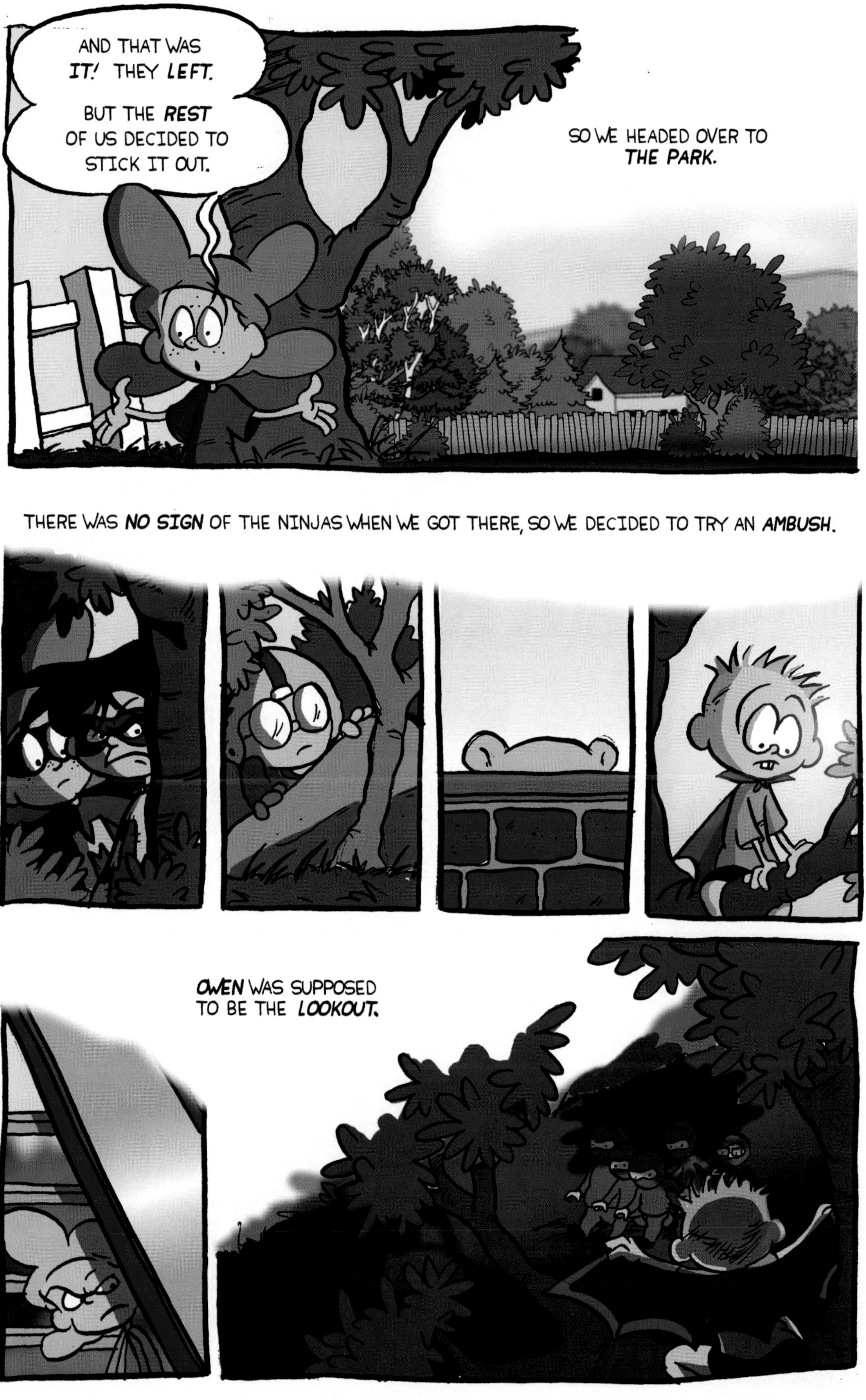
AND THAT WAS IT! THEY LEFT.
BUT THE REST OF US DECIDED TO STICK IT OUT.
SO WE HEADED OVER TO THE PARK.
THERE WAS NO SIGN OF THE NINJAS WHEN WE GOT THERE, SO WE DECIDED TO TRY AN AMBUSH.
OWEN WAS SUPPOSED TO BE THE LOOKOUT.

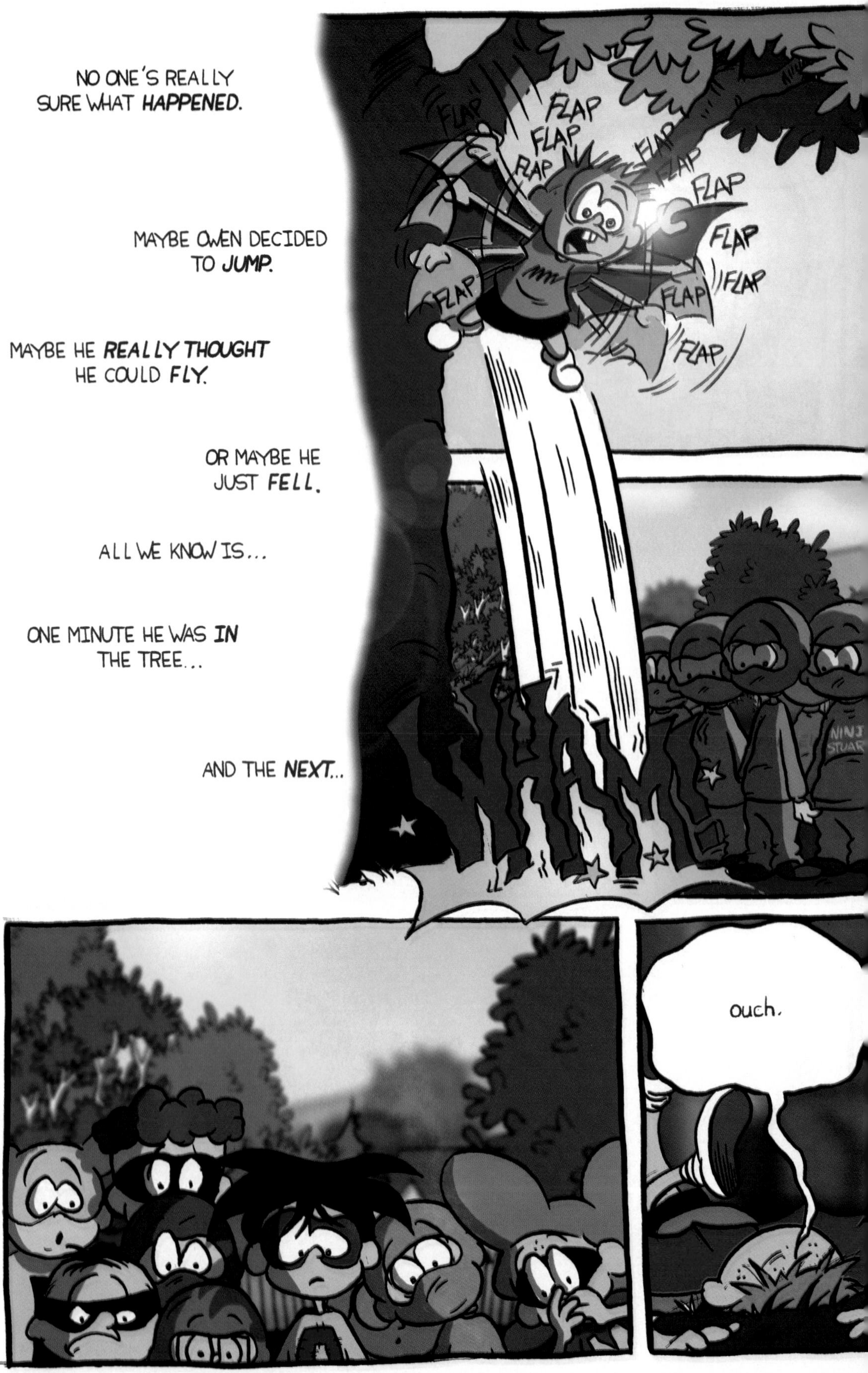
NO ONE'S REALLY SURE WHAT HAPPENED.
FLAP FLAP FLAP FLAP FLAP FLAP FLAP FLAP FLAP FLAP FLAP FLAP
MAYBE OWEN DECIDED TO JUMP.
MAYBE HE REALLY THOUGHT HE COULD FLY.
OR MAYBE HE JUST FELL.
ALL WE KNOW IS...
ONE MINUTE HE WAS IN THE TREE...
AND THE NEXT...
WHAM!
ouch.

Part Four

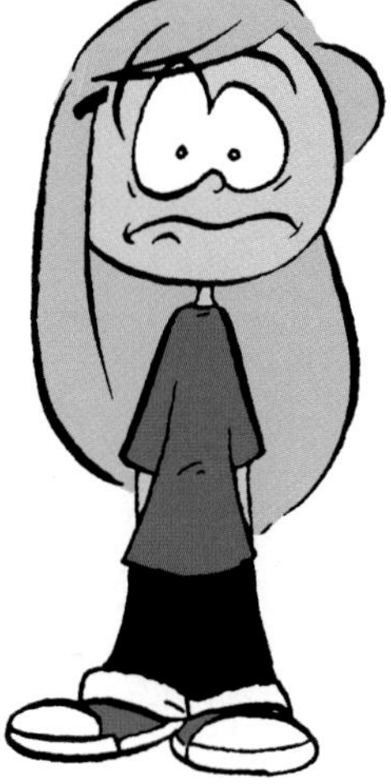

"Rhonda! We're talking about Ninja Kissie! I'll be lucky if I don't get deported."

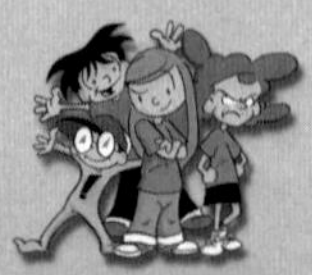

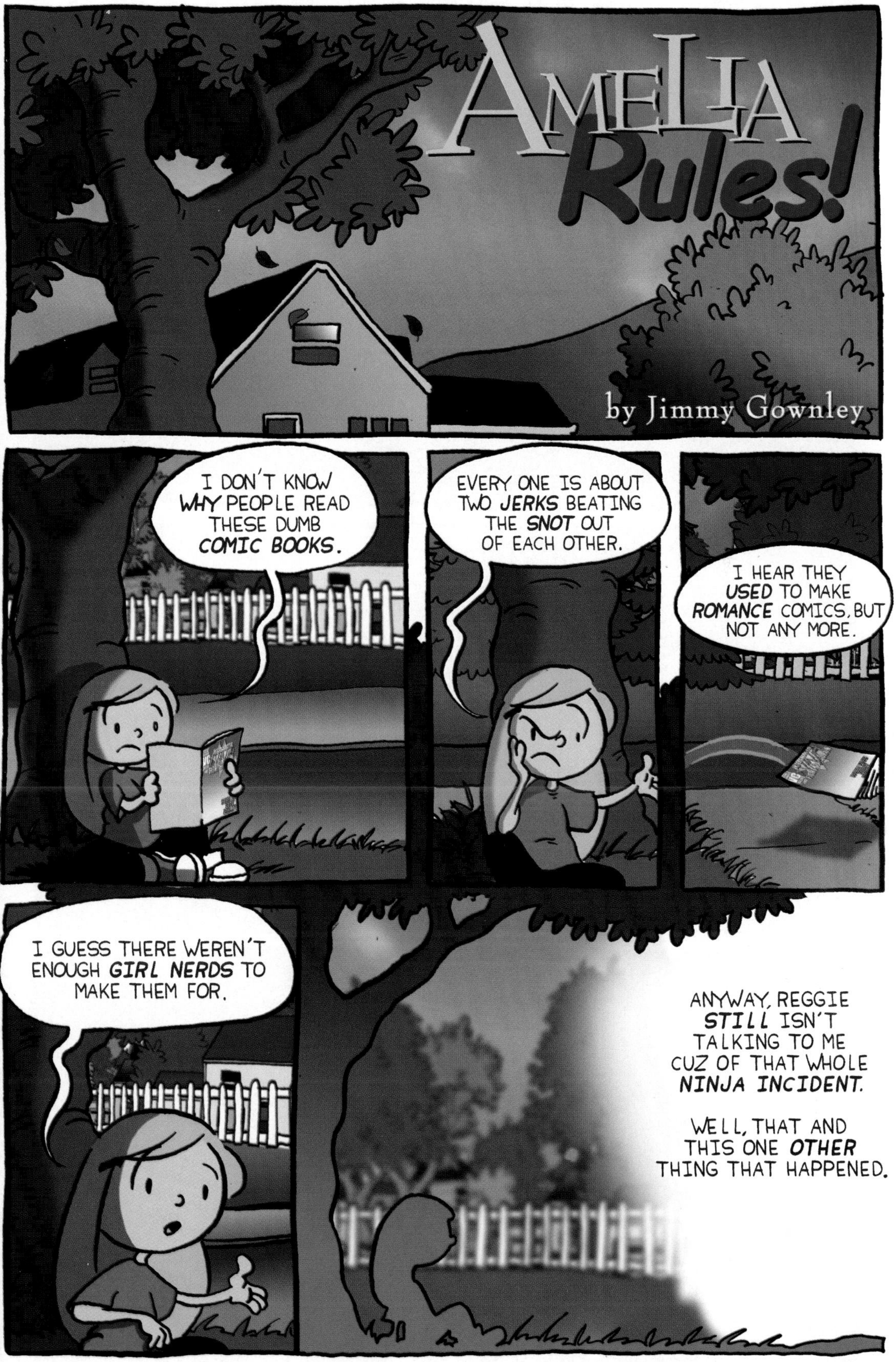
AMELIA Rules!
by Jimmy Gownley
I DON'T KNOW WHY PEOPLE READ THESE DUMB COMIC BOOKS.
EVERY ONE IS ABOUT TWO JERKS BEATING THE SNOT OUT OF EACH OTHER.
I HEAR THEY USED TO MAKE ROMANCE COMICS, BUT NOT ANY MORE.
I GUESS THERE WEREN'T ENOUGH GIRL NERDS TO MAKE THEM FOR.
ANYWAY, REGGIE STILL ISN'T TALKING TO ME CUZ OF THAT WHOLE NINJA INCIDENT.
WELL, THAT AND THIS ONE OTHER THING THAT HAPPENED.

HER THREE KISSES

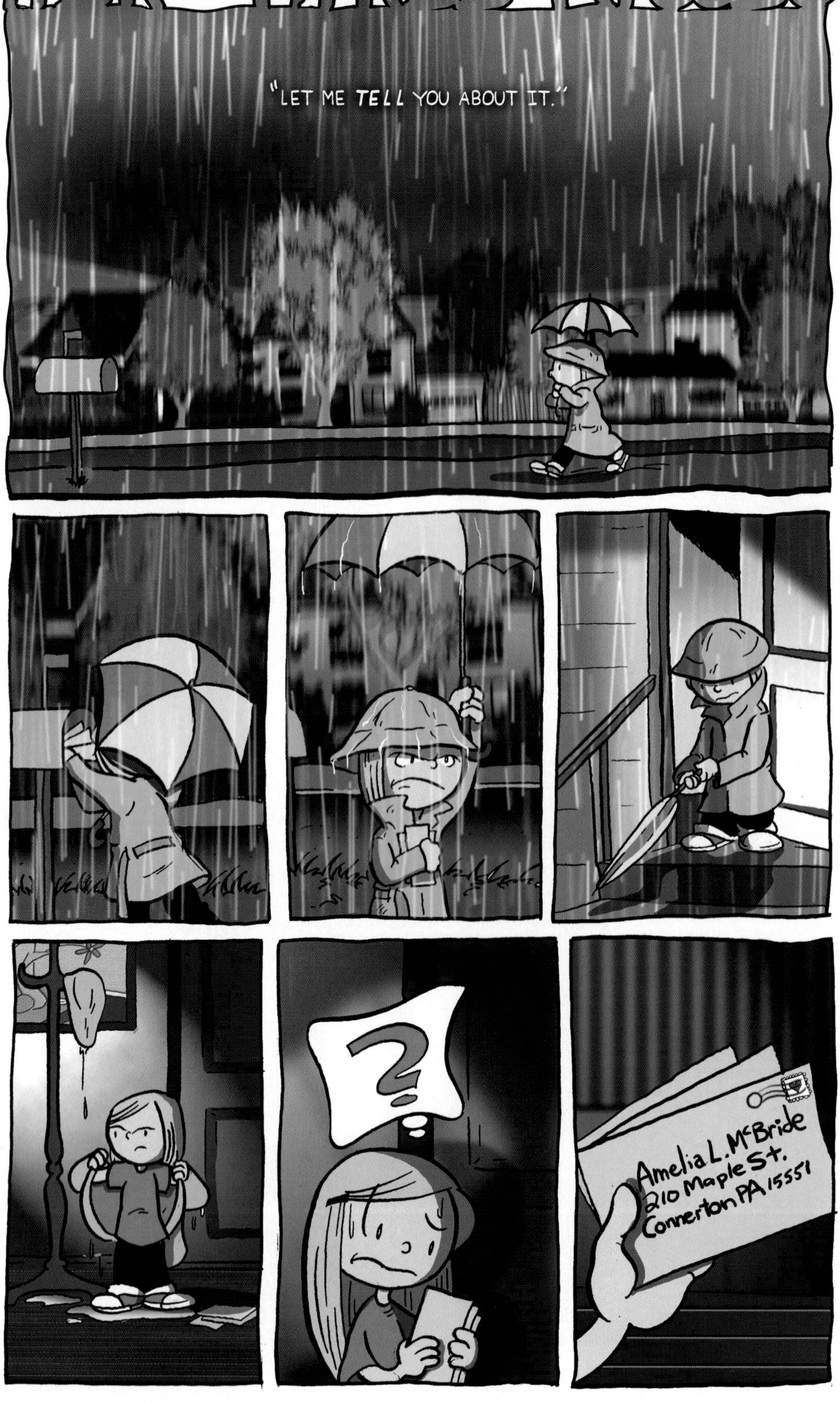
"LET ME TELL YOU ABOUT IT."
?
Amelia L. McBride
210 Maple St.
Connerton PA 15551

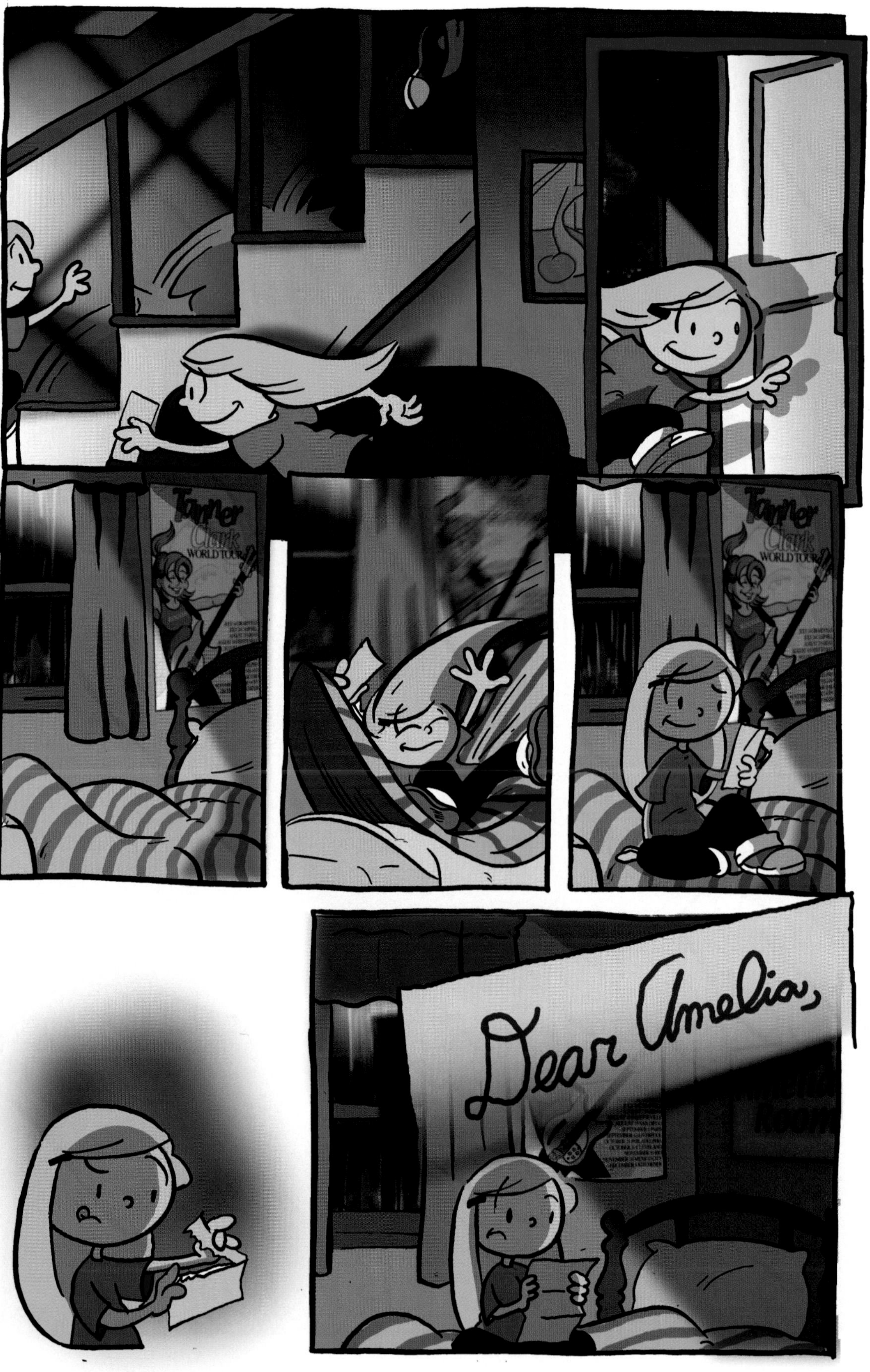
Tanner
Clark
WORLD TOUR
Tanner
Clark
WORLD TOUR
Dear Amelia,

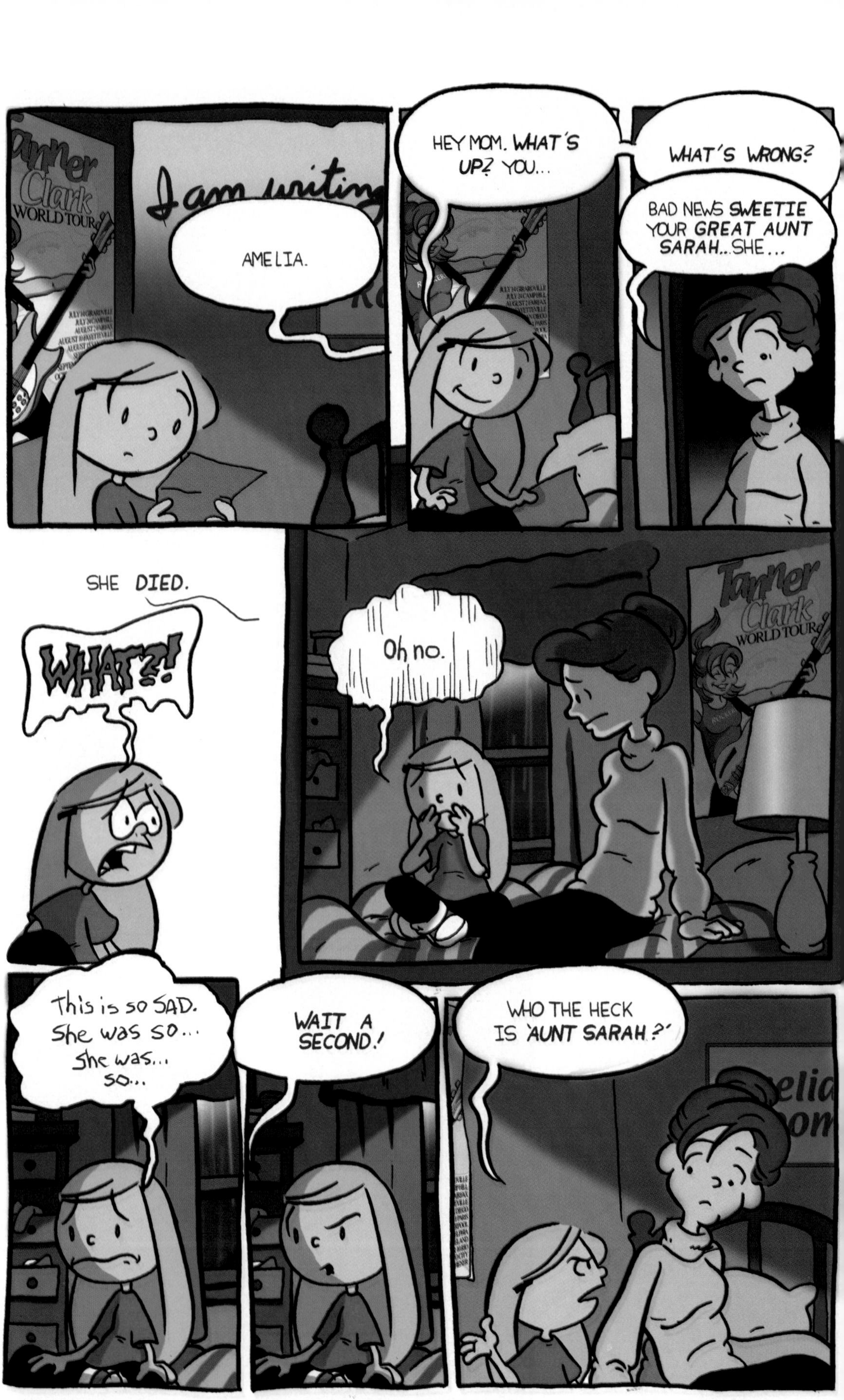

Tanner Clark WORLD TOUR
I am writing
AMELIA.
HEY MOM. WHAT'S UP? YOU...
WHAT'S WRONG?
BAD NEWS SWEETIE YOUR GREAT AUNT SARAH...SHE...
SHE DIED.
WHAT?!
Oh no.
Tanner Clark WORLD TOUR
This is so SAD. She was so... She was... so...
WAIT A SECOND!
WHO THE HECK IS 'AUNT SARAH?'

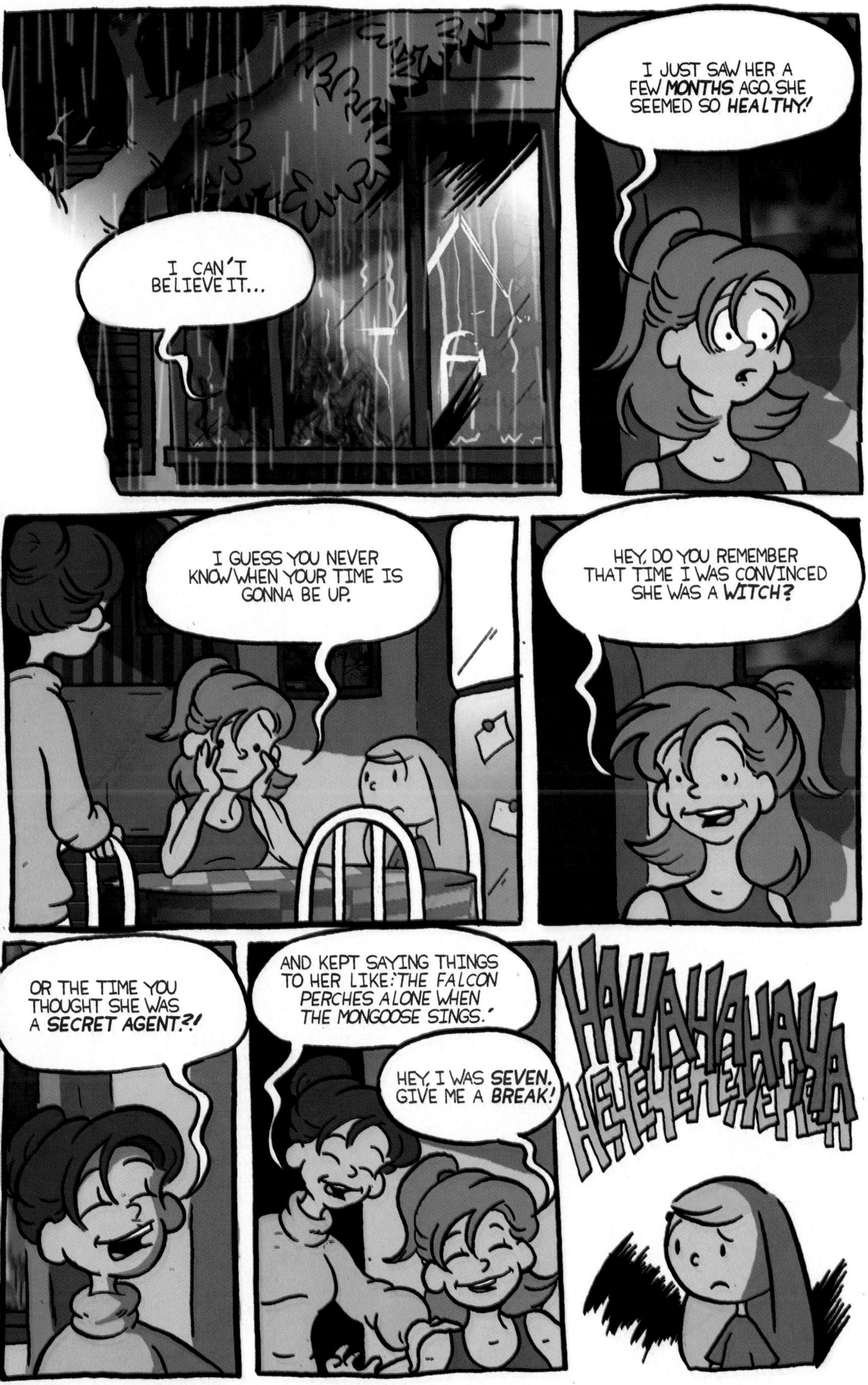
I CAN'T BELIEVE IT...
I JUST SAW HER A FEW MONTHS AGO. SHE SEEMED SO HEALTHY!
I GUESS YOU NEVER KNOW WHEN YOUR TIME IS GONNA BE UP.
HEY, DO YOU REMEMBER THAT TIME I WAS CONVINCED SHE WAS A WITCH?
OR THE TIME YOU THOUGHT SHE WAS A SECRET AGENT?!
AND KEPT SAYING THINGS TO HER LIKE: 'THE FALCON PERCHES ALONE WHEN THE MONGOOSE SINGS.'
HEY, I WAS SEVEN. GIVE ME A BREAK!
HAHAHAHAHAHA
HEHEHEHEHEHEHA

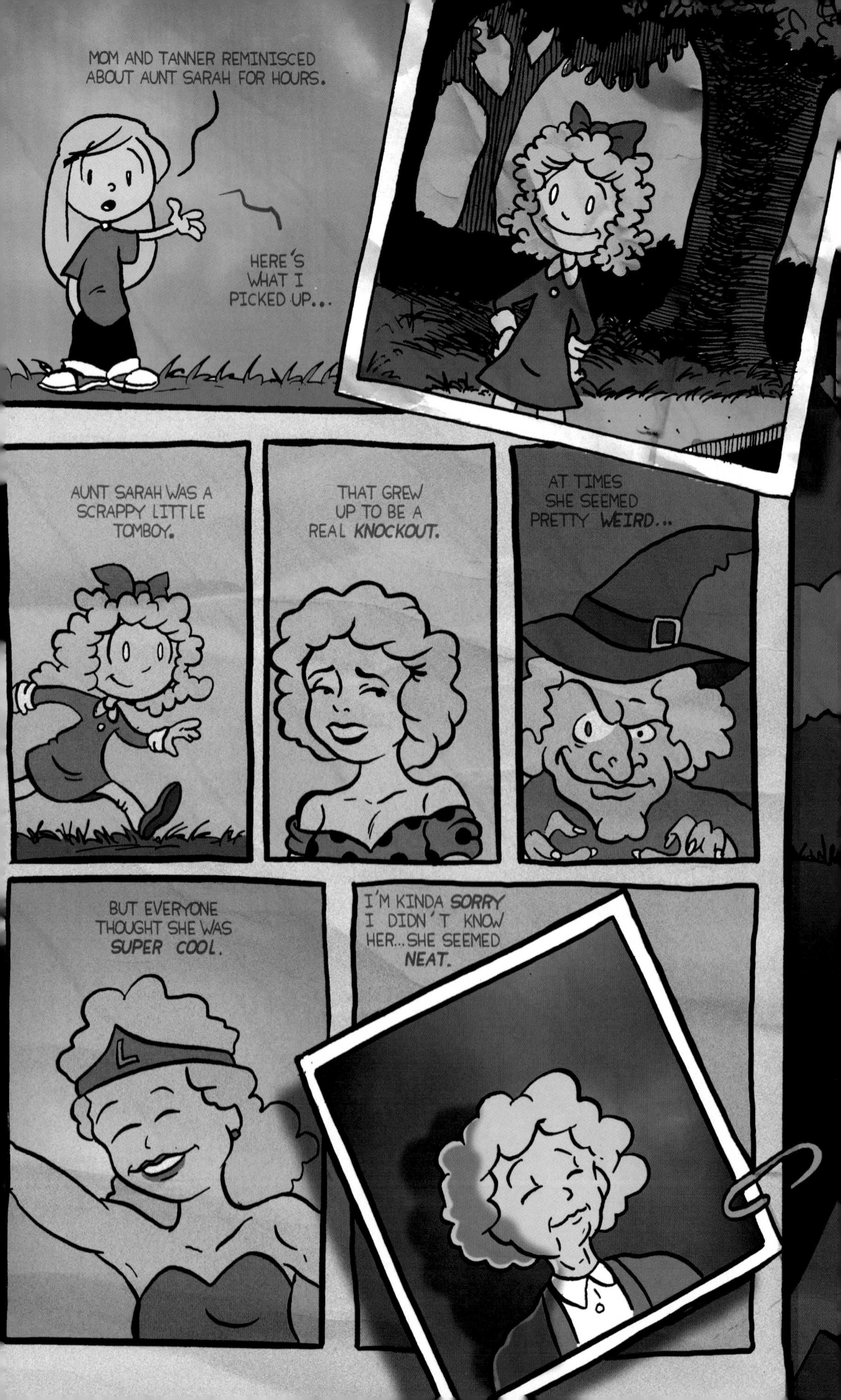
MOM AND TANNER REMINISCED ABOUT AUNT SARAH FOR HOURS.
HERE'S WHAT I PICKED UP...
AUNT SARAH WAS A SCRAPPY LITTLE TOMBOY.
THAT GREW UP TO BE A REAL KNOCKOUT.
AT TIMES SHE SEEMED PRETTY WEIRD...
BUT EVERYONE THOUGHT SHE WAS SUPER COOL.
I'M KINDA SORRY I DIDN'T KNOW HER...SHE SEEMED NEAT.

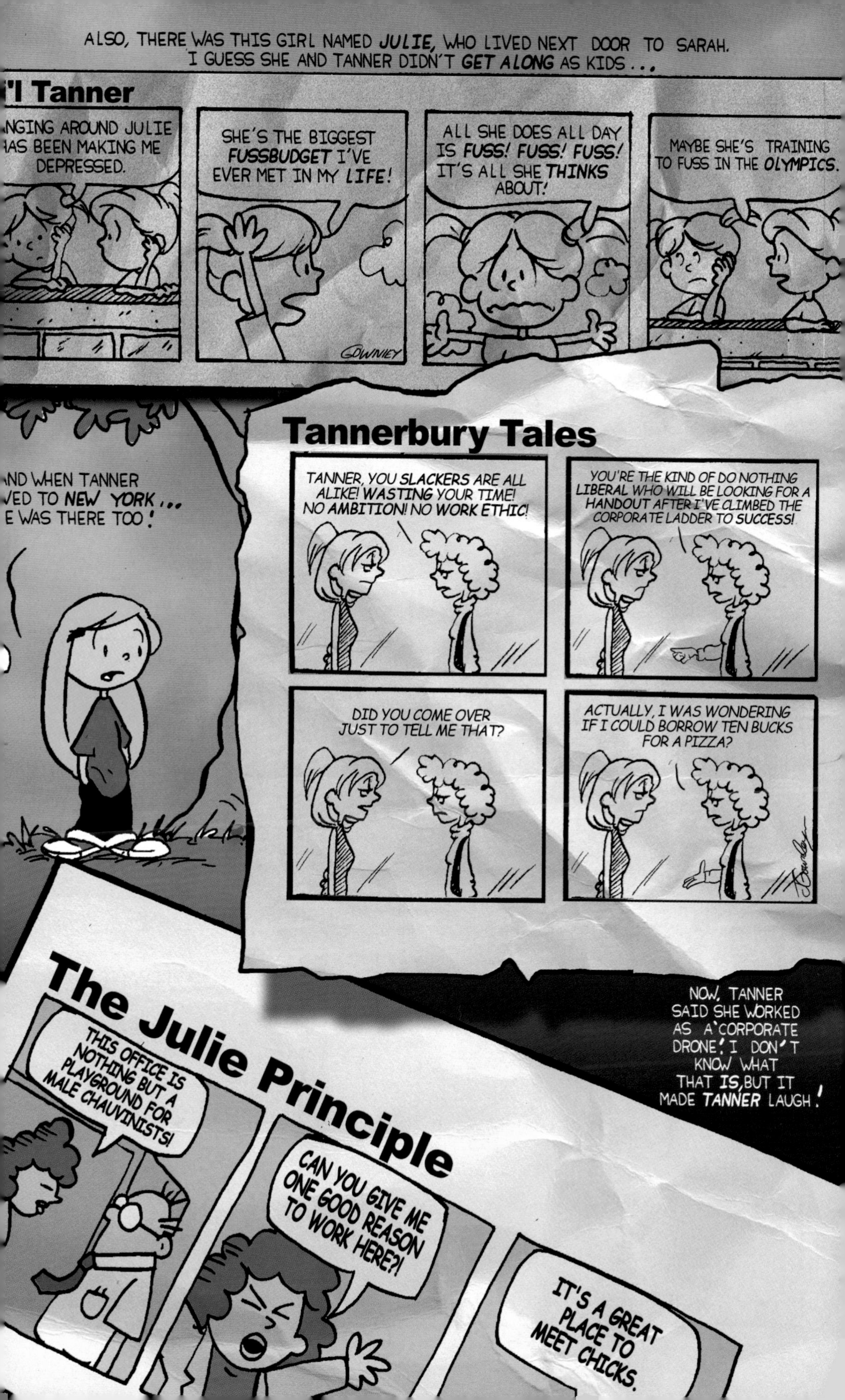
ALSO, THERE WAS THIS GIRL NAMED JULIE, WHO LIVED NEXT DOOR TO SARAH. I GUESS SHE AND TANNER DIDN'T GET ALONG AS KIDS...
'l Tanner
NGING AROUND JULIE HAS BEEN MAKING ME DEPRESSED.
SHE'S THE BIGGEST FUSSBUDGET I'VE EVER MET IN MY LIFE!
ALL SHE DOES ALL DAY IS FUSS! FUSS! FUSS! IT'S ALL SHE THINKS ABOUT!
MAYBE SHE'S TRAINING TO FUSS IN THE OLYMPICS.
AND WHEN TANNER VED TO NEW YORK... E WAS THERE TOO!
Tannerbury Tales
TANNER, YOU SLACKERS ARE ALL ALIKE! WASTING YOUR TIME! NO AMBITION! NO WORK ETHIC!
YOU'RE THE KIND OF DO NOTHING LIBERAL WHO WILL BE LOOKING FOR A HANDOUT AFTER I'VE CLIMBED THE CORPORATE LADDER TO SUCCESS!
DID YOU COME OVER JUST TO TELL ME THAT?
ACTUALLY, I WAS WONDERING IF I COULD BORROW TEN BUCKS FOR A PIZZA?
NOW, TANNER SAID SHE WORKED AS A 'CORPORATE DRONE.' I DON'T KNOW WHAT THAT IS, BUT IT MADE TANNER LAUGH!
The Julie Principle
THIS OFFICE IS NOTHING BUT A PLAYGROUND FOR MALE CHAUVINISTS!
CAN YOU GIVE ME ONE GOOD REASON TO WORK HERE?!
IT'S A GREAT PLACE TO MEET CHICKS.

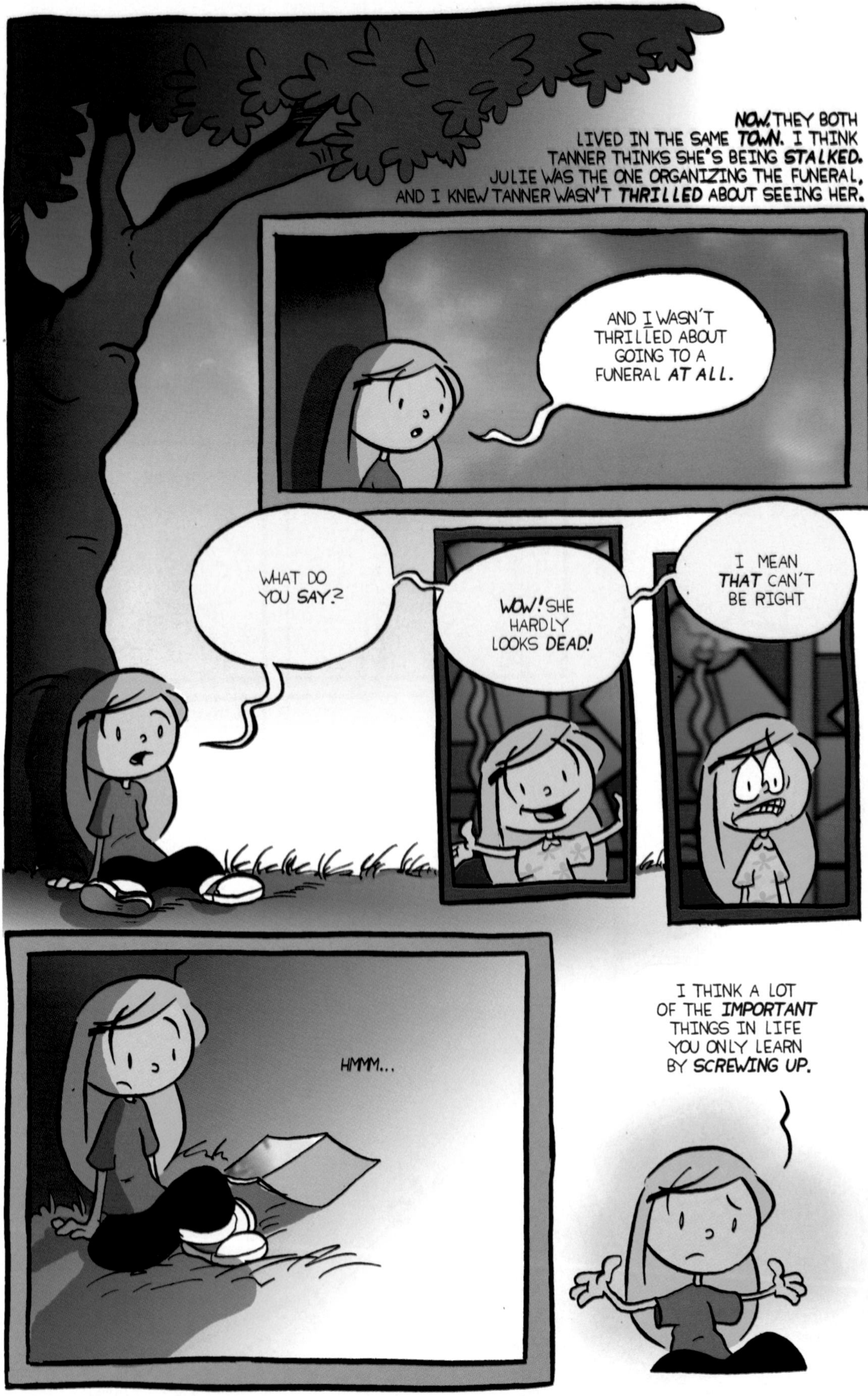
NOW, THEY BOTH LIVED IN THE SAME TOWN. I THINK TANNER THINKS SHE'S BEING STALKED. JULIE WAS THE ONE ORGANIZING THE FUNERAL, AND I KNEW TANNER WASN'T THRILLED ABOUT SEEING HER.
AND I WASN'T THRILLED ABOUT GOING TO A FUNERAL AT ALL.
WHAT DO YOU SAY?
WOW! SHE HARDLY LOOKS DEAD!
I MEAN THAT CAN'T BE RIGHT
HMMM...
I THINK A LOT OF THE IMPORTANT THINGS IN LIFE YOU ONLY LEARN BY SCREWING UP.

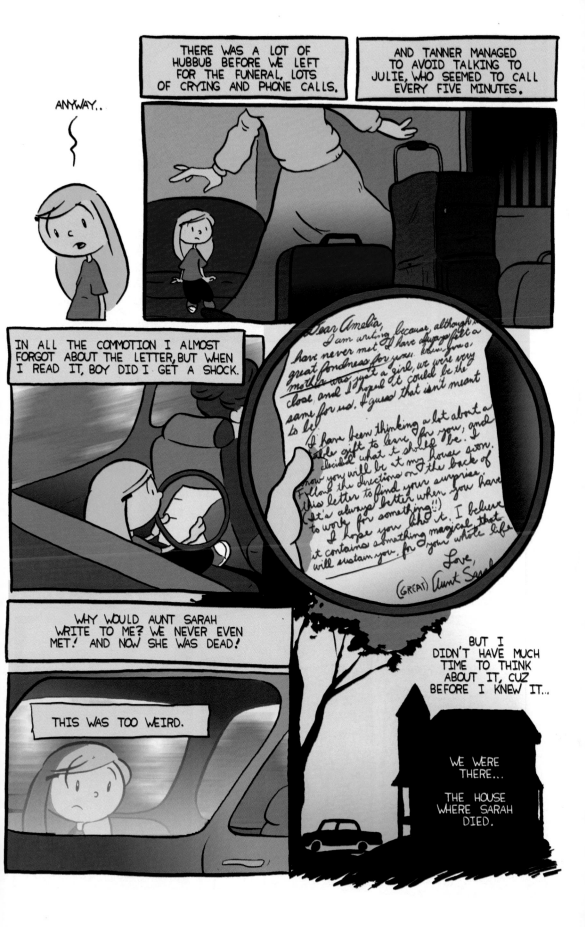

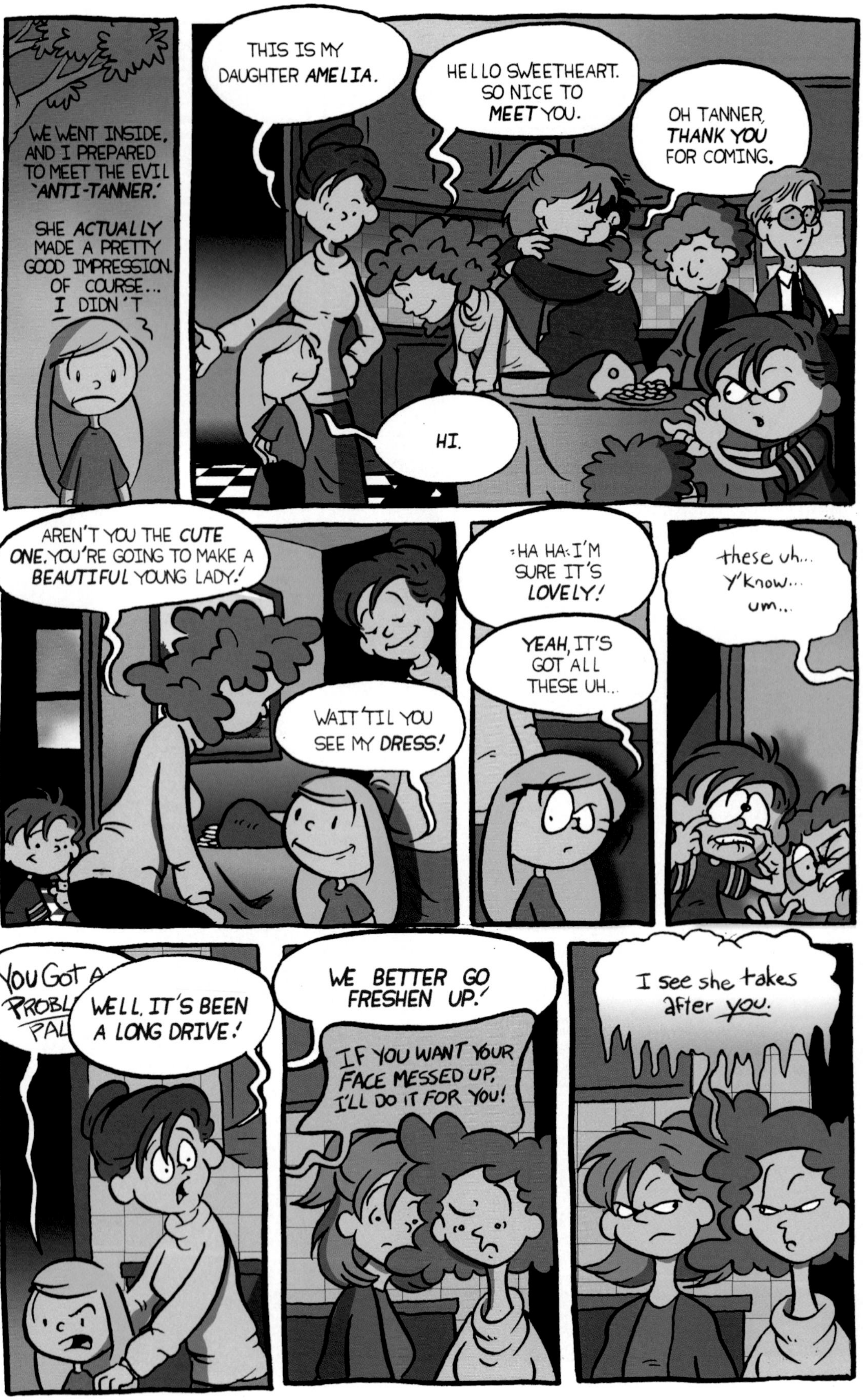
WE WENT INSIDE, AND I PREPARED TO MEET THE EVIL 'ANTI-TANNER.'
SHE ACTUALLY MADE A PRETTY GOOD IMPRESSION. OF COURSE... I DIDN'T
THIS IS MY DAUGHTER AMELIA.
HELLO SWEETHEART. SO NICE TO MEET YOU.
OH TANNER, THANK YOU FOR COMING.
HI.
AREN'T YOU THE CUTE ONE. YOU'RE GOING TO MAKE A BEAUTIFUL YOUNG LADY!
WAIT 'TIL YOU SEE MY DRESS!
HA HA I'M SURE IT'S LOVELY!
YEAH, IT'S GOT ALL THESE UH...
these uh... y'know... um...
YOU GOT A PROBL PAL
WELL, IT'S BEEN A LONG DRIVE!
WE BETTER GO FRESHEN UP!
IF YOU WANT YOUR FACE MESSED UP, I'LL DO IT FOR YOU!
I see she takes after you.

I DON'T KNOW, I WAS ACTUALLY KINDA LOOKING FORWARD TO WEARING A **DRESS**. IT FELT KINDA **GROWN UP**, AND I THOUGHT I'D LOOK... DIFFERENT OR SOMETHING. IT TURNS OUT I JUST LOOK LIKE **ME**, ONLY **PINKER** AND WITH A BOW ON MY **BUTT**.

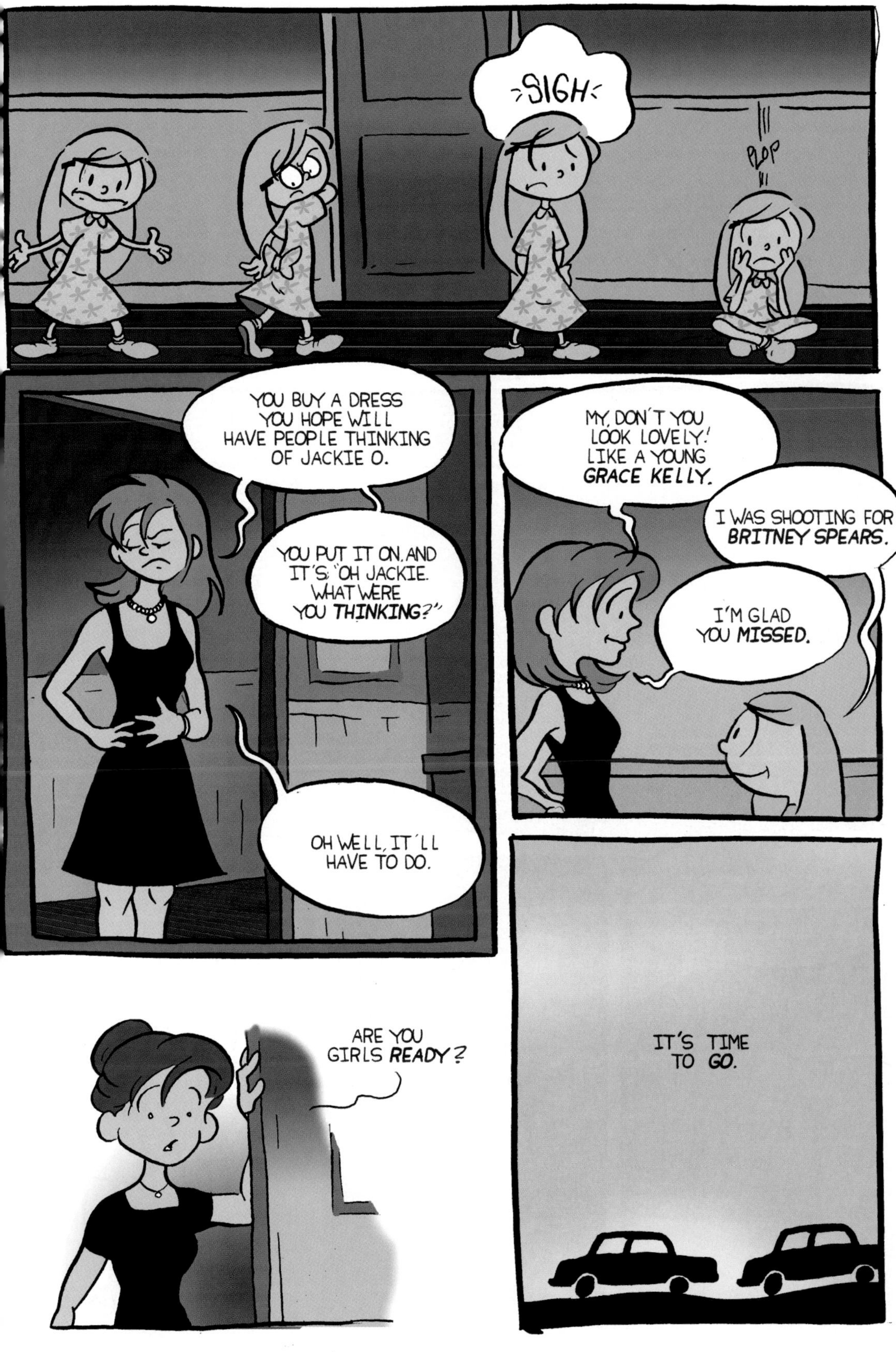
SIGH
PLOP
YOU BUY A DRESS YOU HOPE WILL HAVE PEOPLE THINKING OF JACKIE O.
YOU PUT IT ON, AND IT'S: "OH JACKIE. WHAT WERE YOU THINKING?"
OH WELL, IT'LL HAVE TO DO.
MY, DON'T YOU LOOK LOVELY! LIKE A YOUNG GRACE KELLY.
I WAS SHOOTING FOR BRITNEY SPEARS.
I'M GLAD YOU MISSED.
ARE YOU GIRLS READY?
IT'S TIME TO GO.

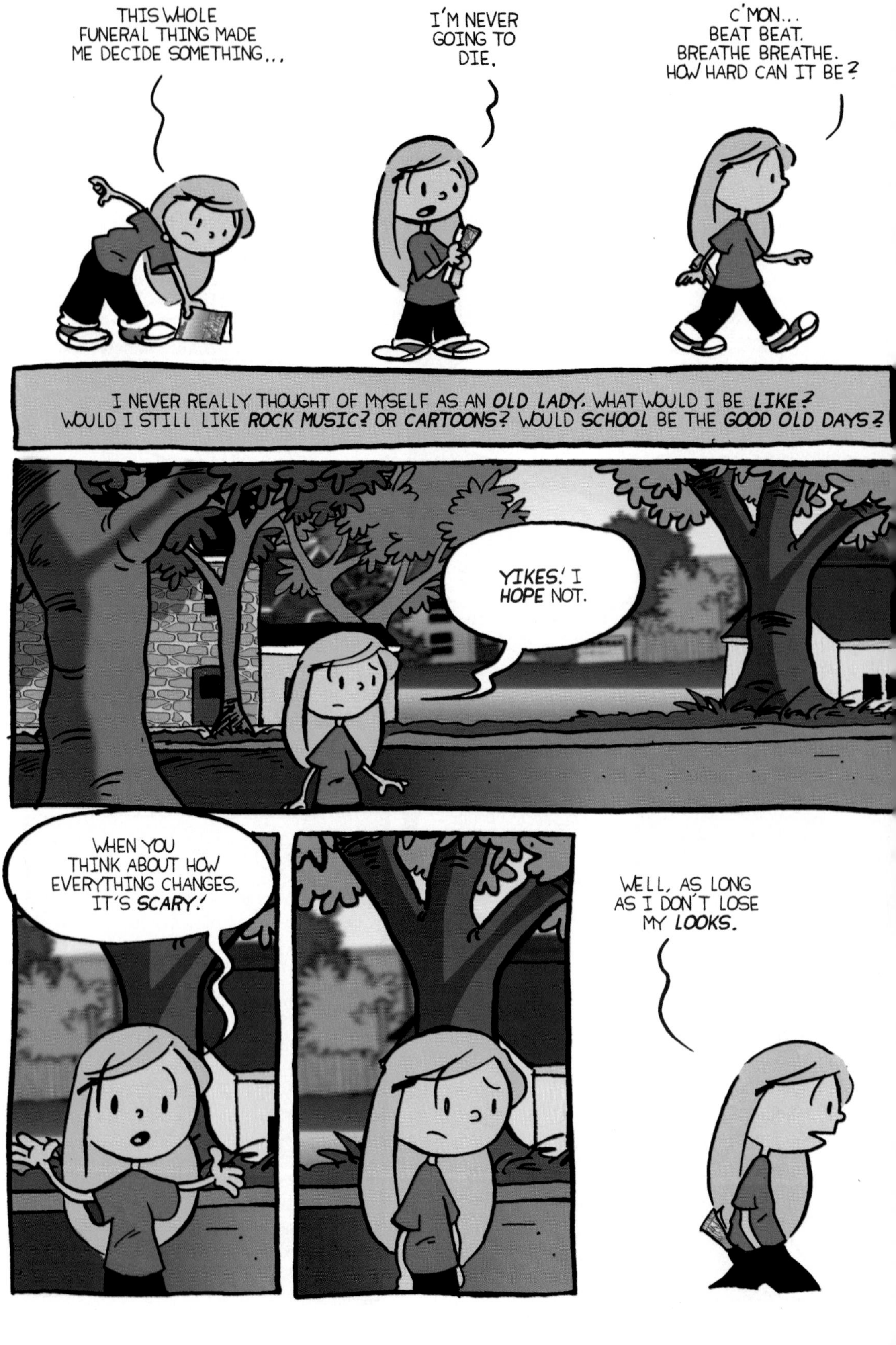

THIS WHOLE FUNERAL THING MADE ME DECIDE SOMETHING...
I'M NEVER GOING TO DIE.
C'MON... BEAT BEAT. BREATHE BREATHE. HOW HARD CAN IT BE?
I NEVER REALLY THOUGHT OF MYSELF AS AN OLD LADY. WHAT WOULD I BE LIKE? WOULD I STILL LIKE ROCK MUSIC? OR CARTOONS? WOULD SCHOOL BE THE GOOD OLD DAYS?
YIKES! I HOPE NOT.
WHEN YOU THINK ABOUT HOW EVERYTHING CHANGES, IT'S SCARY!
WELL, AS LONG AS I DON'T LOSE MY LOOKS.

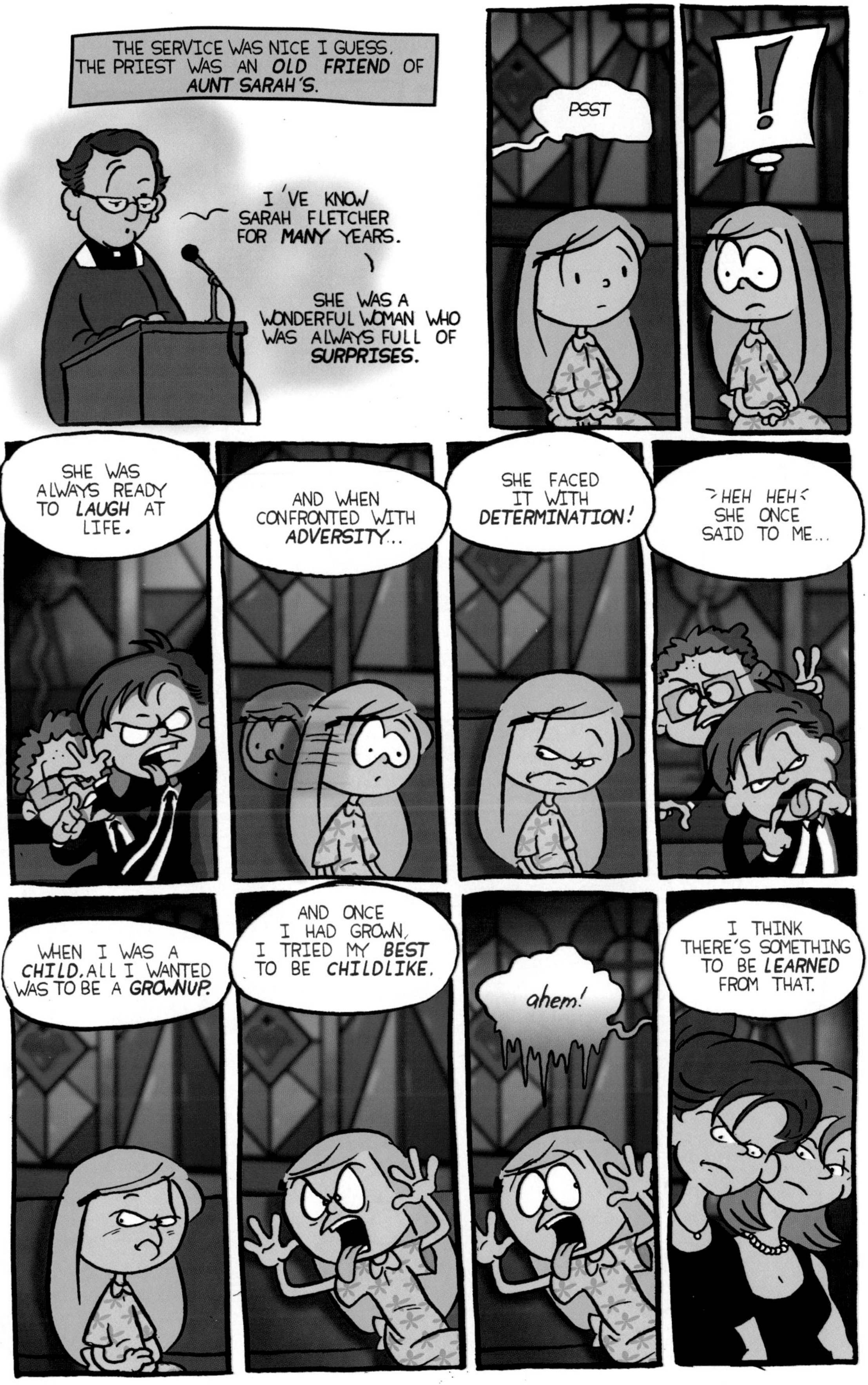
THE SERVICE WAS NICE I GUESS. THE PRIEST WAS AN OLD FRIEND OF AUNT SARAH'S.
I'VE KNOW SARAH FLETCHER FOR MANY YEARS.
SHE WAS A WONDERFUL WOMAN WHO WAS ALWAYS FULL OF SURPRISES.
PSST
!
SHE WAS ALWAYS READY TO LAUGH AT LIFE.
AND WHEN CONFRONTED WITH ADVERSITY...
SHE FACED IT WITH DETERMINATION!
HEH HEH SHE ONCE SAID TO ME...
WHEN I WAS A CHILD, ALL I WANTED WAS TO BE A GROWNUP.
AND ONCE I HAD GROWN, I TRIED MY BEST TO BE CHILDLIKE.
ahem!
I THINK THERE'S SOMETHING TO BE LEARNED FROM THAT.

AFTERWARDS, THERE WAS A RECEPTION AT THE HOUSE. BUT ALL *I* WANTED TO DO WAS GET **CHANGED**, AND **GET AWAY**.

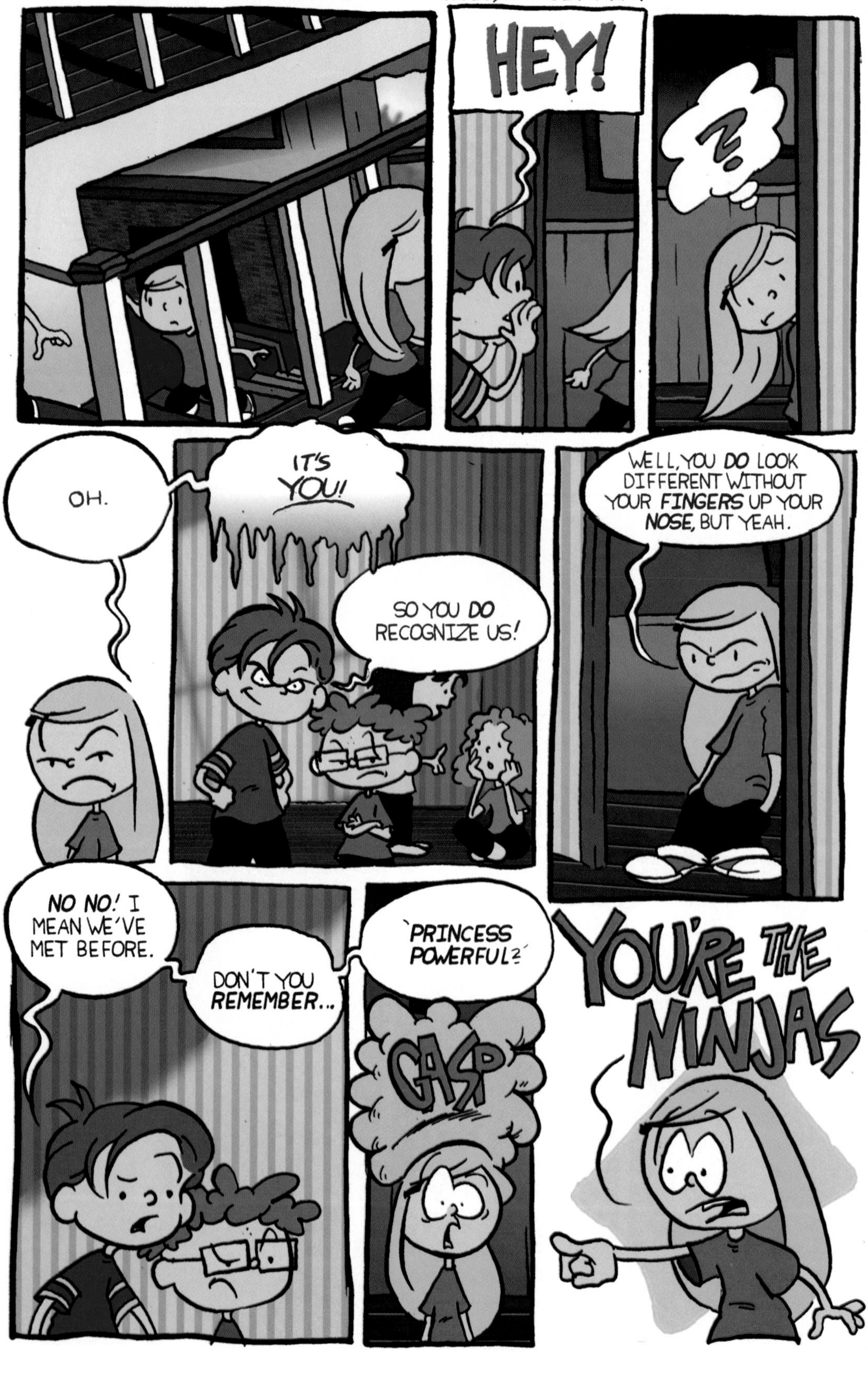

HEY!
?
OH.
IT'S YOU!
SO YOU **DO** RECOGNIZE US!
WELL, YOU **DO** LOOK DIFFERENT WITHOUT YOUR **FINGERS** UP YOUR **NOSE**, BUT YEAH.
NO NO! I MEAN WE'VE MET BEFORE.
DON'T YOU **REMEMBER...**
'**PRINCESS POWERFUL**?'
GASP
YOU'RE THE NINJAS

NINJA *KYLE,* AND *ED!* I NEVER IN A MILLION YEARS THOUGHT I'D RUN INTO THEM *HERE!*

IF REGGIE WAS MAD *BEFORE,* HE'D *FREAK* IF HE KNEW I WAS SHAKING HANDS WITH THE *ENEMY.*

THERE WERE OTHER KIDS TOO, LIKE THIS ONE *WEIRDO* WHO JUST STOOD IN THE *CORNER...*

AND THESE TWO GIRLS, TRISH AND JOANNE (NONE OF THEM WERE NINJAS.)

ALL OF THEM WERE AT THE FUNERAL.

THE *WEIRDEST* THING ABOUT ED AND KYLE IS THAT THEIR MOM IS *JULIE,* THE EVIL *ANTI-TANNER.* I MEAN WHO *KNEW?*

BUT WE STARTED TALKING, AND THEY SEEMED *OKAY.*

IT TURNED OUT *THEIR* PARENTS WERE DIVORCED *TOO.*

DID THEY BUY YOU ANY OF THOSE *CORNY BOOKS* TO 'HELP YOU THROUGH IT?'

LIKE, 'EVEN PENGUINS SOMETIMES PART?'

OR: "WHEN KOALAS CAN'T COMMUNICATE."

OR: "YOUR PARENTS LOVE YOU, THEY JUST HATE EACH OTHER"

OR: "MOMMY'S NEW FRIEND THE MAILMAN"

YIKES! I'M *GLAD* I DIDN'T HAVE TO READ *THAT* ONE!

THIS IS *BORING!*

HAHAHAHAHAHAHAHAHAHA

CAN'T WE PLAY A GAME OR SOMETHING?

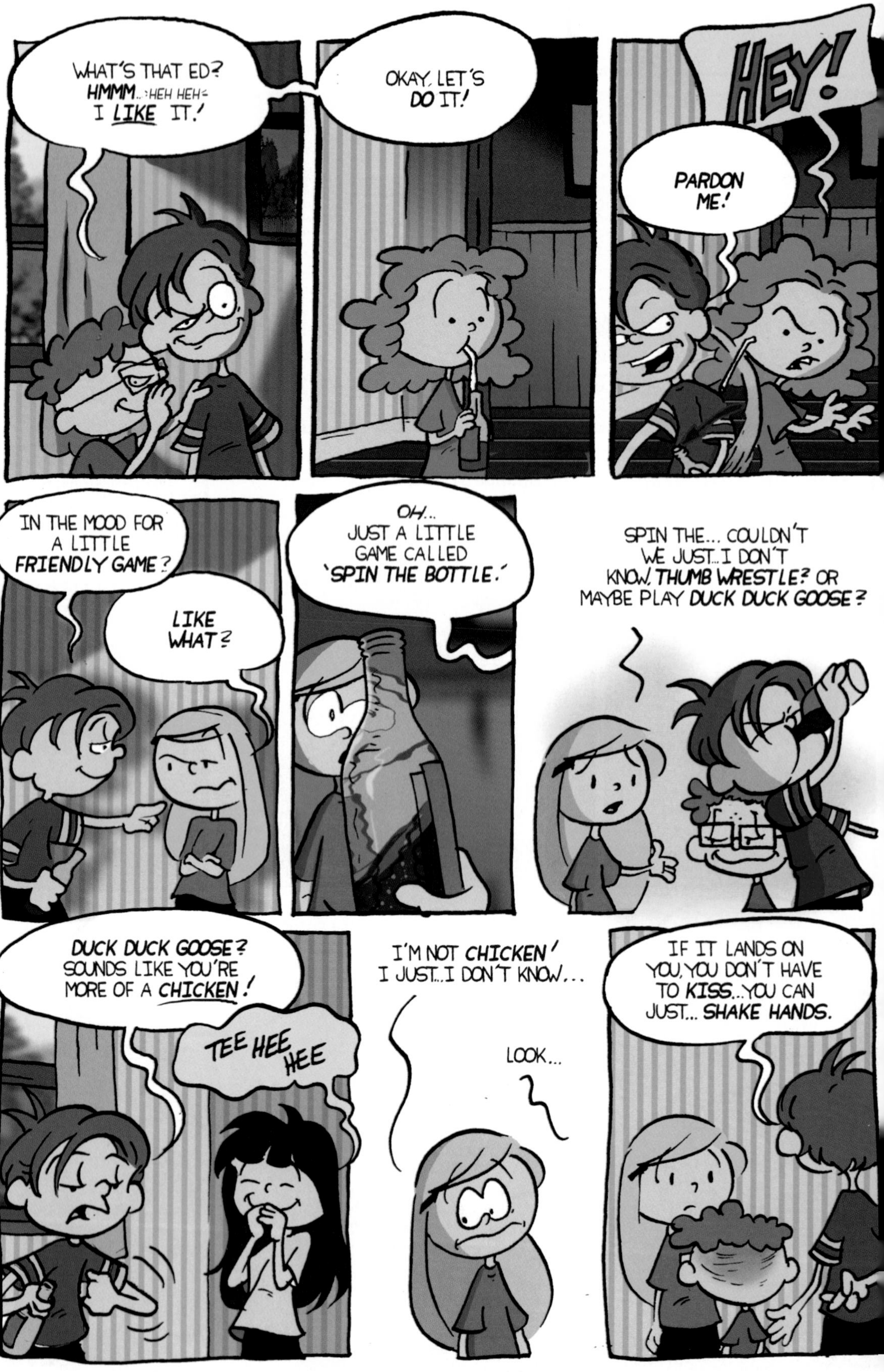

WHAT'S THAT ED? HMMM... HEH HEH I LIKE IT!
OKAY, LET'S DO IT!
HEY!
PARDON ME!
IN THE MOOD FOR A LITTLE FRIENDLY GAME?
LIKE WHAT?
OH... JUST A LITTLE GAME CALLED 'SPIN THE BOTTLE.'
SPIN THE... COULDN'T WE JUST...I DON'T KNOW, THUMB WRESTLE? OR MAYBE PLAY DUCK DUCK GOOSE?
DUCK DUCK GOOSE? SOUNDS LIKE YOU'RE MORE OF A CHICKEN!
TEE HEE HEE
I'M NOT CHICKEN! I JUST...I DON'T KNOW...
LOOK...
IF IT LANDS ON YOU, YOU DON'T HAVE TO KISS...YOU CAN JUST... SHAKE HANDS.

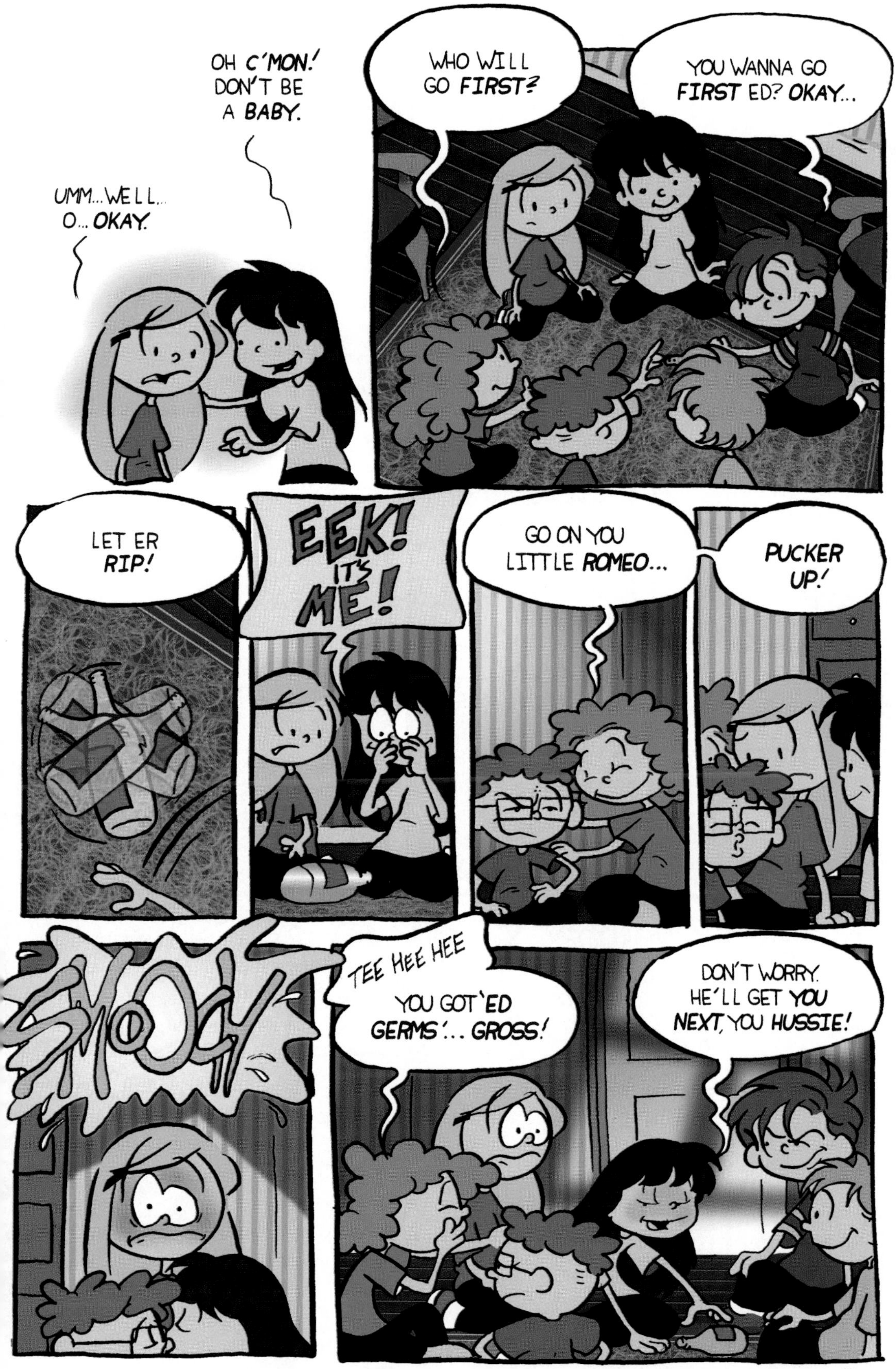
UMM... WELL... O... OKAY.
OH C'MON! DON'T BE A BABY.
WHO WILL GO FIRST?
YOU WANNA GO FIRST ED? OKAY...
LET ER RIP!
EEK! IT'S ME!
GO ON YOU LITTLE ROMEO...
PUCKER UP!
SMOOCH
TEE HEE HEE
YOU GOT 'ED GERMS'... GROSS!
DON'T WORRY. HE'LL GET YOU NEXT, YOU HUSSIE!

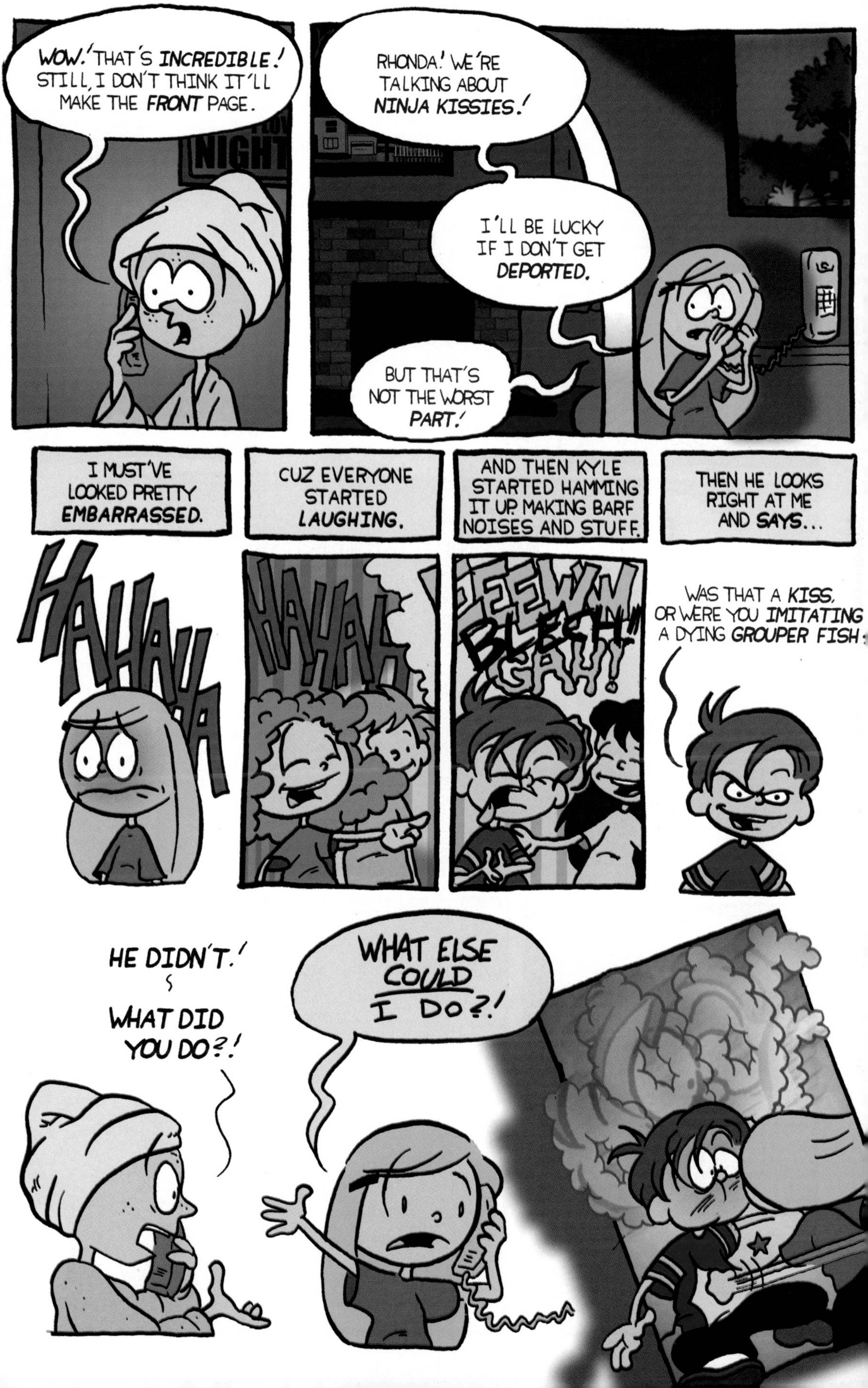
WOW! THAT'S INCREDIBLE! STILL, I DON'T THINK IT'LL MAKE THE FRONT PAGE.
RHONDA! WE'RE TALKING ABOUT NINJA KISSIES!
I'LL BE LUCKY IF I DON'T GET DEPORTED.
BUT THAT'S NOT THE WORST PART!
I MUST'VE LOOKED PRETTY EMBARRASSED.
HAHAHA
CUZ EVERYONE STARTED LAUGHING.
HAHAH
AND THEN KYLE STARTED HAMMING IT UP. MAKING BARF NOISES AND STUFF.
EEEWW BLECH!! GAH!
THEN HE LOOKS RIGHT AT ME AND SAYS...
WAS THAT A KISS, OR WERE YOU IMITATING A DYING GROUPER FISH?
HE DIDN'T! WHAT DID YOU DO?!
WHAT ELSE COULD I DO?!

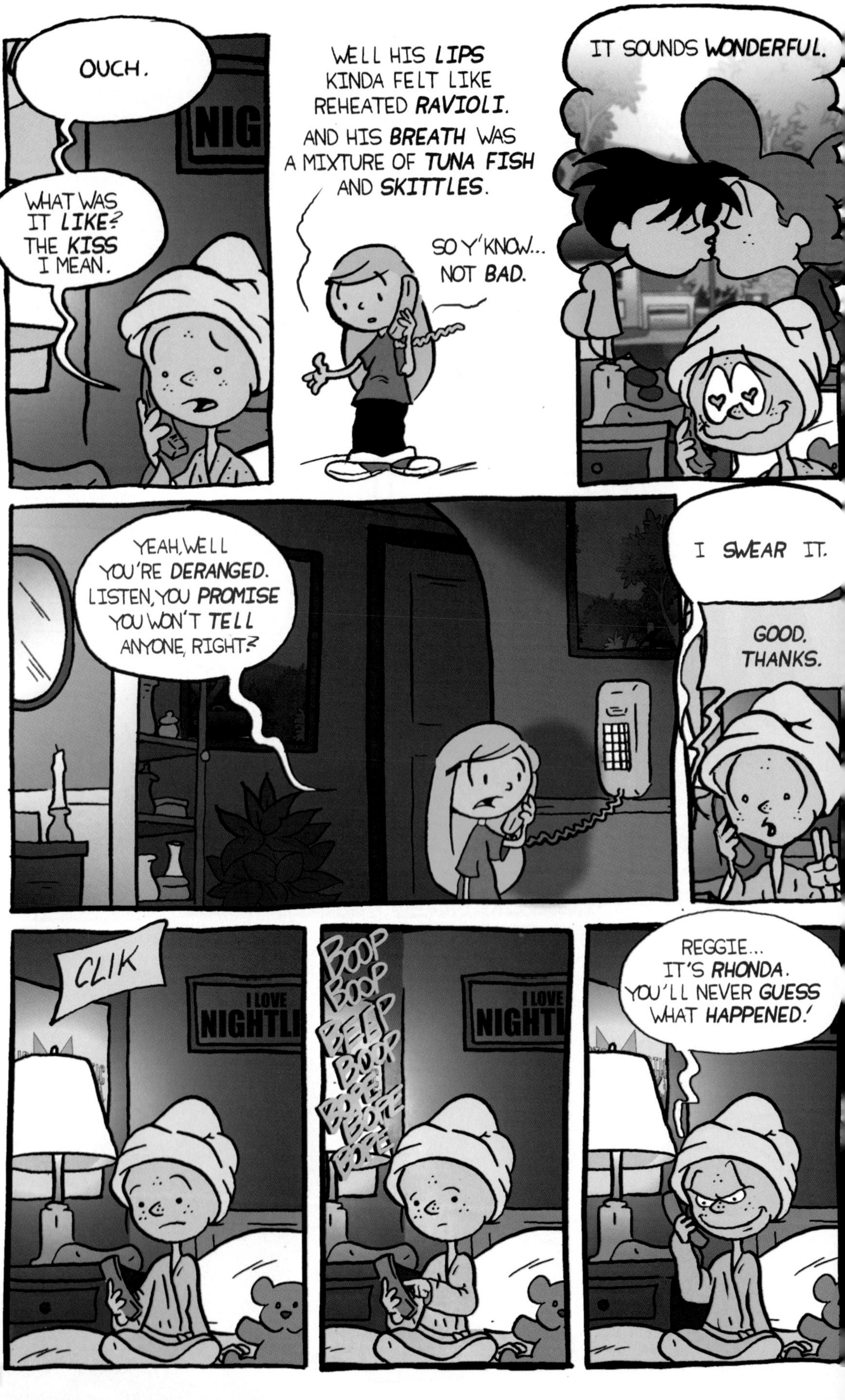
OUCH.
NIG
WHAT WAS IT LIKE? THE KISS I MEAN.
WELL HIS LIPS KINDA FELT LIKE REHEATED RAVIOLI.
AND HIS BREATH WAS A MIXTURE OF TUNA FISH AND SKITTLES.
SO Y'KNOW... NOT BAD.
IT SOUNDS WONDERFUL.
YEAH, WELL YOU'RE DERANGED. LISTEN, YOU PROMISE YOU WON'T TELL ANYONE, RIGHT?
I SWEAR IT.
GOOD. THANKS.
CLIK
I LOVE NIGHTLI
BOOP BOOP BEEP BOOP
I LOVE NIGHTL
REGGIE... IT'S RHONDA. YOU'LL NEVER GUESS WHAT HAPPENED!

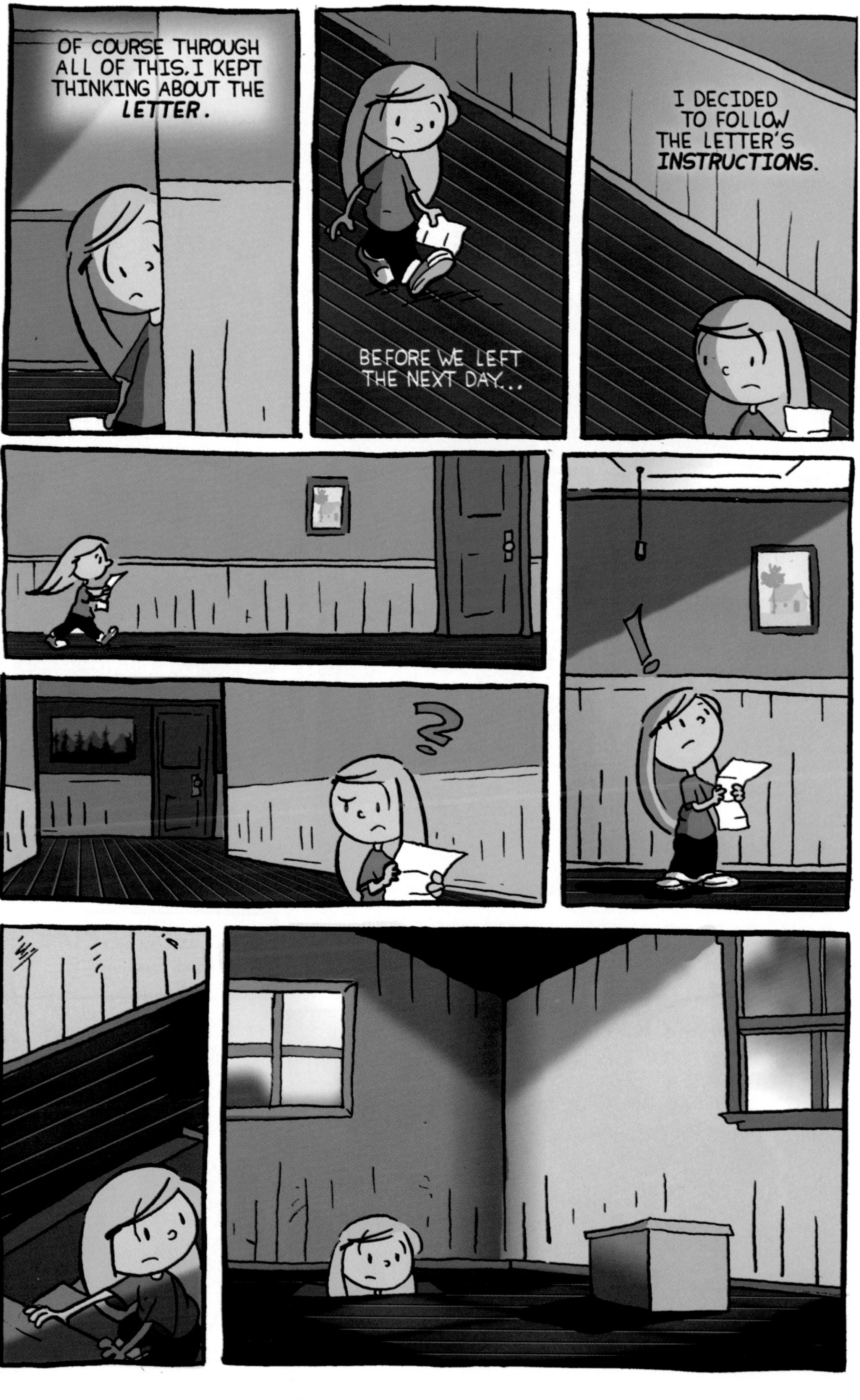
OF COURSE THROUGH ALL OF THIS, I KEPT THINKING ABOUT THE **LETTER**.
BEFORE WE LEFT THE NEXT DAY...
I DECIDED TO FOLLOW THE LETTER'S **INSTRUCTIONS**.

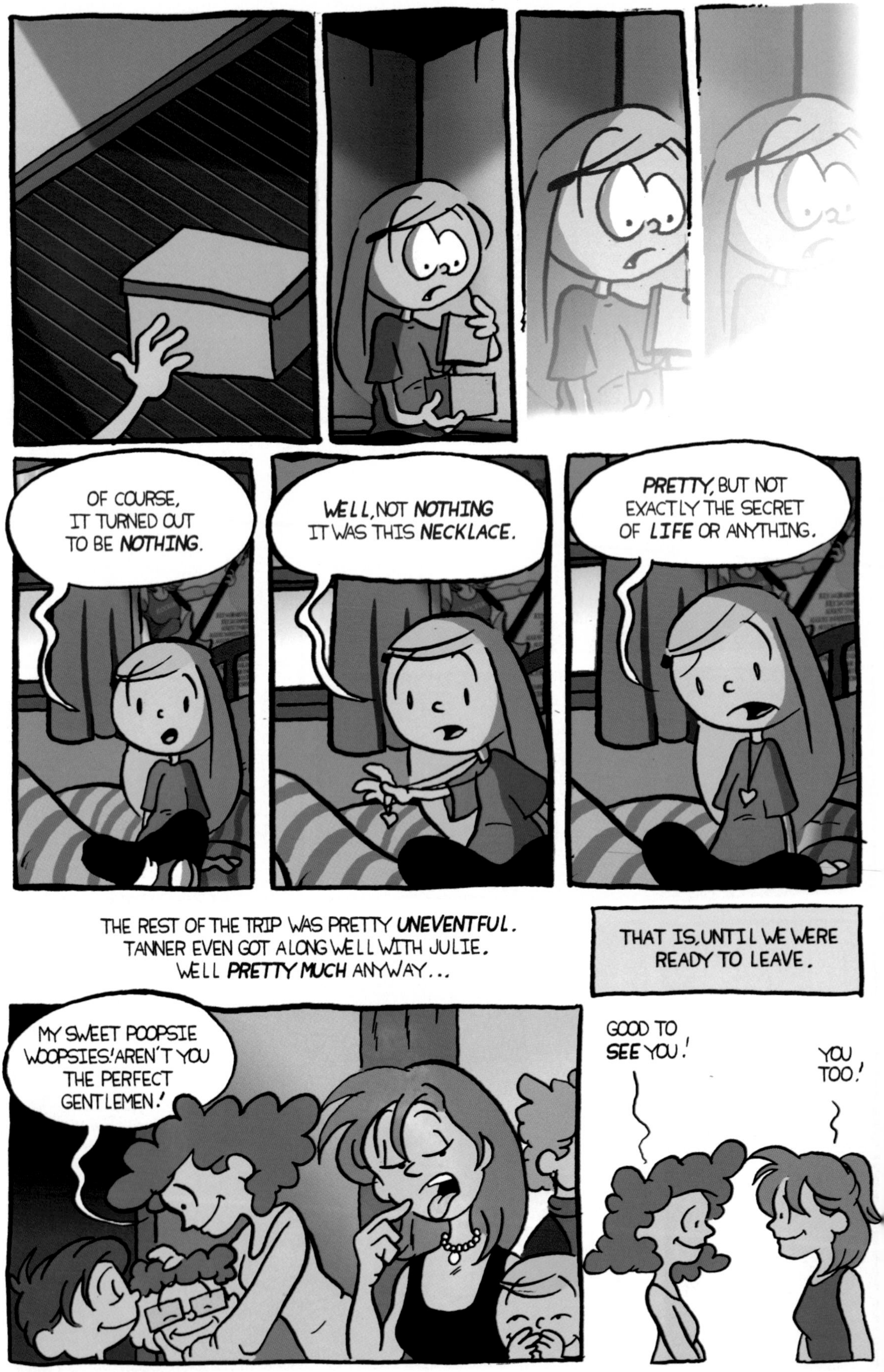
OF COURSE, IT TURNED OUT TO BE NOTHING.
WELL, NOT NOTHING IT WAS THIS NECKLACE.
PRETTY, BUT NOT EXACTLY THE SECRET OF LIFE OR ANYTHING.
THE REST OF THE TRIP WAS PRETTY UNEVENTFUL. TANNER EVEN GOT ALONG WELL WITH JULIE. WELL PRETTY MUCH ANYWAY...
THAT IS, UNTIL WE WERE READY TO LEAVE.
MY SWEET POOPSIE WOOPSIES! AREN'T YOU THE PERFECT GENTLEMEN!
GOOD TO SEE YOU!
YOU TOO!

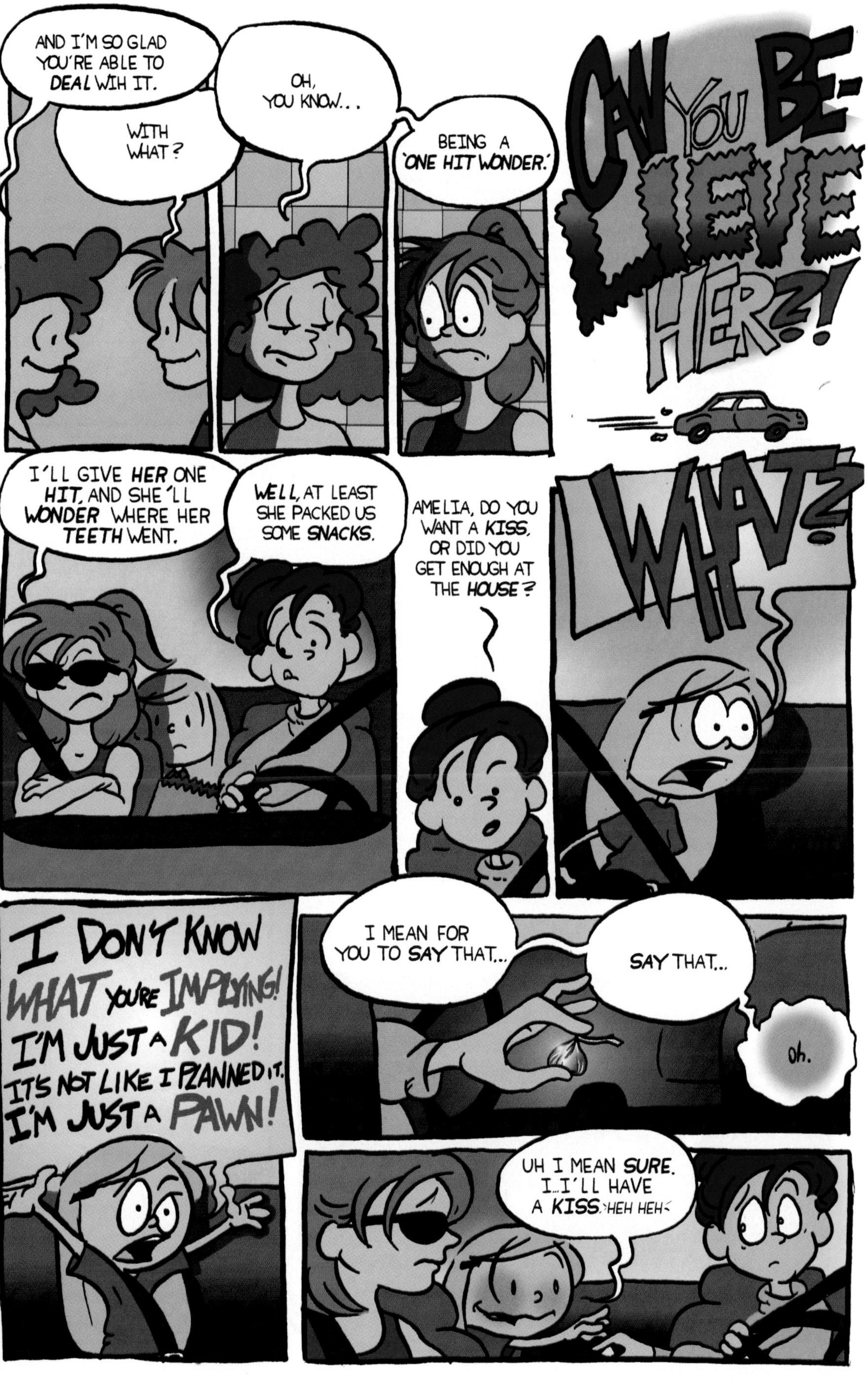
AND I'M SO GLAD YOU'RE ABLE TO DEAL WIH IT.
WITH WHAT?
OH, YOU KNOW...
BEING A 'ONE HIT WONDER.'
CAN YOU BE-LIEVE HER?!
I'LL GIVE HER ONE HIT, AND SHE'LL WONDER WHERE HER TEETH WENT.
WELL, AT LEAST SHE PACKED US SOME SNACKS.
AMELIA, DO YOU WANT A KISS, OR DID YOU GET ENOUGH AT THE HOUSE?
WHAT?
I DON'T KNOW WHAT YOU'RE IMPLYING! I'M JUST A KID! IT'S NOT LIKE I PLANNED IT. I'M JUST A PAWN!
I MEAN FOR YOU TO SAY THAT...
SAY THAT...
Oh.
UH I MEAN SURE. I...I'LL HAVE A KISS. HEH HEH

OBVIOUSLY, I DECIDED TO KEEP MY MOUTH SHUT FOR THE REST OF THE RIDE HOME.

WHEN WE GOT HOME, I DECIDED TO TAKE A WALK OVER TO REGGIE'S. I THOUGHT MAYBE THINGS HAD BLOWN OVER WHILE I WAS GONE.

OR NOT...

No Solicitors
No Loitering
No Amelias

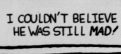

I COULDN'T BELIEVE HE WAS STILL MAD!

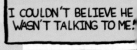

I COULDN'T BELIEVE HE WASN'T TALKING TO ME!"

UP... UP...

AND AWAAAAy!

I COULDN'T BELIEVE I HAD TO APOLOGIZE TO THIS DOOFUS!

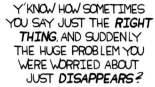

Y'KNOW HOW SOMETIMES YOU SAY JUST THE *RIGHT THING*, AND SUDDENLY THE HUGE PROBLEM YOU WERE WORRIED ABOUT JUST *DISAPPEARS*?

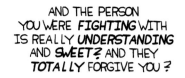

AND THE PERSON YOU WERE *FIGHTING* WITH IS REALLY *UNDERSTANDING* AND *SWEET*? AND THEY *TOTALLY* FORGIVE YOU?

WELL THIS WASN'T LIKE THAT.

Mercy.

Uncle.

WHAT IS WRONG WITH YOU? JUST LEAVE ME ALONE!

GOODBYE.

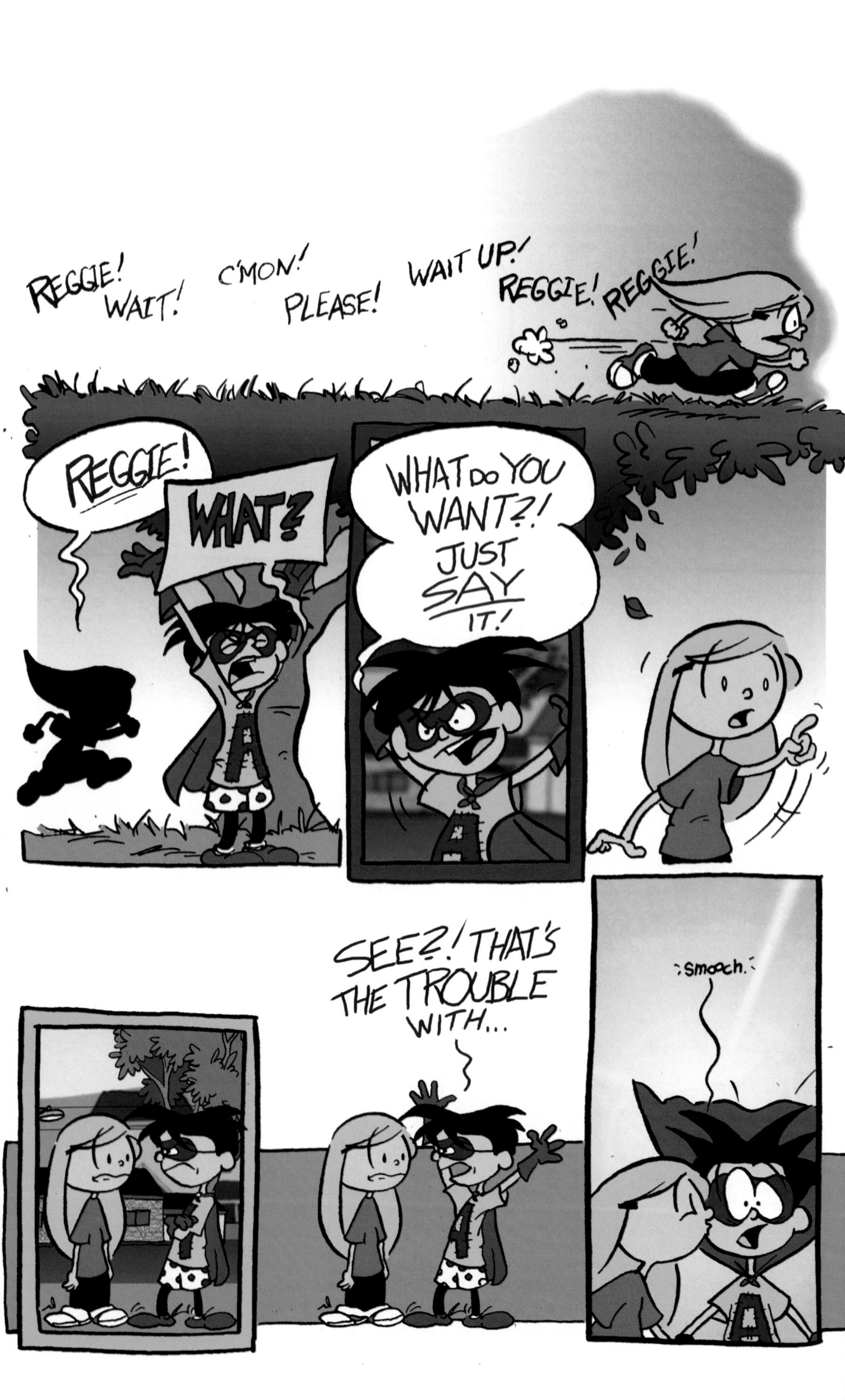

REGGIE!
WAIT!
C'MON!
PLEASE!
WAIT UP!
REGGIE!
REGGIE!
REGGIE!
WHAT?
WHAT DO YOU WANT?! JUST SAY IT!
SEE?! THAT'S THE TROUBLE WITH...
smooch.

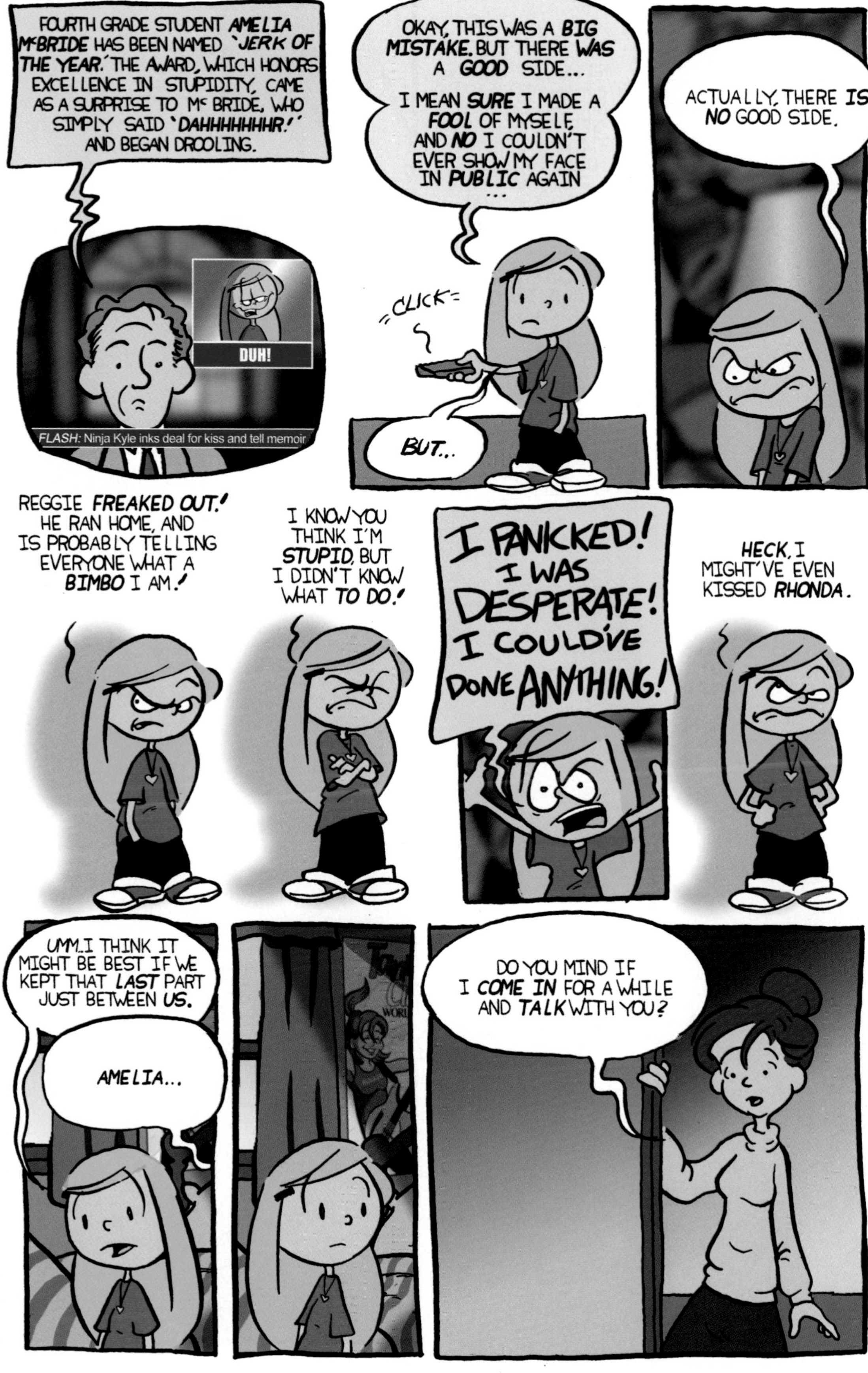
FOURTH GRADE STUDENT AMELIA McBRIDE HAS BEEN NAMED 'JERK OF THE YEAR.' THE AWARD, WHICH HONORS EXCELLENCE IN STUPIDITY, CAME AS A SURPRISE TO McBRIDE, WHO SIMPLY SAID 'DAHHHHHHHR!' AND BEGAN DROOLING.
DUH!
FLASH: Ninja Kyle inks deal for kiss and tell memoir
OKAY, THIS WAS A BIG MISTAKE. BUT THERE WAS A GOOD SIDE...
I MEAN SURE I MADE A FOOL OF MYSELF, AND NO I COULDN'T EVER SHOW MY FACE IN PUBLIC AGAIN ...
CLICK
BUT...
ACTUALLY, THERE IS NO GOOD SIDE.
REGGIE FREAKED OUT! HE RAN HOME, AND IS PROBABLY TELLING EVERYONE WHAT A BIMBO I AM!
I KNOW YOU THINK I'M STUPID, BUT I DIDN'T KNOW WHAT TO DO!
I PANICKED! I WAS DESPERATE! I COULD'VE DONE ANYTHING!
HECK, I MIGHT'VE EVEN KISSED RHONDA.
UMM..I THINK IT MIGHT BE BEST IF WE KEPT THAT LAST PART JUST BETWEEN US.
AMELIA...
DO YOU MIND IF I COME IN FOR A WHILE AND TALK WITH YOU?

MOM SAT DOWN AND REALLY STARTED TALKING ABOUT SARAH, AND HOW *GOOD* SHE'D BEEN TO HER AND TANNER. I REALLY DIDN'T REALIZE HOW *UPSET* MY MOM WAS THAT SHE WAS *GONE*.

SHE SAID IT HAD BEEN OVER TEN YEARS SINCE THEY SAW EACH OTHER.

THEN SHE NOTICED MY *NECKLACE*.

"WHERE DID YOU GET THAT?"

AT FIRST I THOUGHT ABOUT FIBBING, BUT THEN I TOLD HER ALL ABOUT THE *LETTER*, AND THE *BOX*, AND HOW THERE WASN'T ANY *MAGIC*, JUST A DUMB *NECKLACE*.

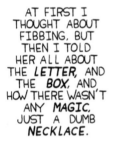

BUT THEN SHE TOOK IT AND OPENED IT UP. I HAD *NO IDEA* THERE WAS ANYTHING *IN IT!* MOM SMILED AND SHOWED ME THAT INSIDE THERE WAS A TINY PICTURE OF HER AND TANNER WHEN THEY WERE JUST LITTLE *KIDS*. I THOUGHT MOM WAS GOING TO CRY.

THEN AFTER A WHILE SHE SAID; 'I GUESS TO FIND MAGIC, YOU HAVE TO KNOW WHERE TO LOOK.' I SMILED AND SHE SAID; 'THAT SEEMS LIKE IT WAS TAKEN *YESTERDAY*.'

'Y'KNOW... ...I HOPE *YOU* DON'T GROW UP AS FAST AS *I* DID.'

AND THEN SHE *KISSED* ME.

MOMMMM

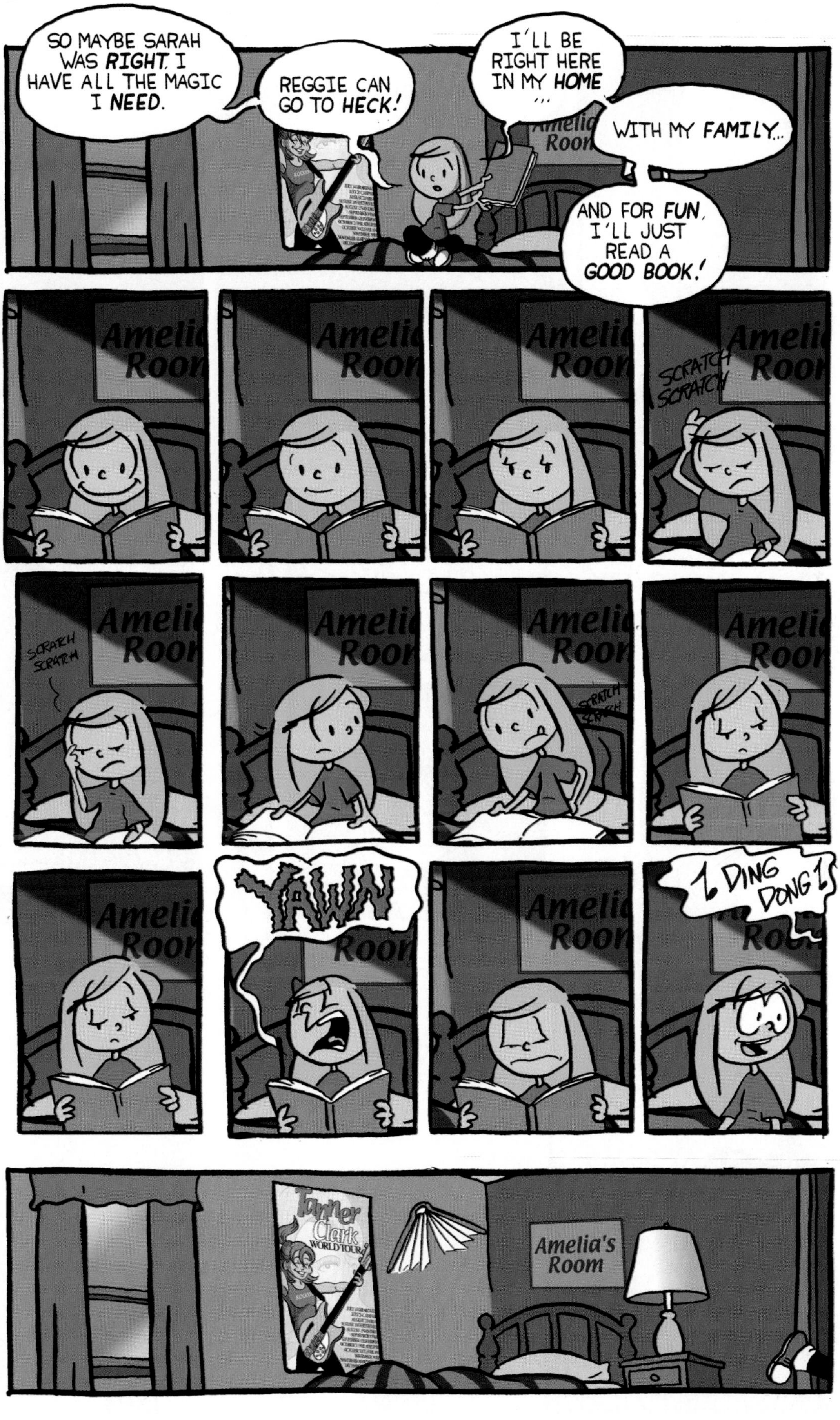
SO MAYBE SARAH WAS RIGHT. I HAVE ALL THE MAGIC I NEED.
REGGIE CAN GO TO HECK!
I'LL BE RIGHT HERE IN MY HOME...
WITH MY FAMILY...
AND FOR FUN, I'LL JUST READ A GOOD BOOK!
SCRATCH SCRATCH
SCRATCH SCRATCH
SCRATCH SCRATCH
YAWN
DING DONG
Tanner Clark WORLD TOUR
Amelia's Room

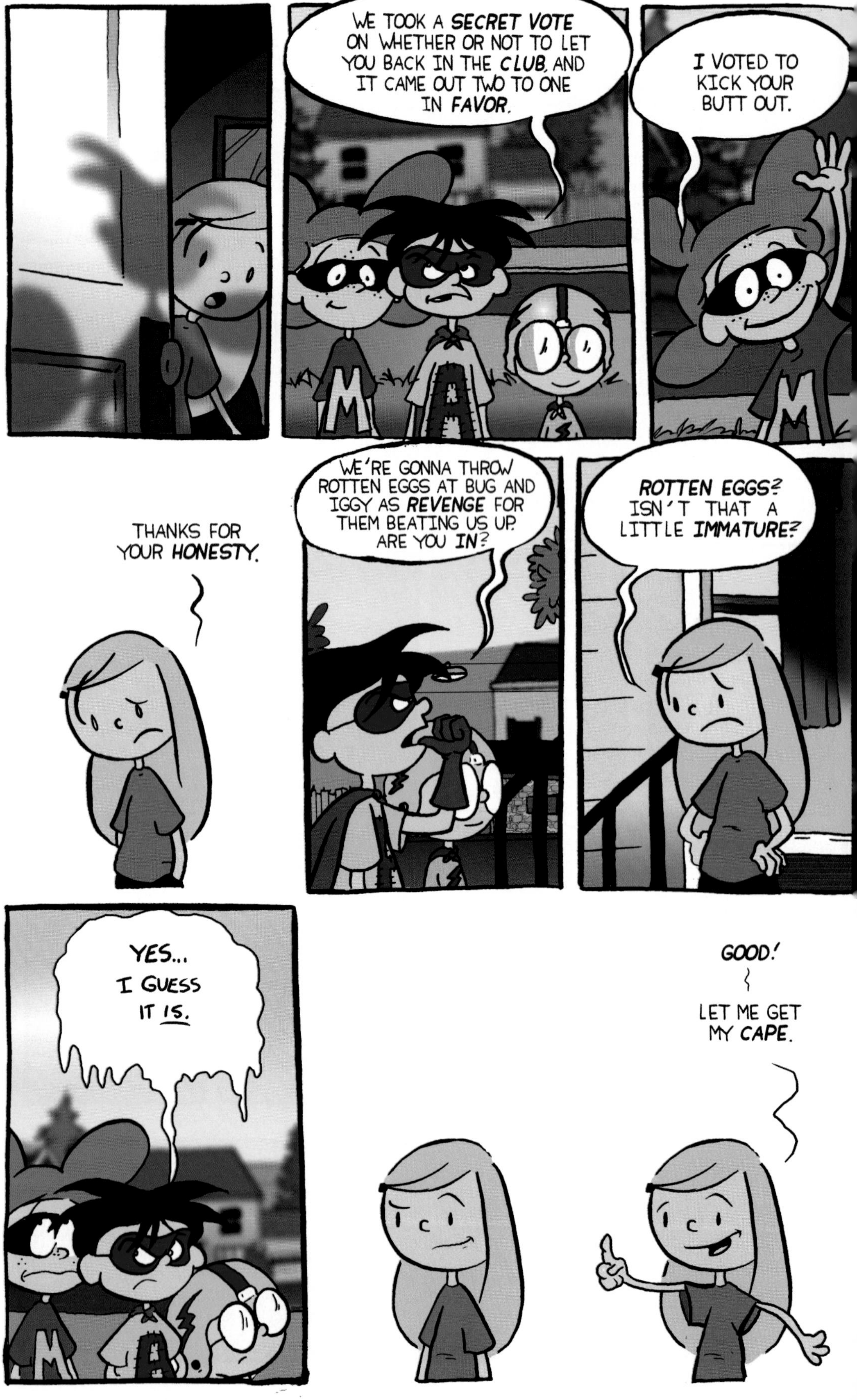

WE TOOK A **SECRET VOTE** ON WHETHER OR NOT TO LET YOU BACK IN THE **CLUB**, AND IT CAME OUT TWO TO ONE IN **FAVOR**.
I VOTED TO KICK YOUR BUTT OUT.
THANKS FOR YOUR **HONESTY**.
WE'RE GONNA THROW ROTTEN EGGS AT BUG AND IGGY AS **REVENGE** FOR THEM BEATING US UP. ARE YOU **IN**?
ROTTEN EGGS? ISN'T THAT A LITTLE **IMMATURE**?
YES... I GUESS IT IS.
GOOD!
LET ME GET MY **CAPE**.

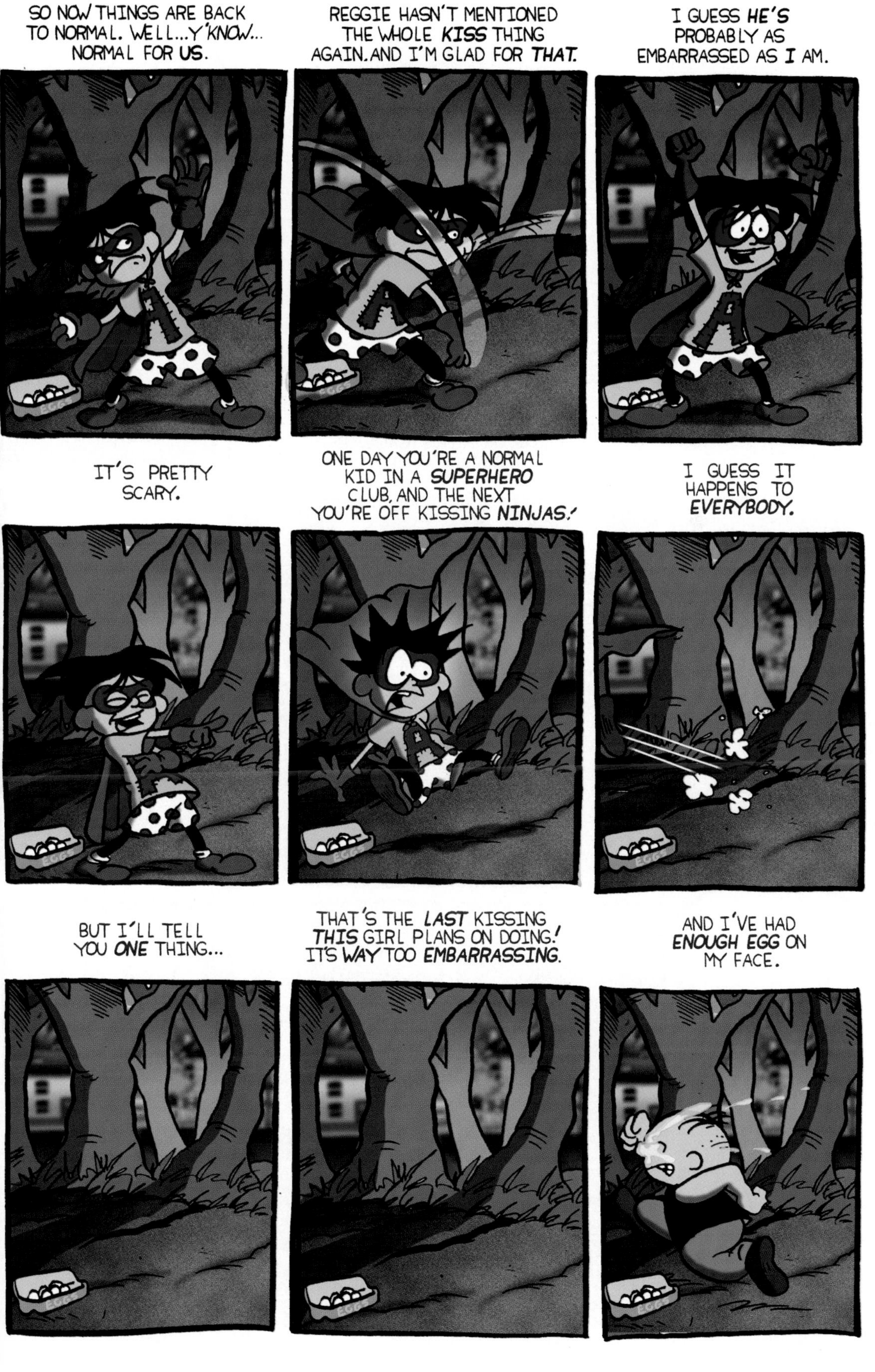
SO NOW THINGS ARE BACK TO NORMAL. WELL...Y'KNOW... NORMAL FOR **US**.
REGGIE HASN'T MENTIONED THE WHOLE **KISS** THING AGAIN. AND I'M GLAD FOR **THAT**.
I GUESS **HE'S** PROBABLY AS EMBARRASSED AS **I** AM.
IT'S PRETTY SCARY.
ONE DAY YOU'RE A NORMAL KID IN A ***SUPERHERO*** CLUB, AND THE NEXT YOU'RE OFF KISSING ***NINJAS!***
I GUESS IT HAPPENS TO ***EVERYBODY.***
BUT I'LL TELL YOU ***ONE*** THING...
THAT'S THE ***LAST*** KISSING ***THIS*** GIRL PLANS ON DOING! IT'S ***WAY*** TOO **EMBARRASSING**.
AND I'VE HAD **ENOUGH EGG** ON MY FACE.

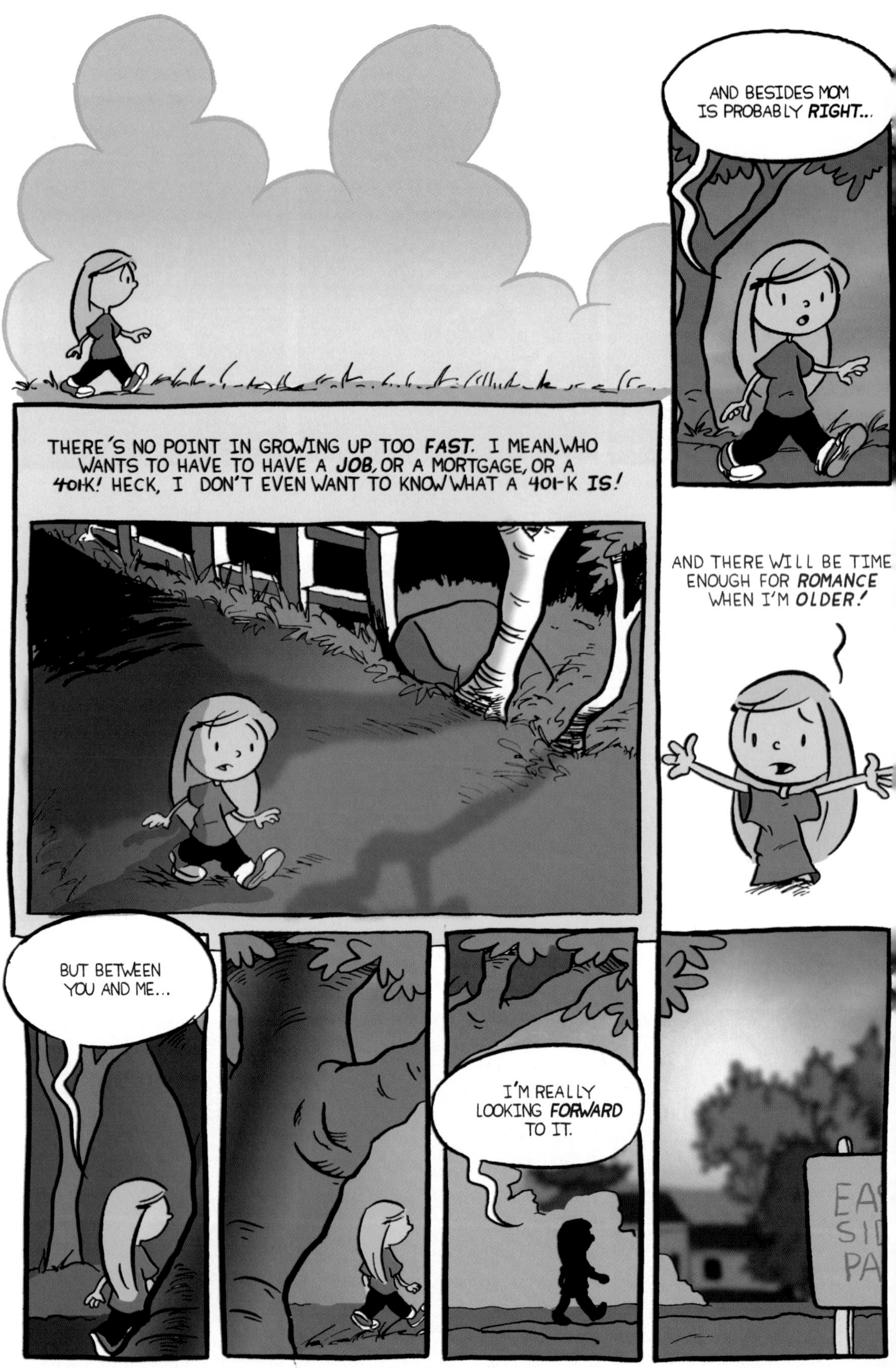

AND BESIDES MOM IS PROBABLY **RIGHT**...
THERE'S NO POINT IN GROWING UP TOO **FAST**. I MEAN, WHO WANTS TO HAVE TO HAVE A **JOB**, OR A MORTGAGE, OR A 401K! HECK, I DON'T EVEN WANT TO KNOW WHAT A 401-K **IS**!
AND THERE WILL BE TIME ENOUGH FOR **ROMANCE** WHEN I'M **OLDER**!
BUT BETWEEN YOU AND ME...
I'M REALLY LOOKING **FORWARD** TO IT.

Part

FivE

5

"I hate you too."

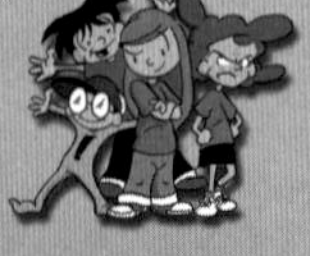

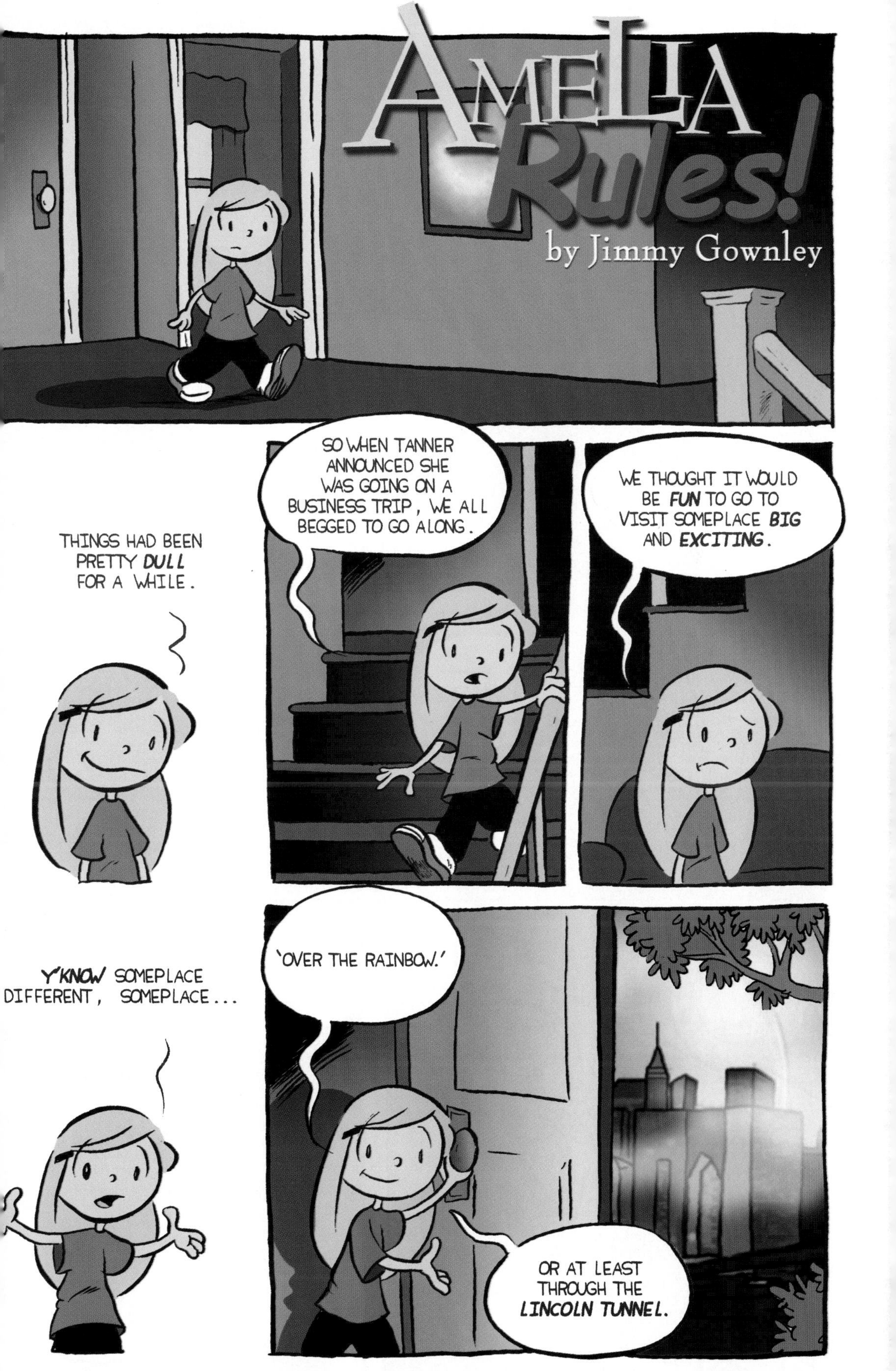
AMELIA Rules!
by Jimmy Gownley
THINGS HAD BEEN PRETTY DULL FOR A WHILE.
SO WHEN TANNER ANNOUNCED SHE WAS GOING ON A BUSINESS TRIP, WE ALL BEGGED TO GO ALONG.
WE THOUGHT IT WOULD BE FUN TO GO TO VISIT SOMEPLACE BIG AND EXCITING.
Y'KNOW SOMEPLACE DIFFERENT, SOMEPLACE...
'OVER THE RAINBOW.'
OR AT LEAST THROUGH THE LINCOLN TUNNEL.

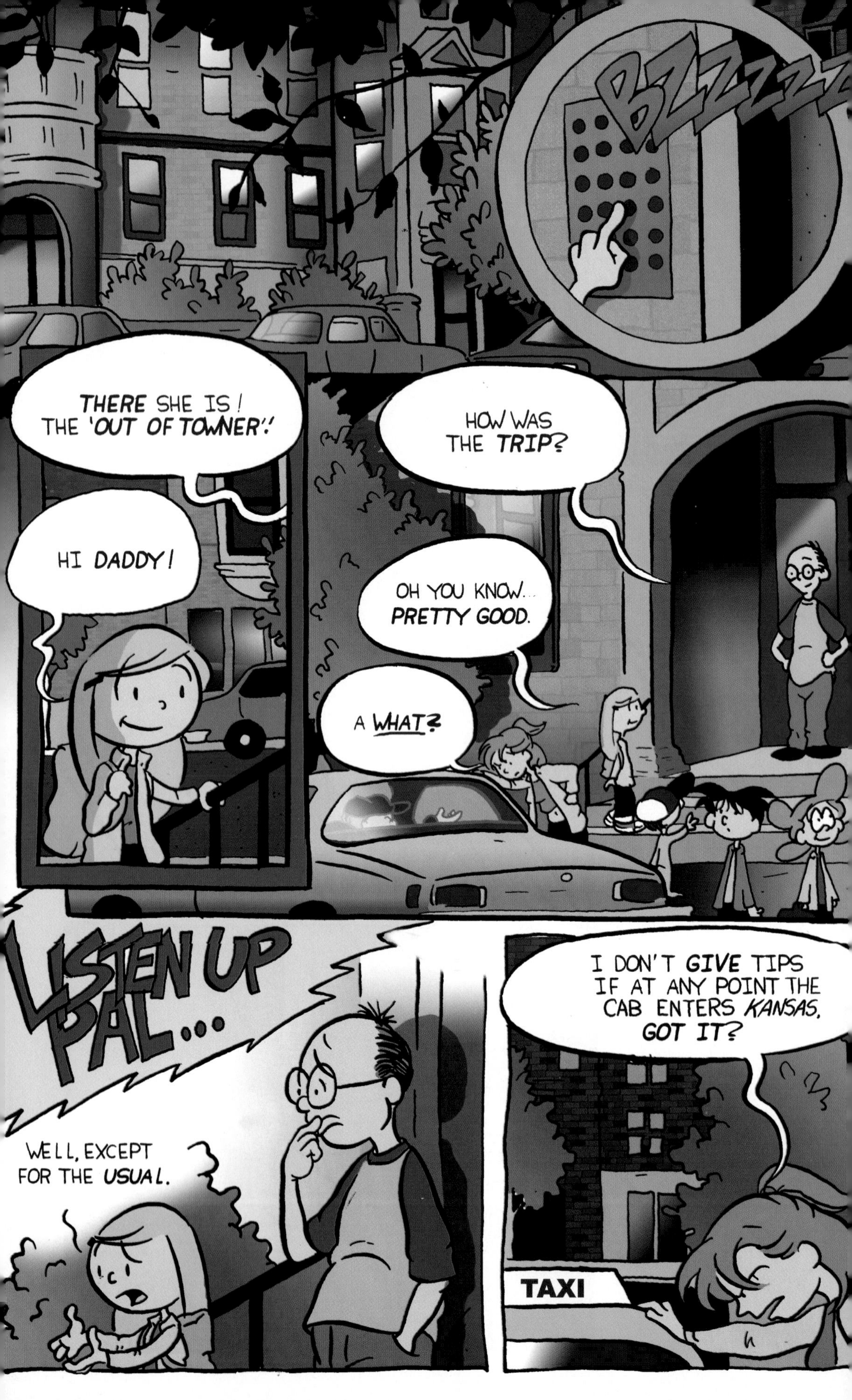
BZZZZZZ
THERE SHE IS! THE 'OUT OF TOWNER'!
HOW WAS THE TRIP?
HI DADDY!
OH YOU KNOW... PRETTY GOOD.
A WHAT?
LISTEN UP PAL...
WELL, EXCEPT FOR THE USUAL.
I DON'T GIVE TIPS IF AT ANY POINT THE CAB ENTERS KANSAS, GOT IT?
TAXI

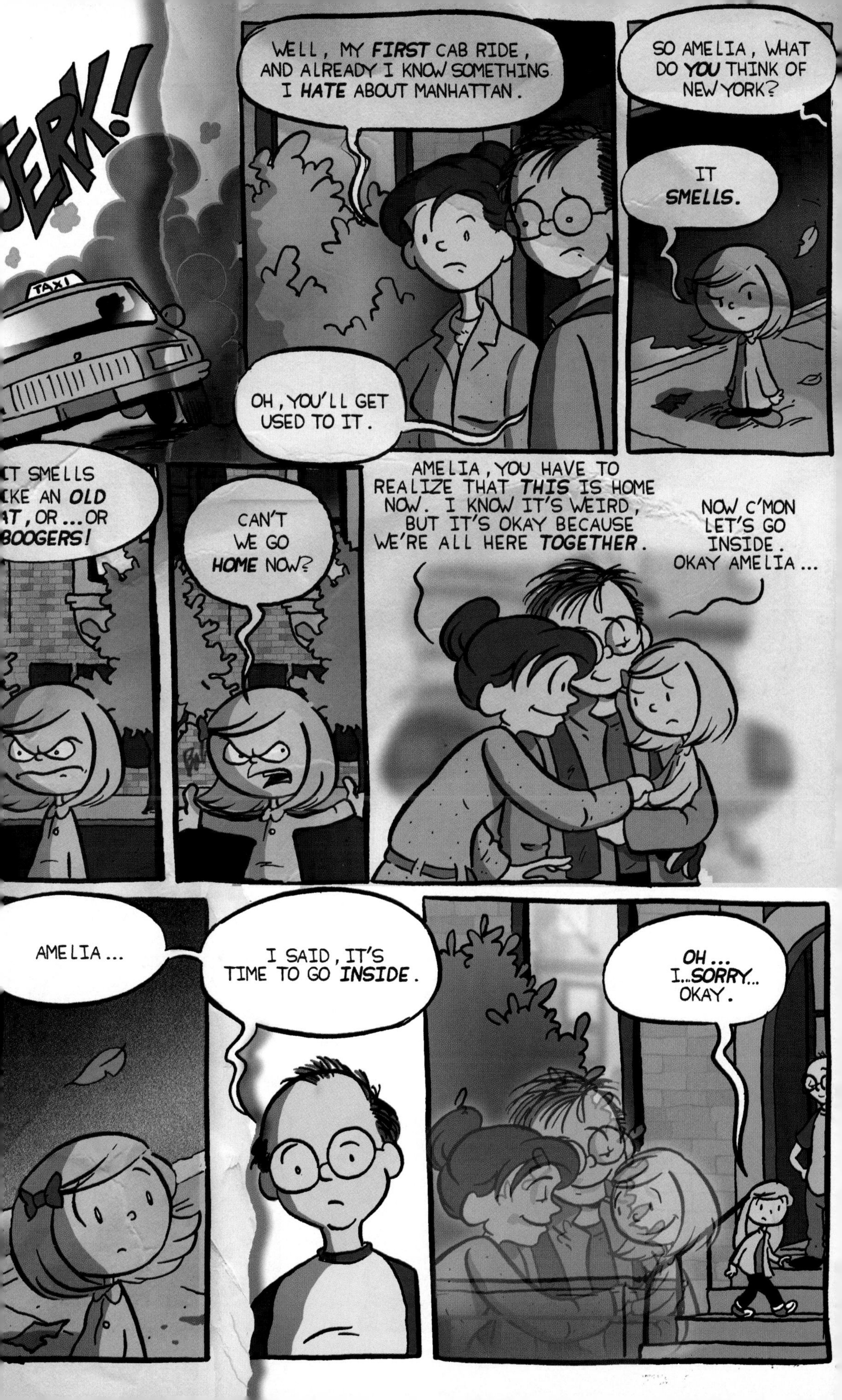

JERK!
TAXI
WELL, MY FIRST CAB RIDE, AND ALREADY I KNOW SOMETHING I HATE ABOUT MANHATTAN.
OH, YOU'LL GET USED TO IT.
SO AMELIA, WHAT DO YOU THINK OF NEW YORK?
IT SMELLS.
IT SMELLS LIKE AN OLD HAT, OR ... OR BOOGERS!
CAN'T WE GO HOME NOW?
AMELIA, YOU HAVE TO REALIZE THAT THIS IS HOME NOW. I KNOW IT'S WEIRD, BUT IT'S OKAY BECAUSE WE'RE ALL HERE TOGETHER.
NOW C'MON LET'S GO INSIDE. OKAY AMELIA ...
AMELIA ...
I SAID, IT'S TIME TO GO INSIDE.
OH ... I...SORRY... OKAY.

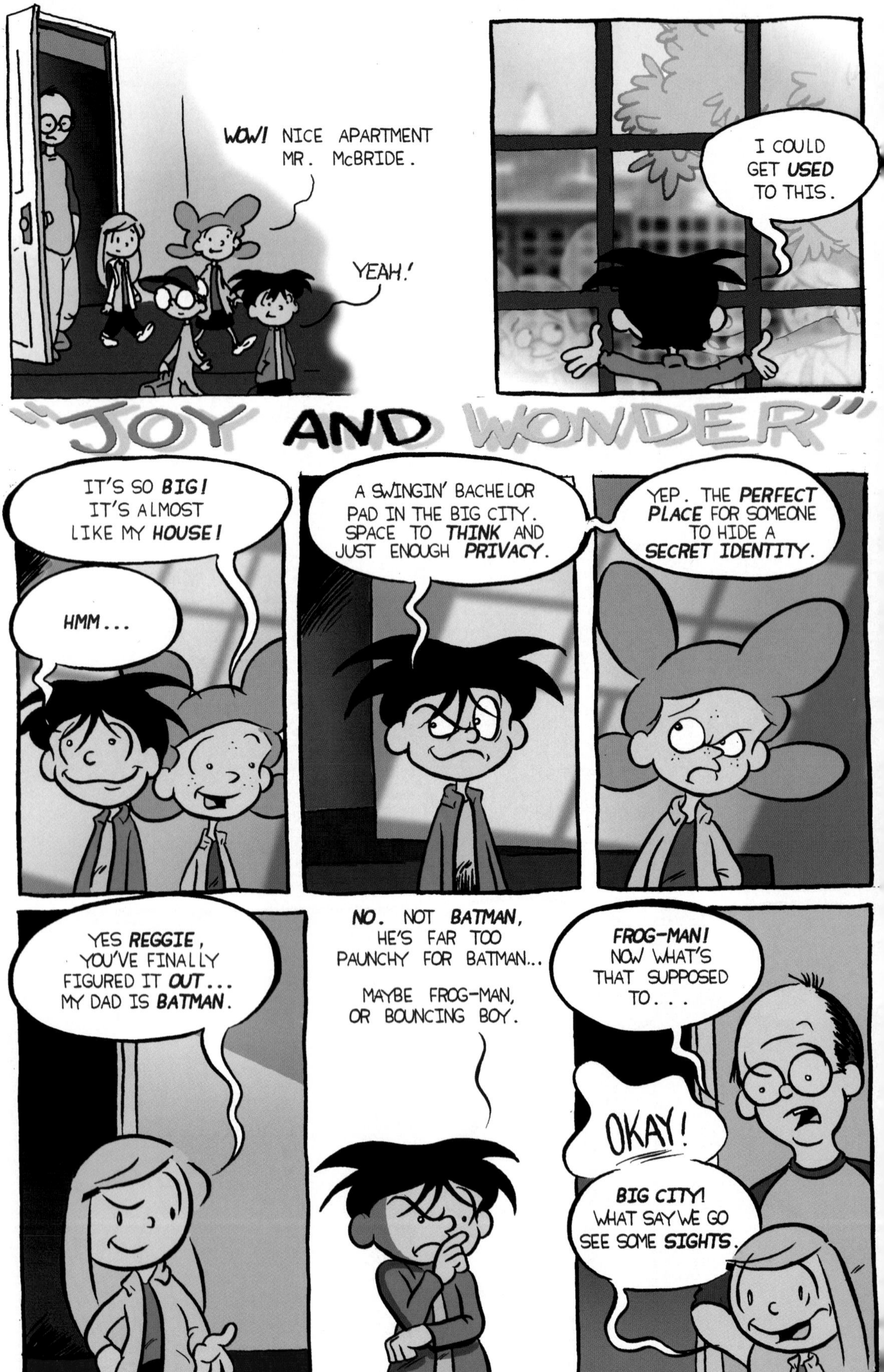

WOW! NICE APARTMENT MR. McBRIDE.
YEAH!
I COULD GET USED TO THIS.
"JOY AND WONDER"
IT'S SO BIG! IT'S ALMOST LIKE MY HOUSE!
HMM...
A SWINGIN' BACHELOR PAD IN THE BIG CITY. SPACE TO THINK AND JUST ENOUGH PRIVACY.
YEP. THE PERFECT PLACE FOR SOMEONE TO HIDE A SECRET IDENTITY.
YES REGGIE, YOU'VE FINALLY FIGURED IT OUT... MY DAD IS BATMAN.
NO. NOT BATMAN, HE'S FAR TOO PAUNCHY FOR BATMAN...
MAYBE FROG-MAN, OR BOUNCING BOY.
FROG-MAN! NOW WHAT'S THAT SUPPOSED TO...
OKAY!
BIG CITY! WHAT SAY WE GO SEE SOME SIGHTS.

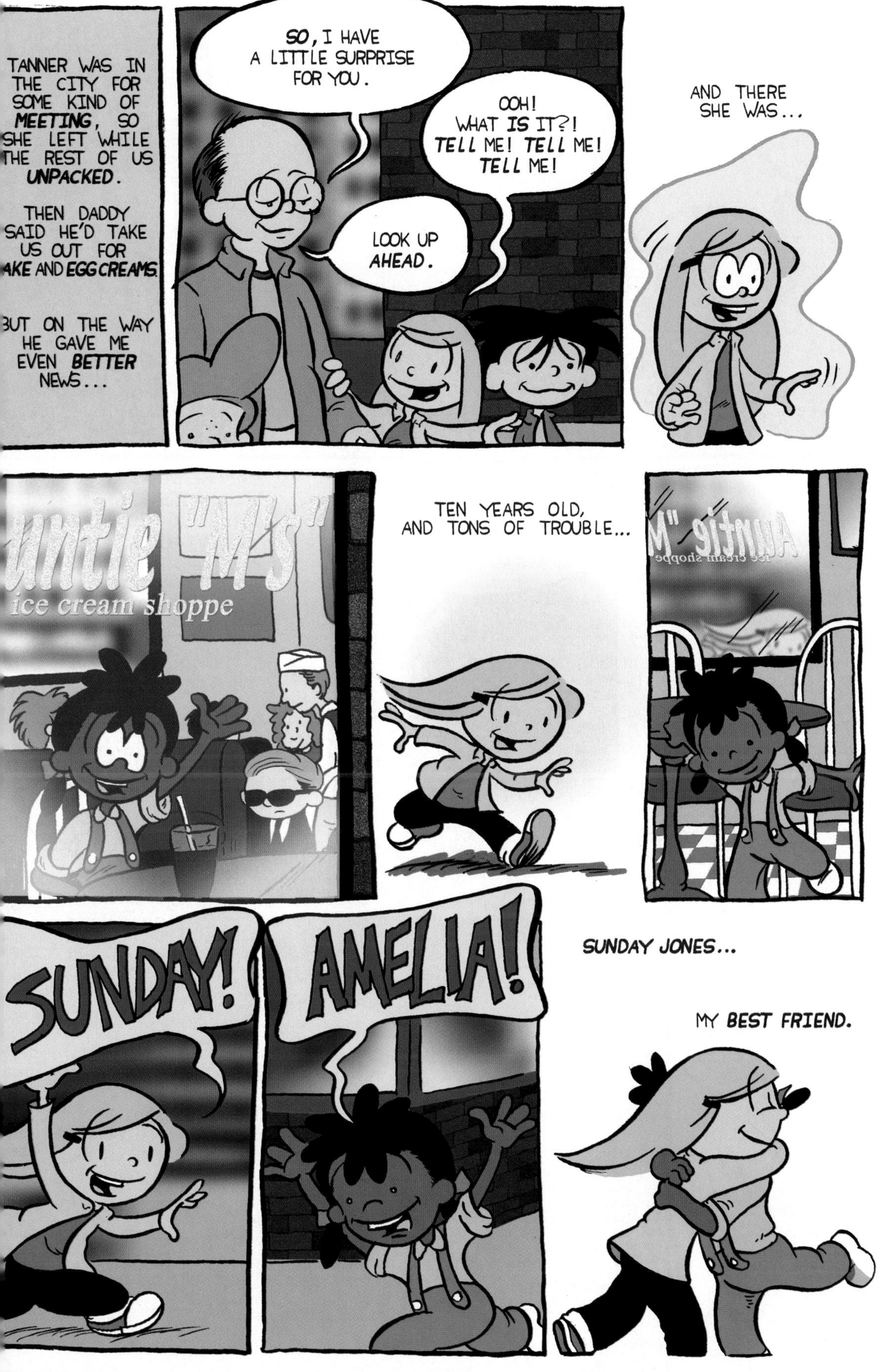
TANNER WAS IN THE CITY FOR SOME KIND OF MEETING, SO SHE LEFT WHILE THE REST OF US UNPACKED.
THEN DADDY SAID HE'D TAKE US OUT FOR AKE AND EGG CREAMS.
BUT ON THE WAY HE GAVE ME EVEN BETTER NEWS...
SO, I HAVE A LITTLE SURPRISE FOR YOU.
OOH! WHAT IS IT?! TELL ME! TELL ME! TELL ME!
LOOK UP AHEAD.
AND THERE SHE WAS...
untie "M's" ice cream shoppe
TEN YEARS OLD, AND TONS OF TROUBLE...
Auntie "M" ice cream shoppe
SUNDAY!
AMELIA!
SUNDAY JONES...
MY BEST FRIEND.

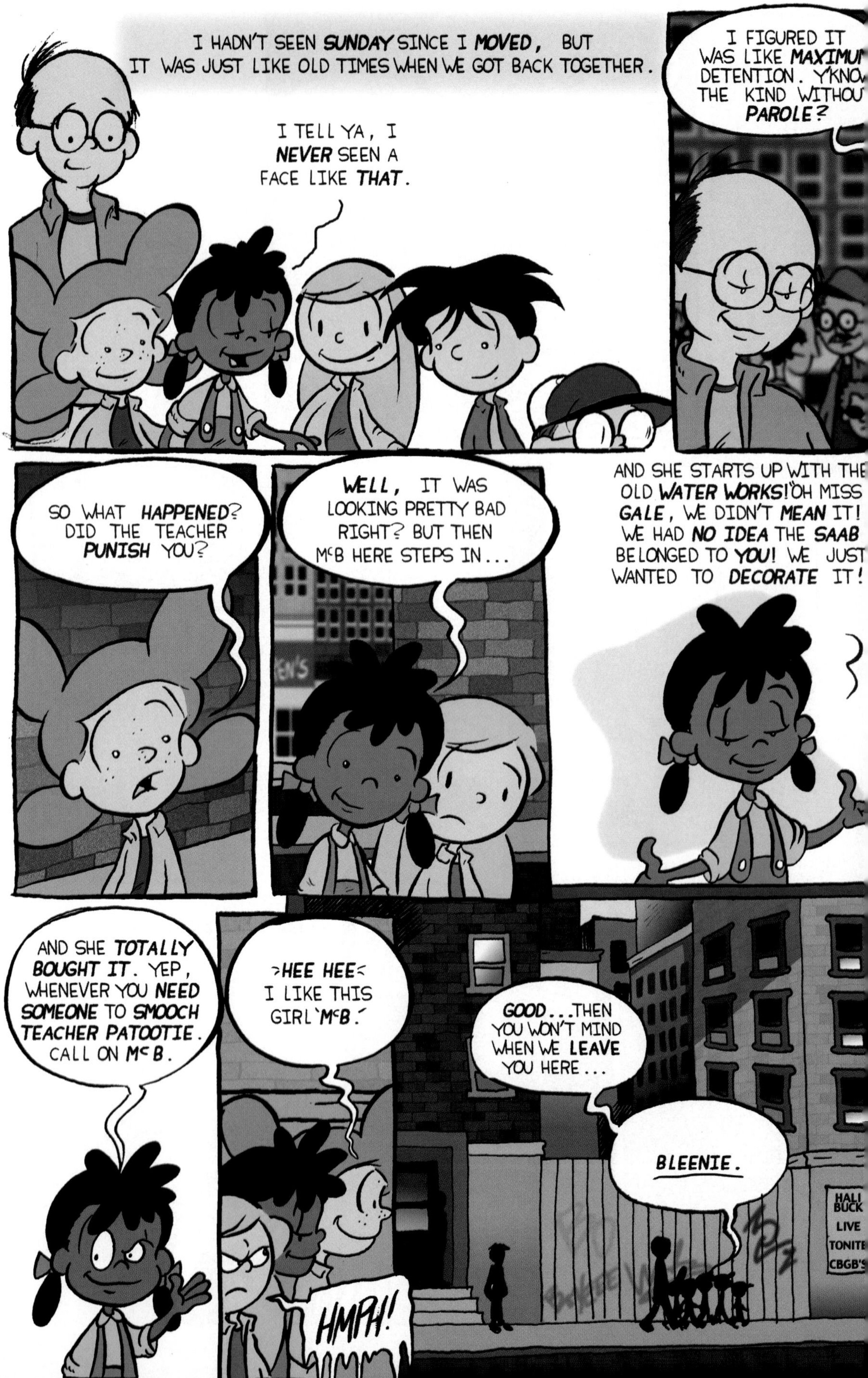
I HADN'T SEEN **SUNDAY** SINCE I **MOVED**, BUT IT WAS JUST LIKE OLD TIMES WHEN WE GOT BACK TOGETHER.
I TELL YA, I **NEVER** SEEN A FACE LIKE **THAT**.
I FIGURED IT WAS LIKE **MAXIMU** DETENTION. Y'KNO THE KIND WITHOU **PAROLE**?
SO WHAT **HAPPENED**? DID THE TEACHER **PUNISH** YOU?
WELL, IT WAS LOOKING PRETTY BAD RIGHT? BUT THEN McB HERE STEPS IN...
AND SHE STARTS UP WITH THE OLD **WATER WORKS**! "OH MISS **GALE**, WE DIDN'T **MEAN** IT! WE HAD **NO IDEA** THE **SAAB** BELONGED TO **YOU**! WE JUST WANTED TO **DECORATE** IT!"
AND SHE **TOTALLY BOUGHT IT**. YEP, WHENEVER YOU **NEED SOMEONE** TO **SMOOCH TEACHER PATOOTIE**. CALL ON McB.
>HEE HEE< I LIKE THIS GIRL 'McB.'
HMPH!
GOOD...THEN YOU WON'T MIND WHEN WE **LEAVE** YOU HERE...
BLEENIE.
HALL BUCK LIVE TONITE CBGB'S

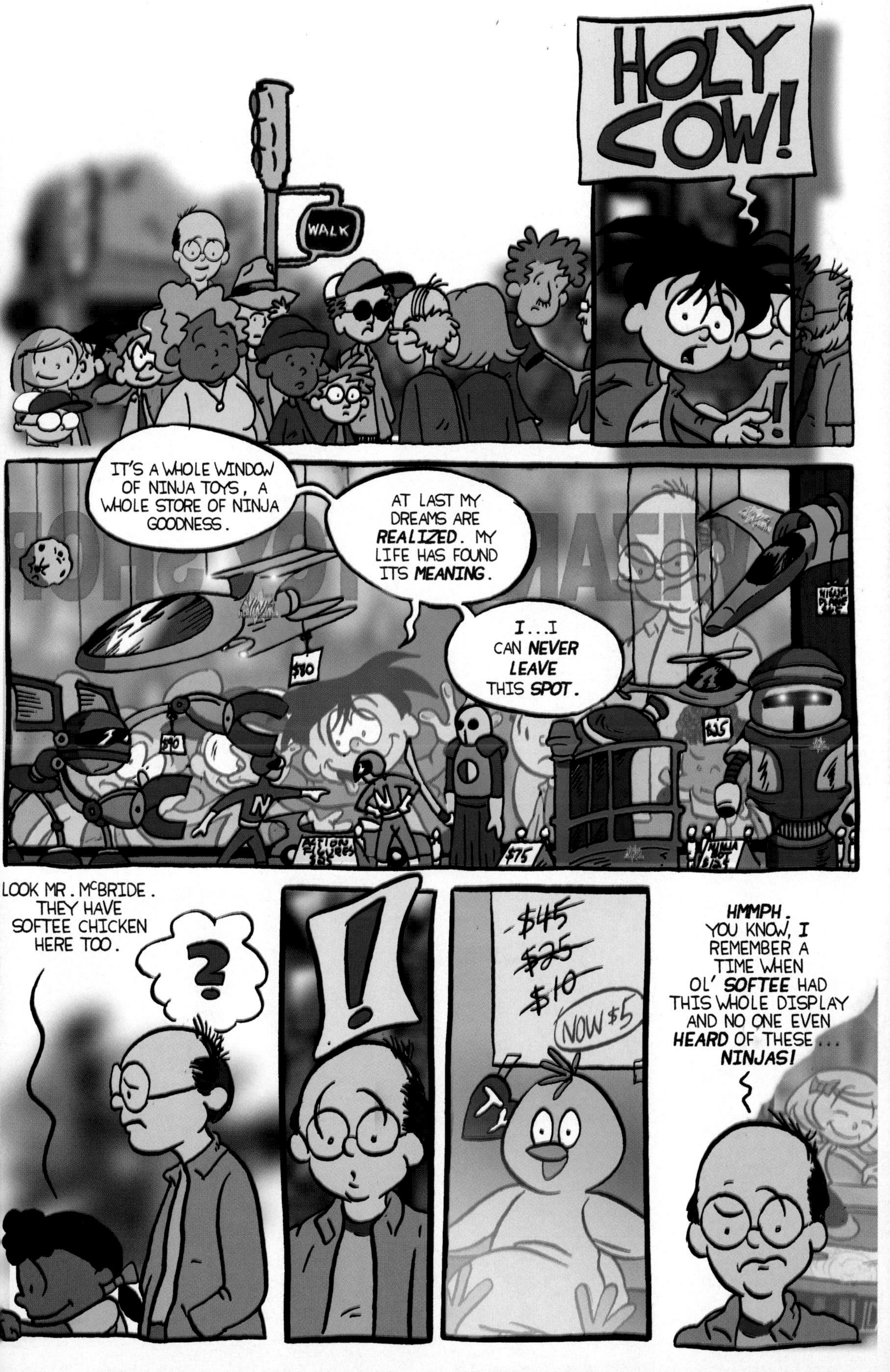
WALK
HOLY COW!
IT'S A WHOLE WINDOW OF NINJA TOYS, A WHOLE STORE OF NINJA GOODNESS.
AT LAST MY DREAMS ARE REALIZED. MY LIFE HAS FOUND ITS MEANING.
I...I CAN NEVER LEAVE THIS SPOT.
$80
$90
$35
$75
LOOK MR. McBRIDE. THEY HAVE SOFTEE CHICKEN HERE TOO.
?
!
$45
$25
$10
NOW $5
HMMPH. YOU KNOW, I REMEMBER A TIME WHEN OL' SOFTEE HAD THIS WHOLE DISPLAY AND NO ONE EVEN HEARD OF THESE.... NINJAS!

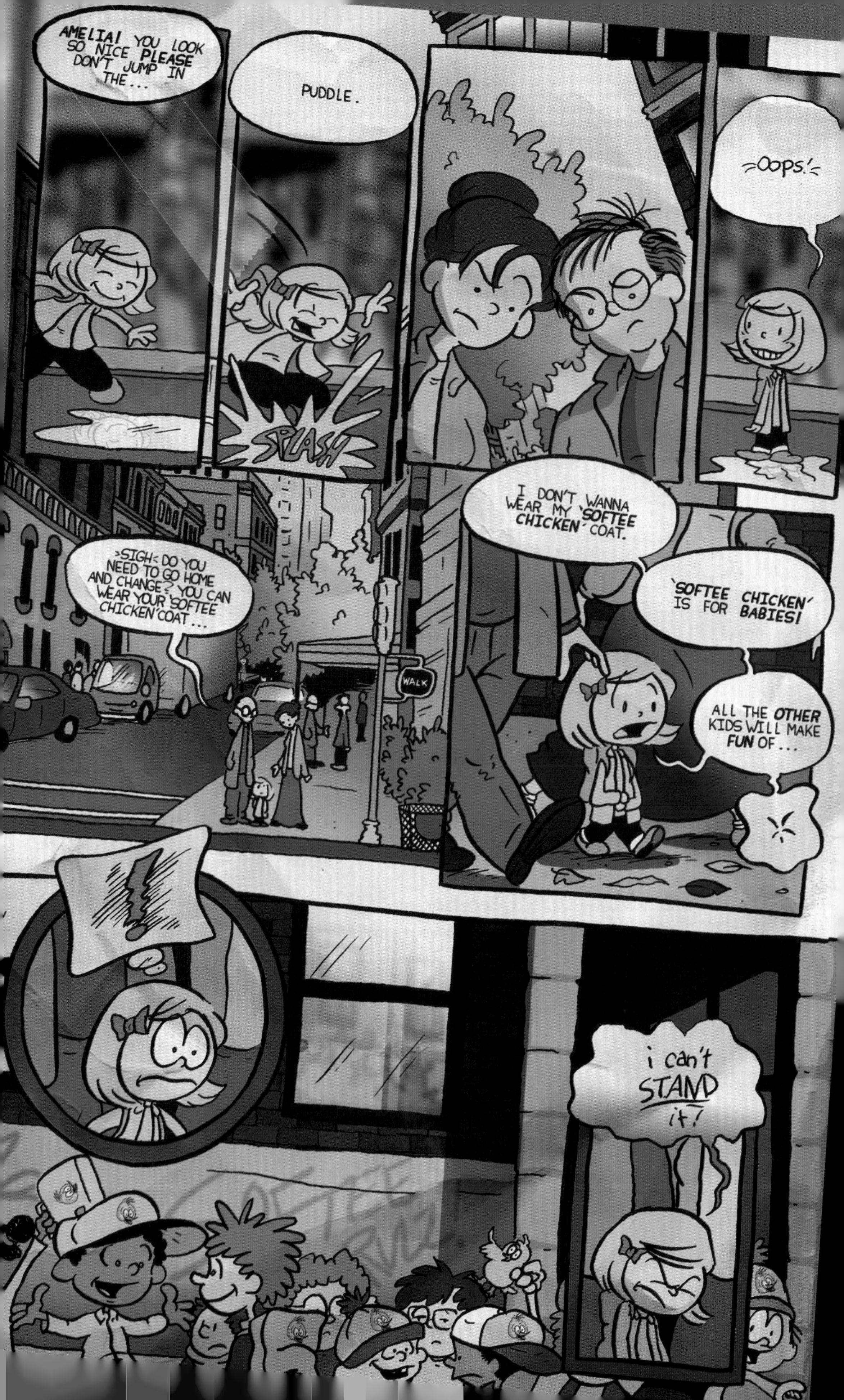
AMELIA! YOU LOOK SO NICE PLEASE DON'T JUMP IN THE...
PUDDLE.
SPLASH
=Oops!=
>SIGH< DO YOU NEED TO GO HOME AND CHANGE? YOU CAN WEAR YOUR 'SOFTEE CHICKEN' COAT...
WALK
I DON'T WANNA WEAR MY 'SOFTEE CHICKEN' COAT.
'SOFTEE CHICKEN' IS FOR BABIES!
ALL THE OTHER KIDS WILL MAKE FUN OF...
i can't STAND it!

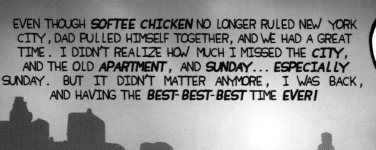

EVEN THOUGH **SOFTEE CHICKEN** NO LONGER RULED NEW YORK CITY, DAD PULLED HIMSELF TOGETHER, AND WE HAD A GREAT TIME. I DIDN'T REALIZE HOW MUCH I MISSED THE **CITY**, AND THE OLD **APARTMENT**, AND **SUNDAY**... **ESPECIALLY** SUNDAY. BUT IT DIDN'T MATTER ANYMORE, I WAS BACK, AND HAVING THE **BEST-BEST-BEST** TIME **EVER!**

AND THE DAY WASN'T OVER. WE STILL HAD ALL NIGHT TO DO ANYTHING WE WANTED IN MANHATTAN...

THE BEST CITY IN THE **WORLD** AND **YOU** WANT TO WATCH **TV**.

HAVE YOU **SEEN** ALL THE CHANNELS?

THERE'S A GOOD **NIGHTLINE** ON TONIGHT, BUT I'M HAVING MY PARENTS 'TIVO' IT.

OOOH... **WAIT!** STOP **FLIPPING**, THAT'S MY **FAVORITE**.

The WIZARD of OZ

UH OH Mᶜ B! **FLYING MONKEYS!**

SUNDAY! PLEASE! NOT THE 'FLYING MONKEY' STORY.

OOH! WILL THIS STORY EMABARRASS AMELIA IN FRONT OF ALL OF US? I **HOPE!** I **HOPE!**

NO I'M SURE IT **WON'T**.

WELL **MAYBE**... OKAY, YES.

SO **HERE** GOES...

It was back in 1st Grade. See, by the time McB. came to town, school had already been rolling for awhile. And let's just say I had already made my rep. What I hadn't made was, y'know, any friends. And on top of that, we had this teacher, Miss Hamilton. She was a real witch, and she had it in for me, BIG TIME.

And really, it was for no reason. I mean, sure...there were one or two little things, but the fire department was barely involved. And besides they couldn't prove anyth....

uh...anyway...

So when Amelia joined the class, I barely even noticed. She was just this quiet shy girl who kept to herself and...

Rhonda? Rhonda? What's so funny? Are you okay? Breathe girl! *BREATHE!*

So like I said, I pretty much ignored her. Then one day I noticed something.

If there was one person Miss Hamilton liked less than me, it was Amelia Louise McBride.

See, that's even what she called her... Amelia Louise... never just Amelia, she always stuck on Louise. Only it sounded like this...

Leweeeeeeeeez.

Like she just stepped in something nasty.

Rhonda, if you can't control the laughing, we'll have to ask you to leave.

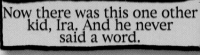

So...since we had something in common, we started to hang out.

Now there was this one other kid, Ira. And he never said a word.

Can you imagine that? A kid who went all day without eve saying...Oh...yeah...I guess you can. Anyway, it seemed lik the three of us were invisible to the rest of the class.

One day Miss Hamilton says the class is gonna do a play "The Wizard of Oz" right? So everyone gets real excited and she starts handin' out the parts.

Cowardly Lion.

Auntie Em

Scarecrow

Wicked Witch

Soon, it seems like all the parts are given out.

But the three of us were left hangin'.

then, she laid it on us...

FLYING.

MONKE

This was not exactly a compliment, y'know? I mean it's not like she picked her favorite students and said; "Ah yes...You shall be my monkeys." It was more like; "Let's put these numbskulls where they can do the least amount of damage."

I think Mr. and Mrs. McBride felt bad for us. They invited us over a bunch of times, so we could "rehearse" with Amelia. Not that there was much to rehearse. We pretty much just ran around the apartment going "Eek! Eek!" But y'know, it was fun.

The best part was when Amelia's mom made us these way cool monkey costumes. They had wings, and ears, and big ol' monkey tails. We were stylin! I think, that's when we started getting into it. I came up with this name "The Flying Monkey Society," and we ran around calling ourselves that. Whenever someone would ask what time it was, we'd yell "IT'S MONKEY TIME!" (Well, me and McB. would. Ira still wasn't talking), and then we'd jump around like rejects.

It must've looked like fun, 'cuz pretty soon everyone wanted to be a "Flying Monkey." Of course we wouldn't let them. Heh Heh...It was pretty cool.

So anyway, the day of the big show finally comes, and everyone is freaking out. Even Miss Hamilton is kinda goin' wonky. And the more wonky she got, the more freaked out we got. It was a scene.

Then, things really went downhill, first the girl who was playing "Dorothy" forgot the words to "Over the Rainbow." Then the Tin Man got the hiccups, which wouldn't have been so bad, if it didn't make Carlos, the kid playing Scarecrow, laugh. He laughed so hard, he fell of the stage. By the time we came on, it was a massacre. People were leaving. I'm pretty sure I even heard another teacher "Boo" us.

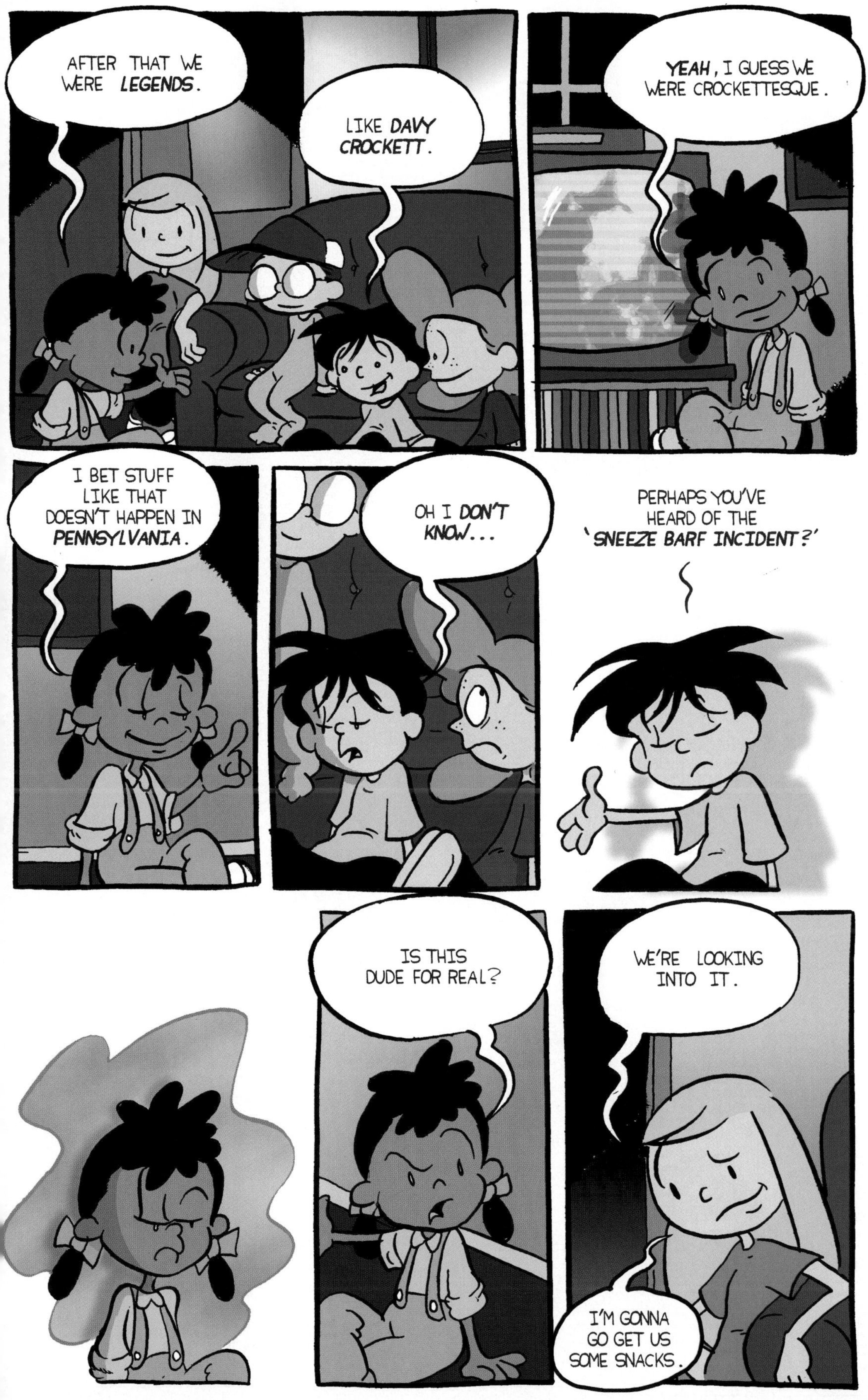
AFTER THAT WE WERE LEGENDS.
LIKE DAVY CROCKETT.
YEAH, I GUESS WE WERE CROCKETTESQUE.
I BET STUFF LIKE THAT DOESN'T HAPPEN IN PENNSYLVANIA.
OH I DON'T KNOW...
PERHAPS YOU'VE HEARD OF THE 'SNEEZE BARF INCIDENT?'
IS THIS DUDE FOR REAL?
WE'RE LOOKING INTO IT.
I'M GONNA GO GET US SOME SNACKS.

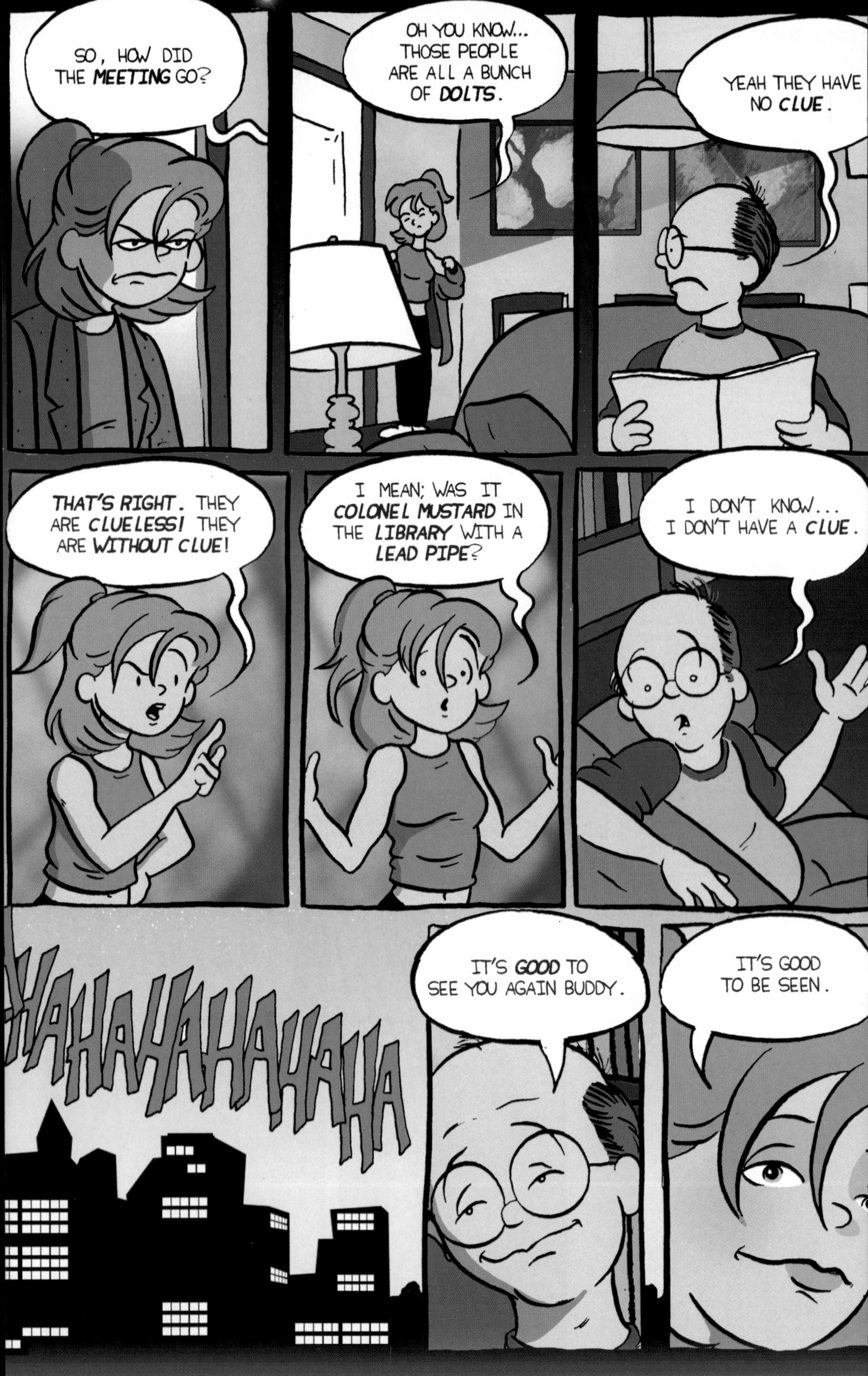
SO, HOW DID THE MEETING GO?
OH YOU KNOW... THOSE PEOPLE ARE ALL A BUNCH OF DOLTS.
YEAH THEY HAVE NO CLUE.
THAT'S RIGHT. THEY ARE CLUELESS! THEY ARE WITHOUT CLUE!
I MEAN; WAS IT COLONEL MUSTARD IN THE LIBRARY WITH A LEAD PIPE?
I DON'T KNOW... I DON'T HAVE A CLUE.
HAHAHAHAHAHAHA
IT'S GOOD TO SEE YOU AGAIN BUDDY.
IT'S GOOD TO BE SEEN.

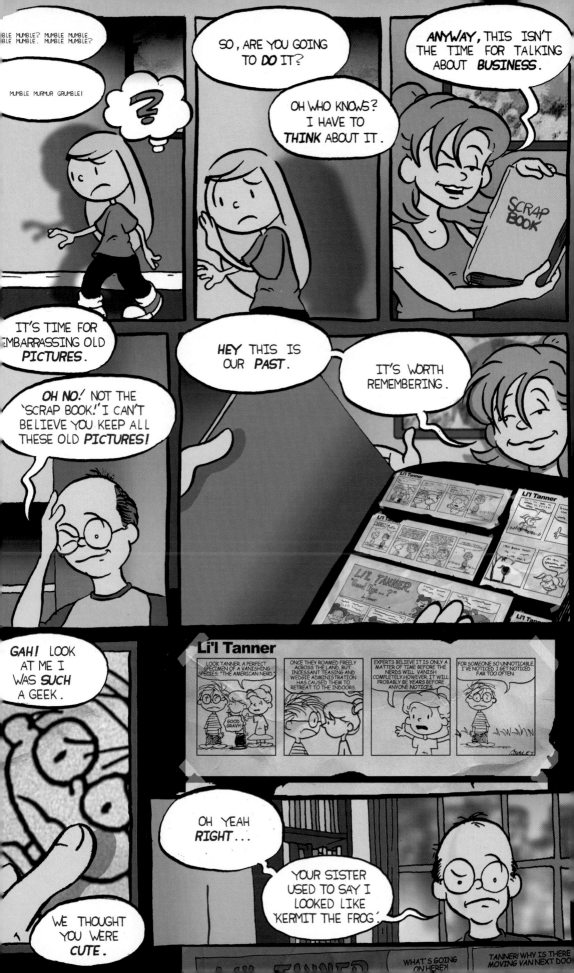

WELL, *KERMIT'S* KINDA CUTE.

I REMEMBER THE *FIRST TIME* I SAW YOUR SISTER. I THOUGHT SHE LOOKED LIKE AN *ANGEL*.

WHICH IS *IRONIC*, CONSIDERING SHE PUT ME THROUGH ...

DON'T SAY IT.

ANYWAY, SHE PROBABLY DIDN'T EVEN NOTICE WHEN I MOVED *AWAY*.

Li'l Tanner

I'M TRYING TO BECOME A KINDER PERSON.

OH? HOW SO?

WELL, I WAS GOING TO INVITE YOU TO THIS PARTY I'M HAVING, BUT THEN I REMEMBERED HOW NO ONE LIKES YOU, AND HOW YOU DON'T FIT IN, AND HOW WE TEASE YOU UNMERCIFULLY.

IT MADE ME REALIZE WHAT A MISERABLE TIME YOU WOULD HAVE SEEING ALL THOSE OTHER PEOPLE HAVE FUN, AND SO I DECIDED TO DO THE *KIND* THING AND *NOT INVITE* YOU!

SOMETIMES I THINK ALL THIS *KINDNESS* IS KILLING ME.

`WELL, I HAPPEN TO KNOW THAT SHE *DID* NOTICE, AND I THINK SHE FELT *PRETTY BAD* ABOUT THE WAY SHE USED TO *TREAT* YOU.`

I MEAN *RELATIVELY SPEAKING* ANYWAY.

LI'L TANNER. in "Good Bye ... ?" by GOWNLEY

WHAT'S GOING ON HERE?!

TANNER! WHY IS THERE A MOVING VAN NEXT DOOR?!

THE MCBRIDES ARE MOVING AWAY. YOU KNEW THAT!

YES, BUT I DIDN'T REALLY BELIEVE IT!

BUT NOW HE'S *GONE*, AND I NEVER EVEN GOT TO SAY *GOODBYE*!

YOU DIDN'T EVEN LIKE HIM!

THAT'S NOT *TRUE*!

WE MAY HAVE HAD OUR *DIFFERENCES*, BUT DEEP DOWN WE WERE REALLY *CLOSE*.

YES SIR, I'M SURE GONNA MISS GOOD OL'... GOOD OL'.

WHAT WAS HIS NAME AGAIN?

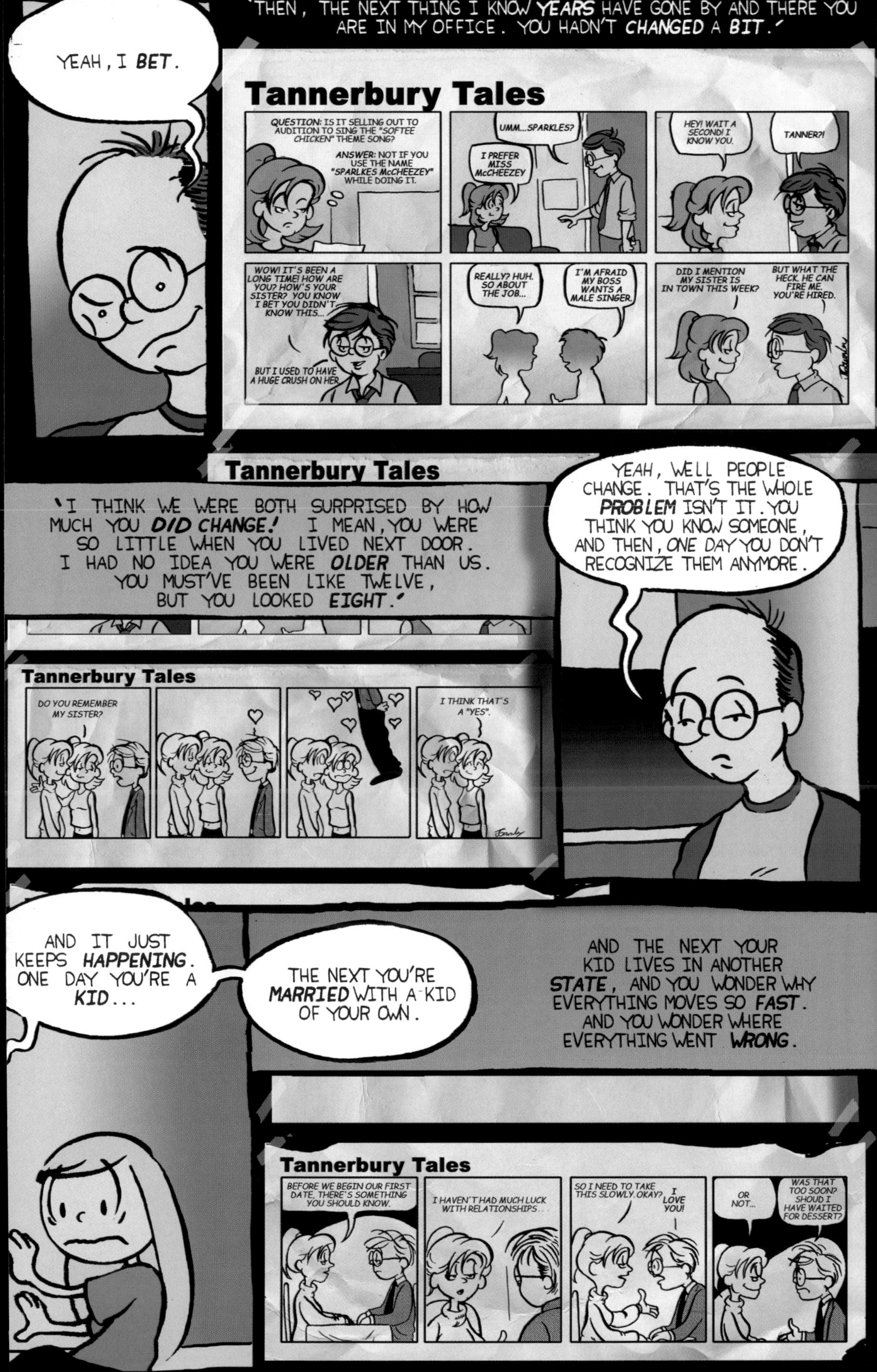

YEAH, I *BET.*

THEN, THE NEXT THING I KNOW *YEARS* HAVE GONE BY AND THERE YOU ARE IN MY OFFICE. YOU HADN'T *CHANGED* A *BIT.'*

Tannerbury Tales

QUESTION: IS IT SELLING OUT TO AUDITION TO SING THE "SOFTEE CHICKEN" THEME SONG?

ANSWER: NOT IF YOU USE THE NAME "SPARLKES McCHEEZEY" WHILE DOING IT.

UMM...SPARKLES?

I PREFER MISS McCHEEZEY

HEY! WAIT A SECOND! I KNOW YOU.

TANNER?!

WOW! IT'S BEEN A LONG TIME! HOW ARE YOU? HOW'S YOUR SISTER? YOU KNOW I BET YOU DIDN'T KNOW THIS...

BUT I USED TO HAVE A HUGE CRUSH ON HER

REALLY? HUH. SO ABOUT THE JOB...

I'M AFRAID MY BOSS WANTS A MALE SINGER.

DID I MENTION MY SISTER IS IN TOWN THIS WEEK?

BUT WHAT THE HECK. HE CAN FIRE ME. YOU'RE HIRED.

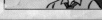

Tannerbury Tales

'I THINK WE WERE BOTH SURPRISED BY HOW MUCH YOU *DID CHANGE!* I MEAN, YOU WERE SO LITTLE WHEN YOU LIVED NEXT DOOR. I HAD NO IDEA YOU WERE *OLDER* THAN US. YOU MUST'VE BEEN LIKE TWELVE, BUT YOU LOOKED *EIGHT.'*

YEAH, WELL PEOPLE CHANGE. THAT'S THE WHOLE *PROBLEM* ISN'T IT. YOU THINK YOU KNOW SOMEONE, AND THEN, ONE DAY YOU DON'T RECOGNIZE THEM ANYMORE.

Tannerbury Tales

DO YOU REMEMBER MY SISTER?

I THINK THAT'S A "YES".

AND IT JUST KEEPS *HAPPENING.* ONE DAY YOU'RE A *KID*...

THE NEXT YOU'RE *MARRIED* WITH A KID OF YOUR OWN.

AND THE NEXT YOUR KID LIVES IN ANOTHER *STATE,* AND YOU WONDER WHY EVERYTHING MOVES SO *FAST.* AND YOU WONDER WHERE EVERYTHING WENT *WRONG.*

Tannerbury Tales

BEFORE WE BEGIN OUR FIRST DATE, THERE'S SOMETHING YOU SHOULD KNOW.

I HAVEN'T HAD MUCH LUCK WITH RELATIONSHIPS...

SO I NEED TO TAKE THIS SLOWLY. OKAY?

I LOVE YOU!

OR NOT...

WAS THAT TOO SOON? SHOUD I HAVE WAITED FOR DESSERT?

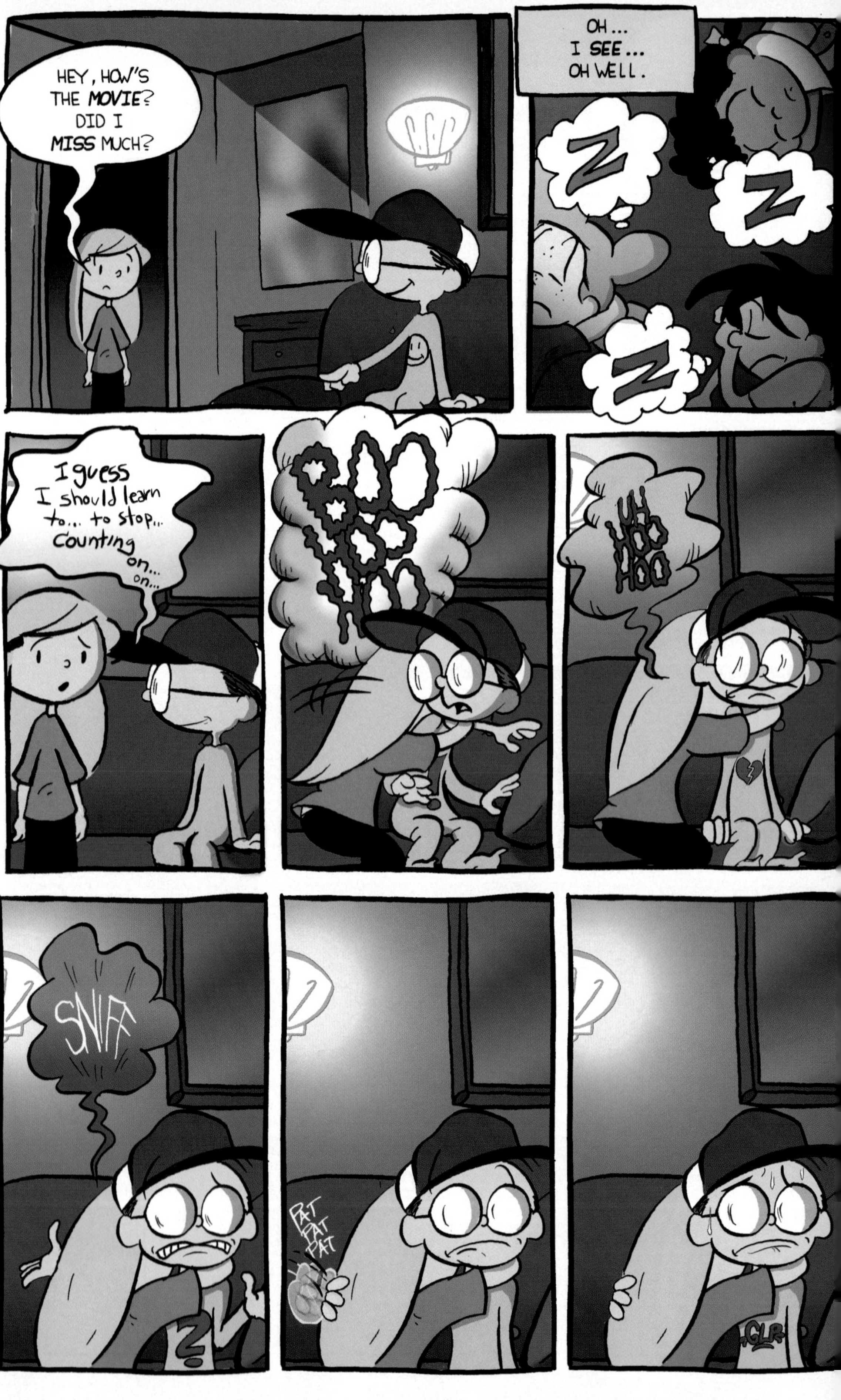
HEY, HOW'S THE MOVIE? DID I MISS MUCH?
OH... I SEE... OH WELL.
Z
Z
Z
I guess I should learn to... to stop... counting on... on...
BOO HOO HOO
UH HOO HOO
SNIFF
PAT PAT PAT
GLR

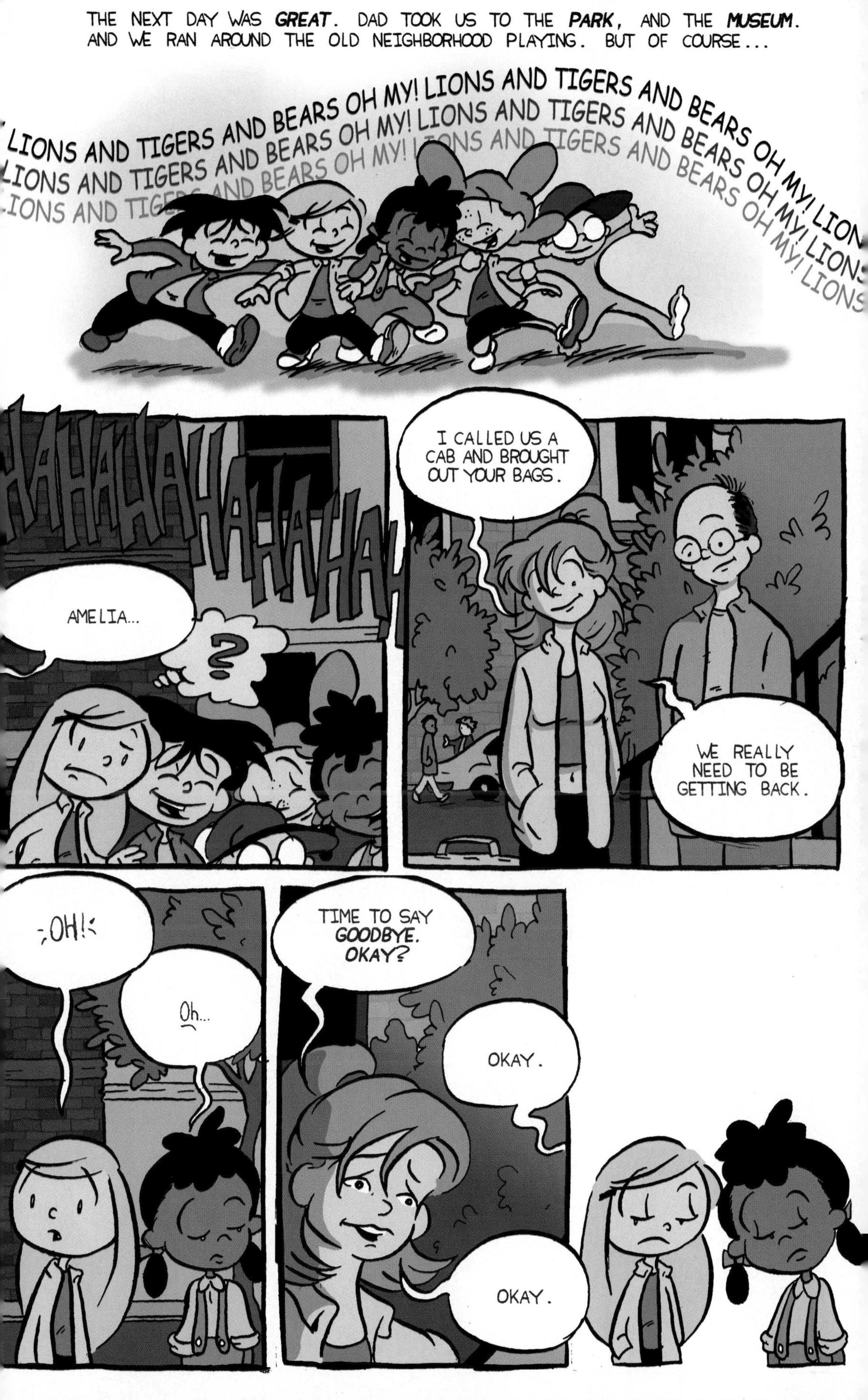
THE NEXT DAY WAS **GREAT**. DAD TOOK US TO THE **PARK**, AND THE **MUSEUM**. AND WE RAN AROUND THE OLD NEIGHBORHOOD PLAYING. BUT OF COURSE...
LIONS AND TIGERS AND BEARS OH MY! LIONS AND TIGERS AND BEARS OH MY! LIONS
LIONS AND TIGERS AND BEARS OH MY! LIONS AND TIGERS AND BEARS OH MY! LIONS
HAHAHAHAHAHAHAHAHAH
AMELIA...
?
I CALLED US A CAB AND BROUGHT OUT YOUR BAGS.
WE REALLY NEED TO BE GETTING BACK.
OH!
Oh...
TIME TO SAY **GOODBYE. OKAY?**
OKAY.
OKAY.

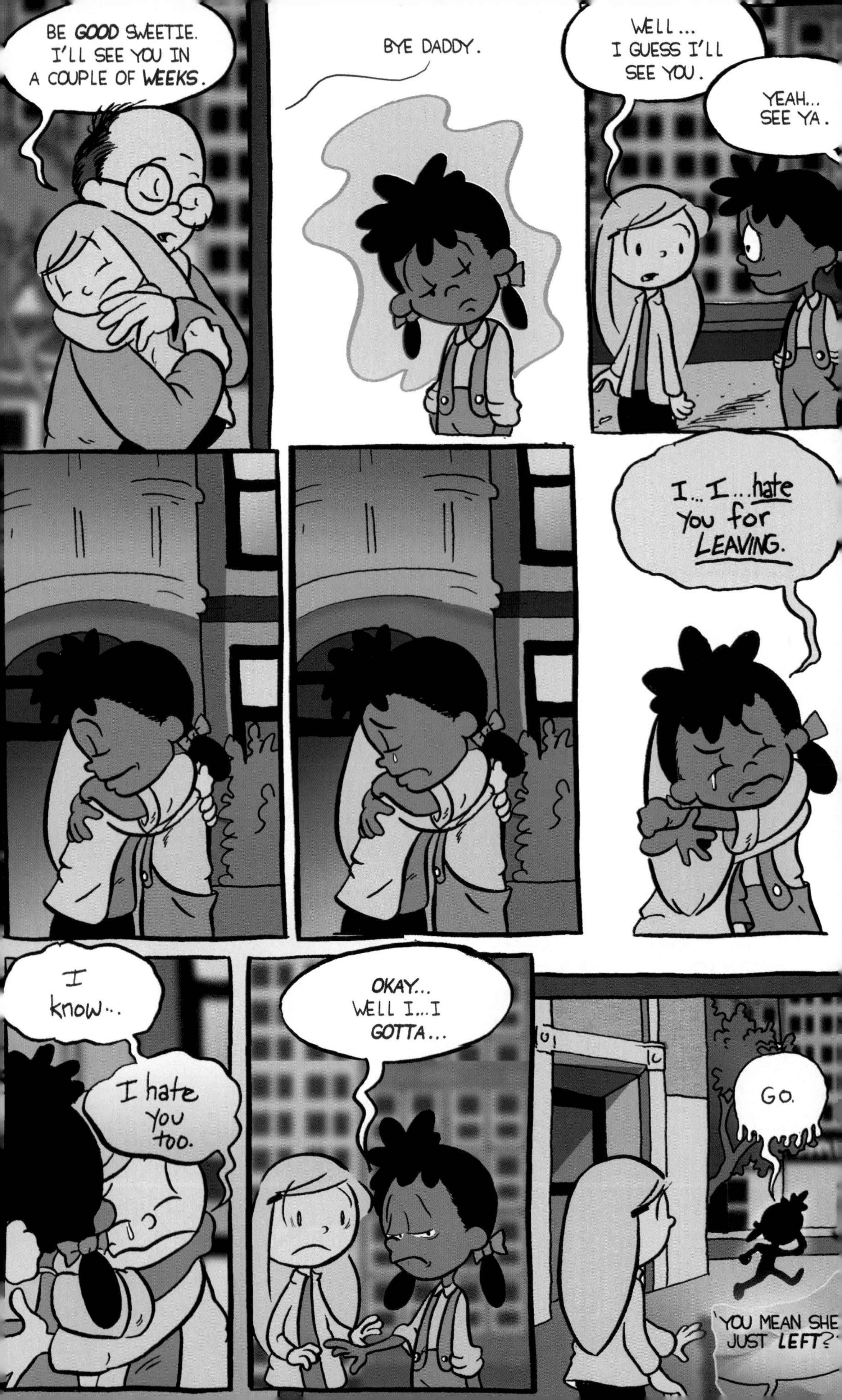
BE GOOD SWEETIE. I'LL SEE YOU IN A COUPLE OF WEEKS.
BYE DADDY.
WELL... I GUESS I'LL SEE YOU.
YEAH... SEE YA.
I... I... hate you for LEAVING.
I know...
I hate you too.
OKAY... WELL I...I GOTTA...
GO.
YOU MEAN SHE JUST LEFT?

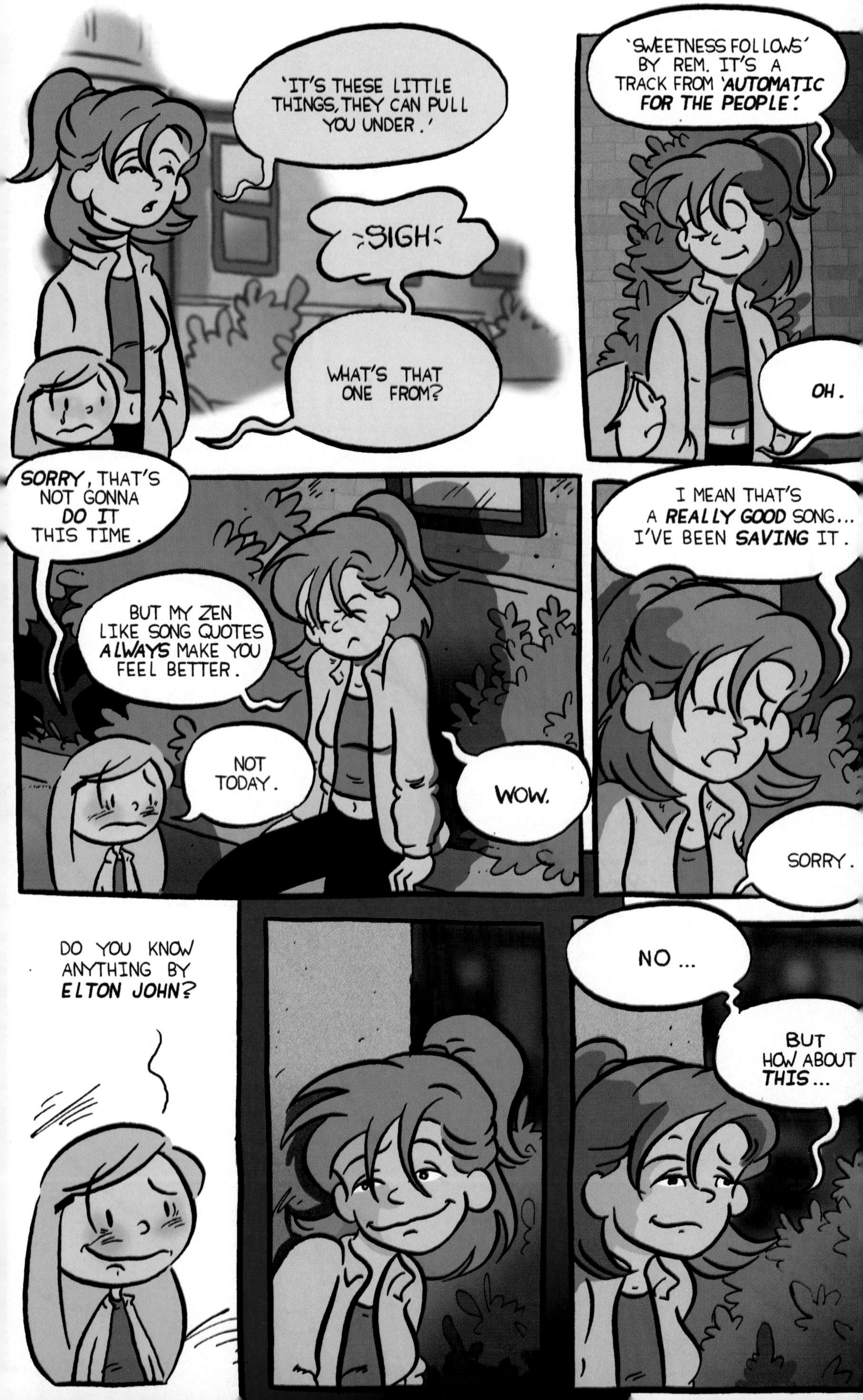
'IT'S THESE LITTLE THINGS, THEY CAN PULL YOU UNDER.'
SIGH
WHAT'S THAT ONE FROM?
'SWEETNESS FOLLOWS' BY REM. IT'S A TRACK FROM 'AUTOMATIC FOR THE PEOPLE.'
OH.
SORRY, THAT'S NOT GONNA DO IT THIS TIME.
BUT MY ZEN LIKE SONG QUOTES ALWAYS MAKE YOU FEEL BETTER.
NOT TODAY.
WOW.
I MEAN THAT'S A REALLY GOOD SONG... I'VE BEEN SAVING IT.
SORRY.
DO YOU KNOW ANYTHING BY ELTON JOHN?
NO...
BUT HOW ABOUT THIS...

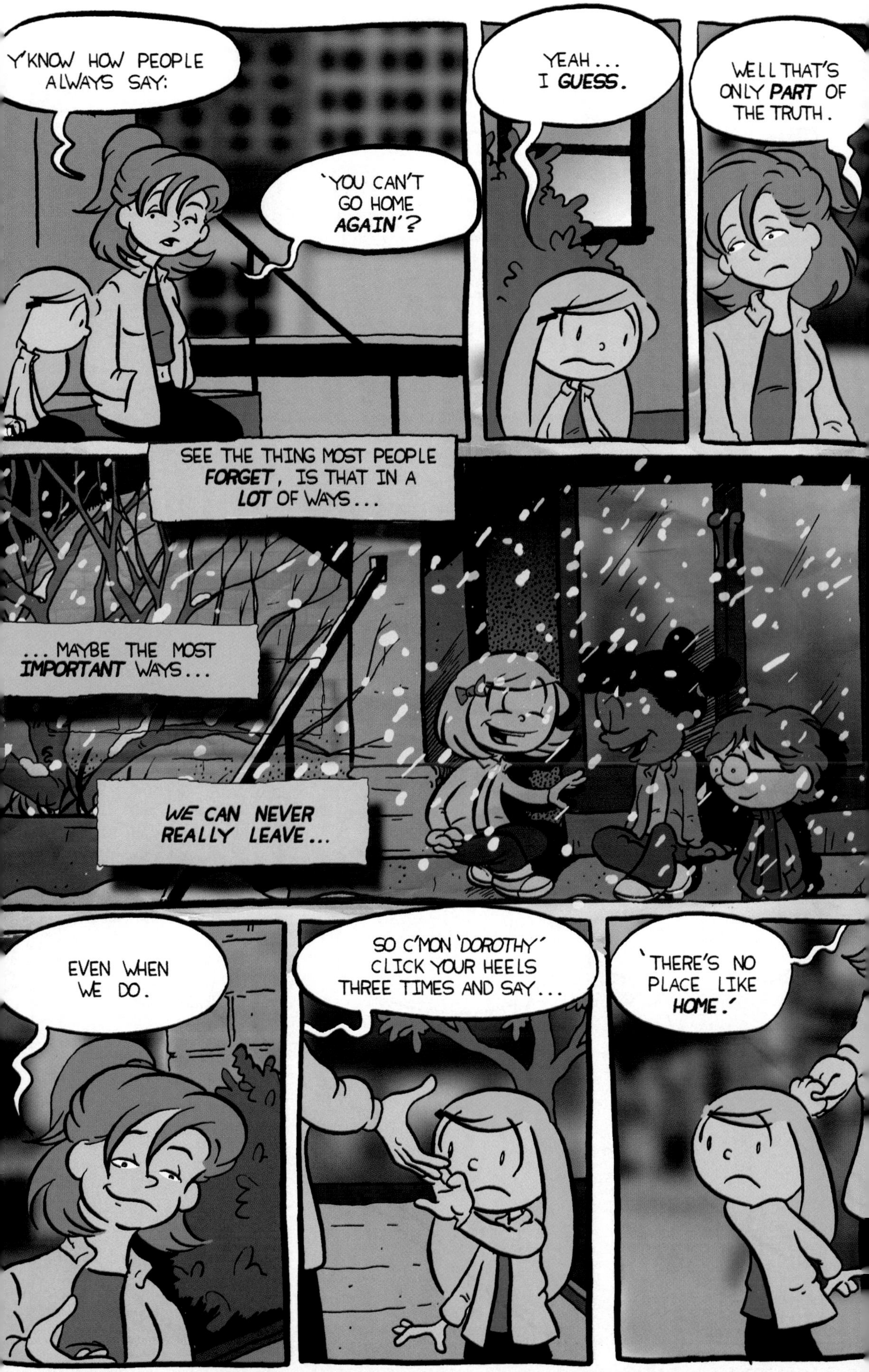
Y'KNOW HOW PEOPLE ALWAYS SAY:
`YOU CAN'T GO HOME AGAIN'?
YEAH... I GUESS.
WELL THAT'S ONLY PART OF THE TRUTH.
SEE THE THING MOST PEOPLE FORGET, IS THAT IN A LOT OF WAYS...
...MAYBE THE MOST IMPORTANT WAYS...
WE CAN NEVER REALLY LEAVE...
EVEN WHEN WE DO.
SO C'MON 'DOROTHY' CLICK YOUR HEELS THREE TIMES AND SAY...
`THERE'S NO PLACE LIKE HOME.'

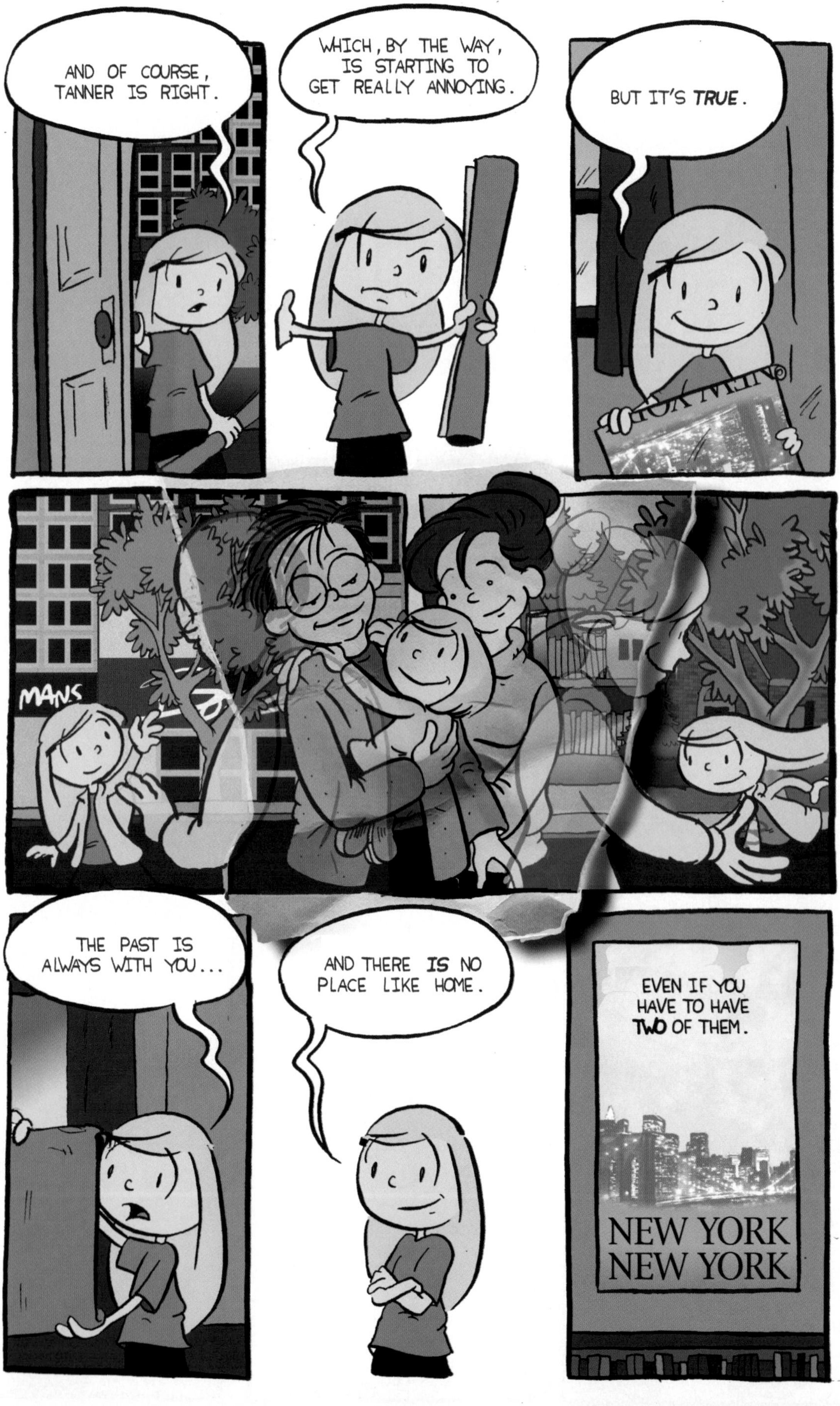
AND OF COURSE, TANNER IS RIGHT.
WHICH, BY THE WAY, IS STARTING TO GET REALLY ANNOYING.
BUT IT'S TRUE.
MANS
THE PAST IS ALWAYS WITH YOU...
AND THERE IS NO PLACE LIKE HOME.
EVEN IF YOU HAVE TO HAVE TWO OF THEM.
NEW YORK NEW YORK

Part

Six

"Rhonda and I are just saying No."

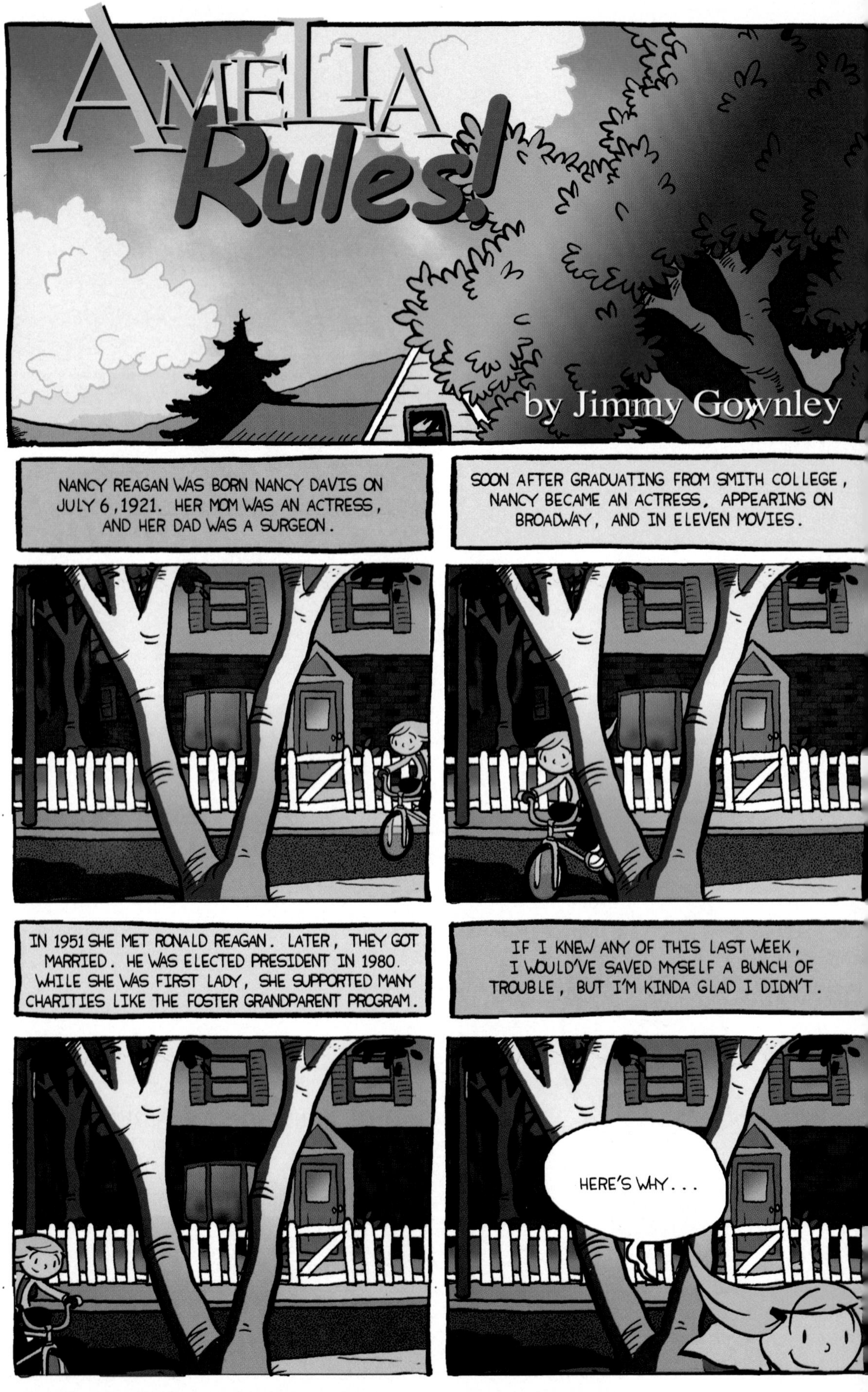
Amelia Rules!
by Jimmy Gownley
NANCY REAGAN WAS BORN NANCY DAVIS ON JULY 6, 1921. HER MOM WAS AN ACTRESS, AND HER DAD WAS A SURGEON.
SOON AFTER GRADUATING FROM SMITH COLLEGE, NANCY BECAME AN ACTRESS, APPEARING ON BROADWAY, AND IN ELEVEN MOVIES.
IN 1951 SHE MET RONALD REAGAN. LATER, THEY GOT MARRIED. HE WAS ELECTED PRESIDENT IN 1980. WHILE SHE WAS FIRST LADY, SHE SUPPORTED MANY CHARITIES LIKE THE FOSTER GRANDPARENT PROGRAM.
IF I KNEW ANY OF THIS LAST WEEK, I WOULD'VE SAVED MYSELF A BUNCH OF TROUBLE, BUT I'M KINDA GLAD I DIDN'T.
HERE'S WHY...

“FOR THE HEROES AND VILLAINS”

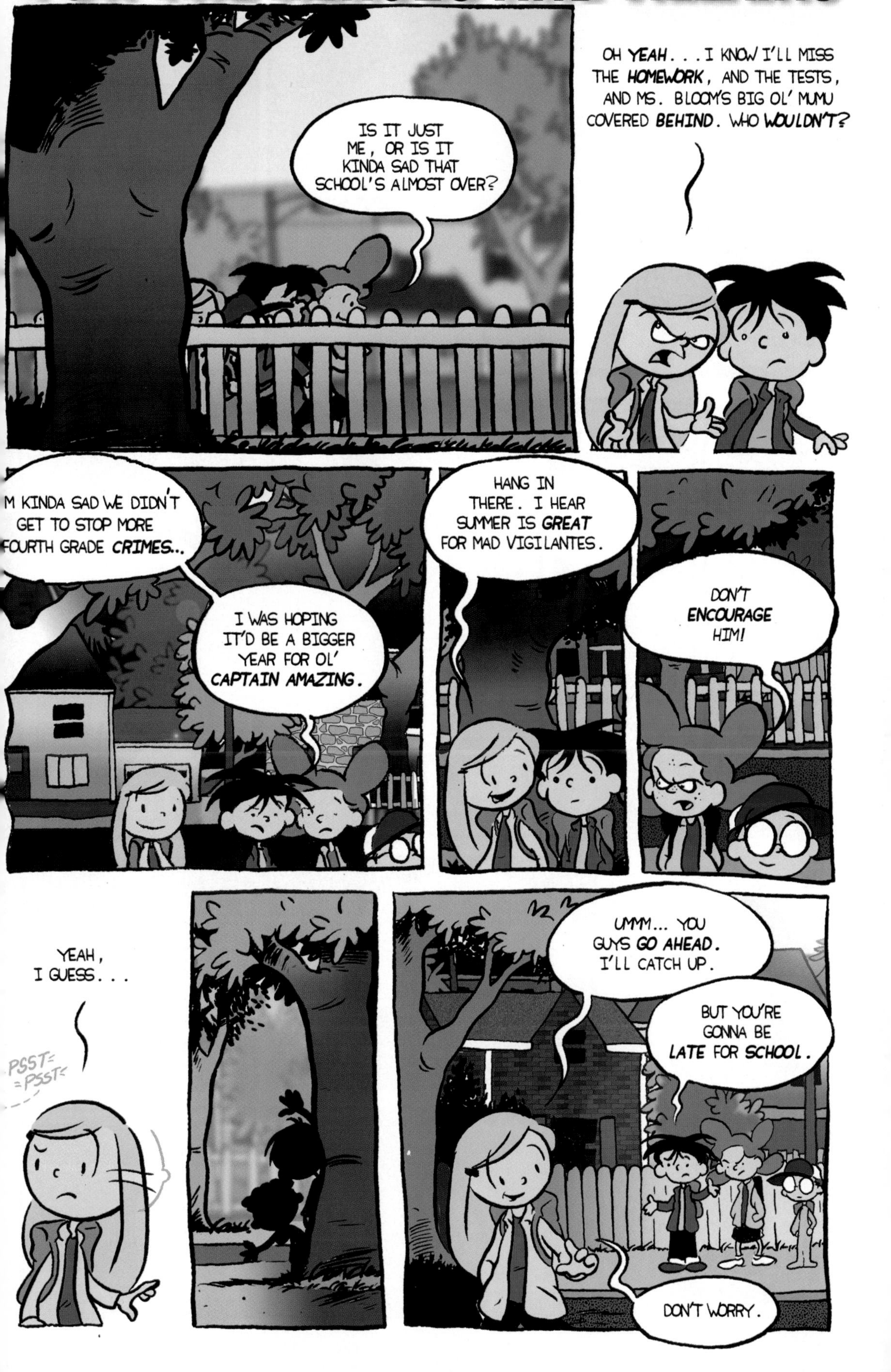
IS IT JUST ME, OR IS IT KINDA SAD THAT SCHOOL'S ALMOST OVER?
OH YEAH. . . I KNOW I'LL MISS THE HOMEWORK, AND THE TESTS, AND MS. BLOOM'S BIG OL' MUMU COVERED BEHIND. WHO WOULDN'T?
M KINDA SAD WE DIDN'T GET TO STOP MORE FOURTH GRADE CRIMES...
I WAS HOPING IT'D BE A BIGGER YEAR FOR OL' CAPTAIN AMAZING.
HANG IN THERE. I HEAR SUMMER IS GREAT FOR MAD VIGILANTES.
DON'T ENCOURAGE HIM!
YEAH, I GUESS. . .
PSST PSST
UMM... YOU GUYS GO AHEAD. I'LL CATCH UP.
BUT YOU'RE GONNA BE LATE FOR SCHOOL.
DON'T WORRY.

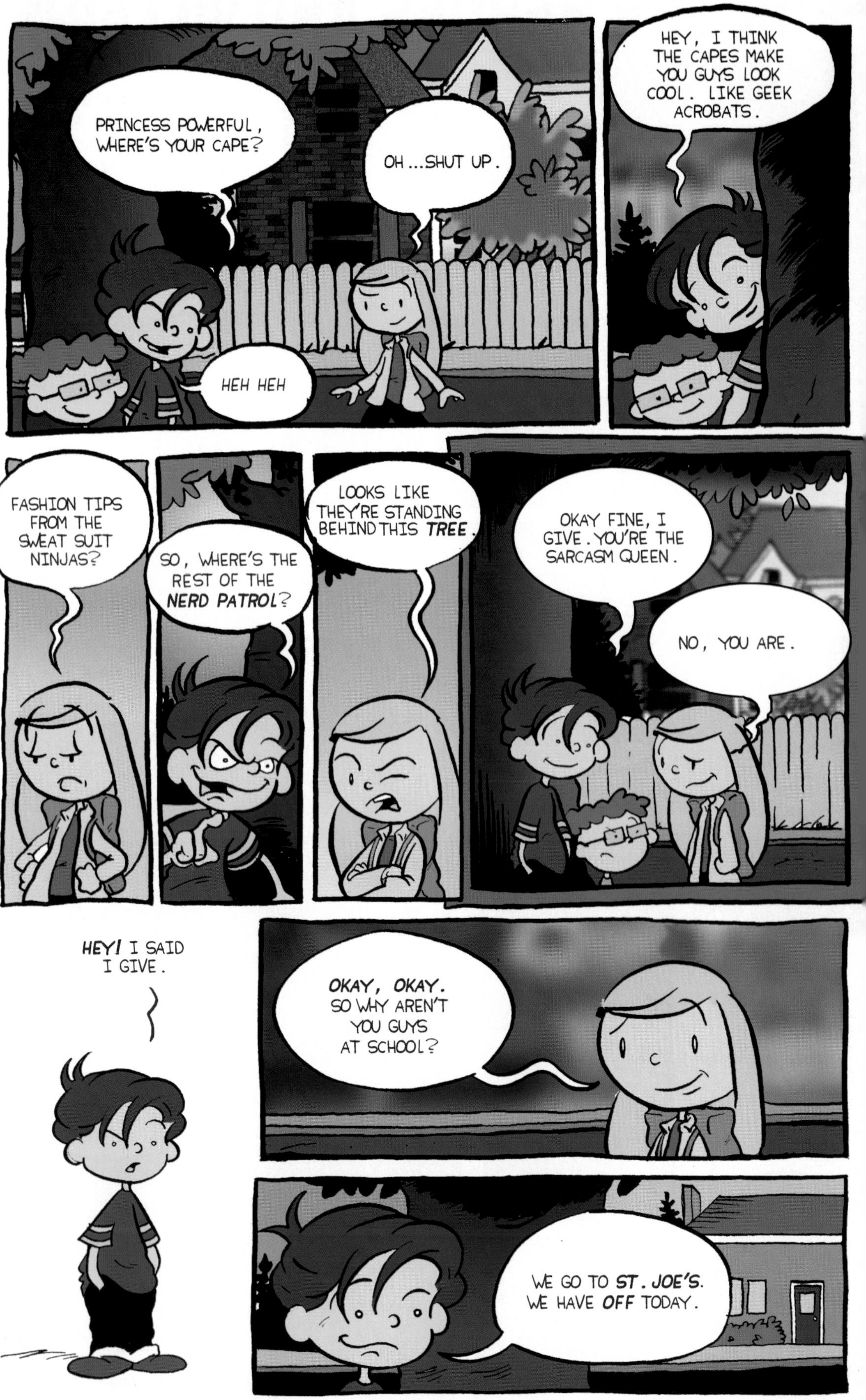
PRINCESS POWERFUL, WHERE'S YOUR CAPE?
HEH HEH
OH ...SHUT UP.
HEY, I THINK THE CAPES MAKE YOU GUYS LOOK COOL. LIKE GEEK ACROBATS.
FASHION TIPS FROM THE SWEAT SUIT NINJAS?
SO, WHERE'S THE REST OF THE NERD PATROL?
LOOKS LIKE THEY'RE STANDING BEHIND THIS TREE.
OKAY FINE, I GIVE. YOU'RE THE SARCASM QUEEN.
NO, YOU ARE.
HEY! I SAID I GIVE.
OKAY, OKAY. SO WHY AREN'T YOU GUYS AT SCHOOL?
WE GO TO ST. JOE'S. WE HAVE OFF TODAY.

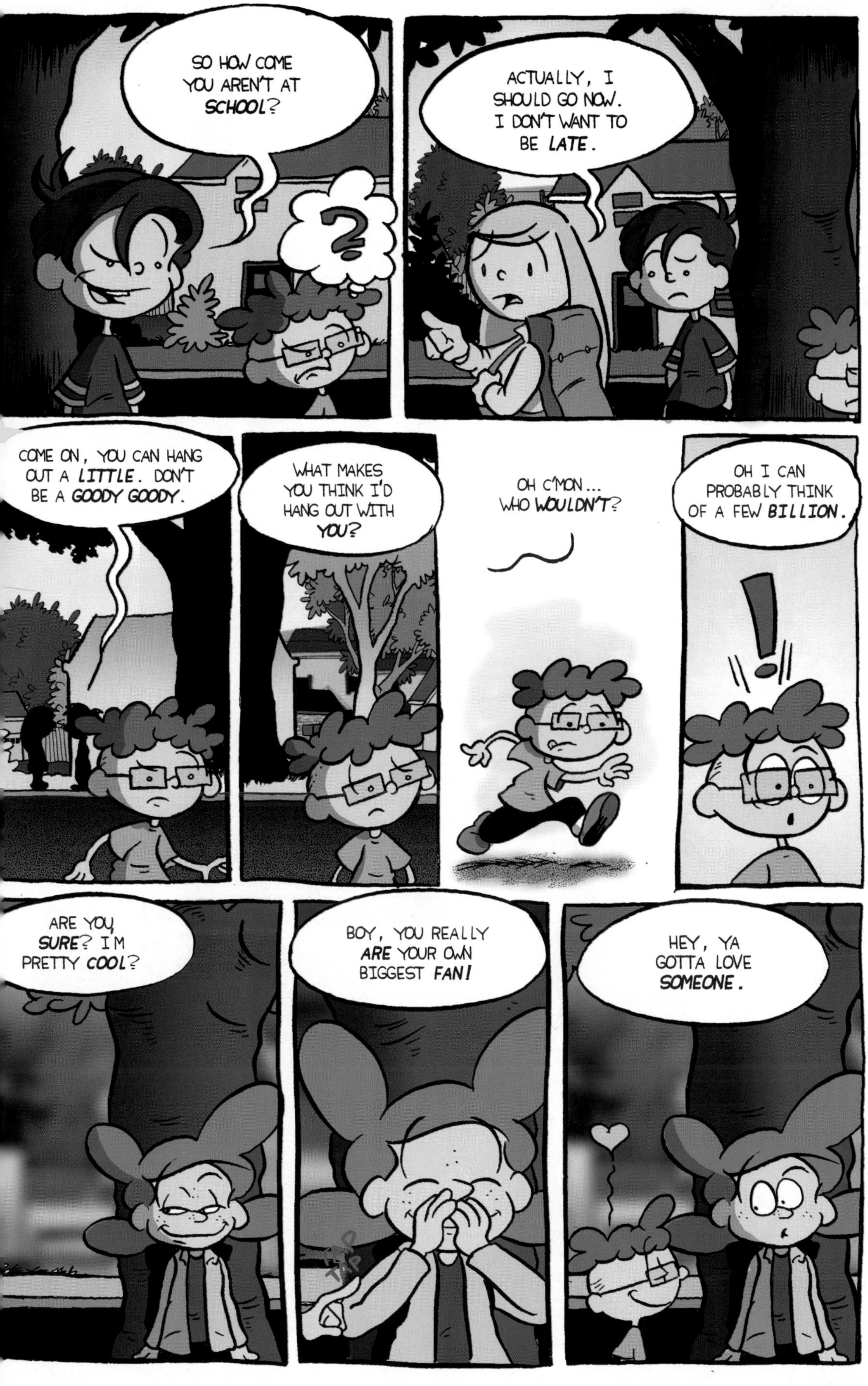
SO HOW COME YOU AREN'T AT SCHOOL?
?
ACTUALLY, I SHOULD GO NOW. I DON'T WANT TO BE LATE.
COME ON, YOU CAN HANG OUT A LITTLE. DON'T BE A GOODY GOODY.
WHAT MAKES YOU THINK I'D HANG OUT WITH YOU?
OH C'MON... WHO WOULDN'T?
OH I CAN PROBABLY THINK OF A FEW BILLION.
!
ARE YOU SURE? I'M PRETTY COOL?
BOY, YOU REALLY ARE YOUR OWN BIGGEST FAN!
TAP TAP
HEY, YA GOTTA LOVE SOMEONE.

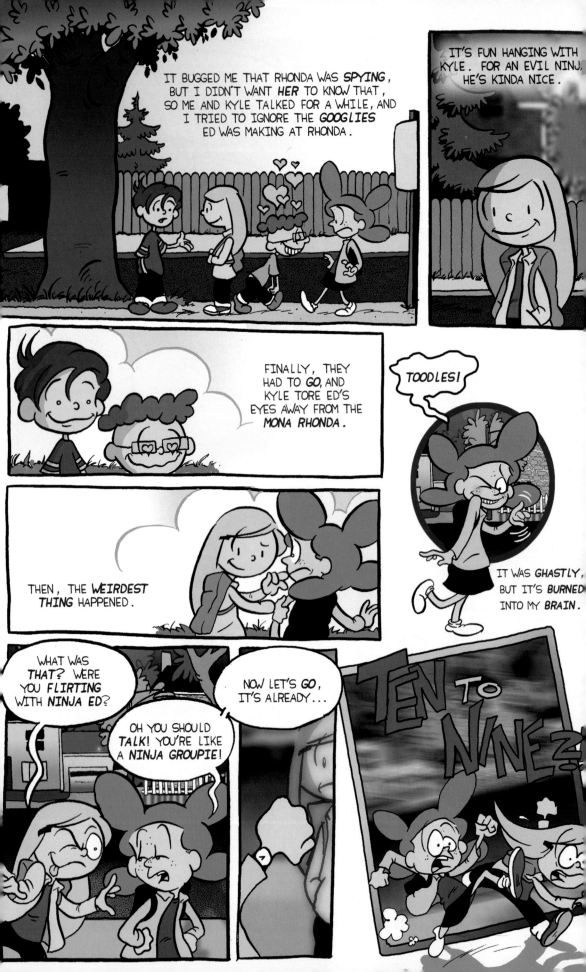

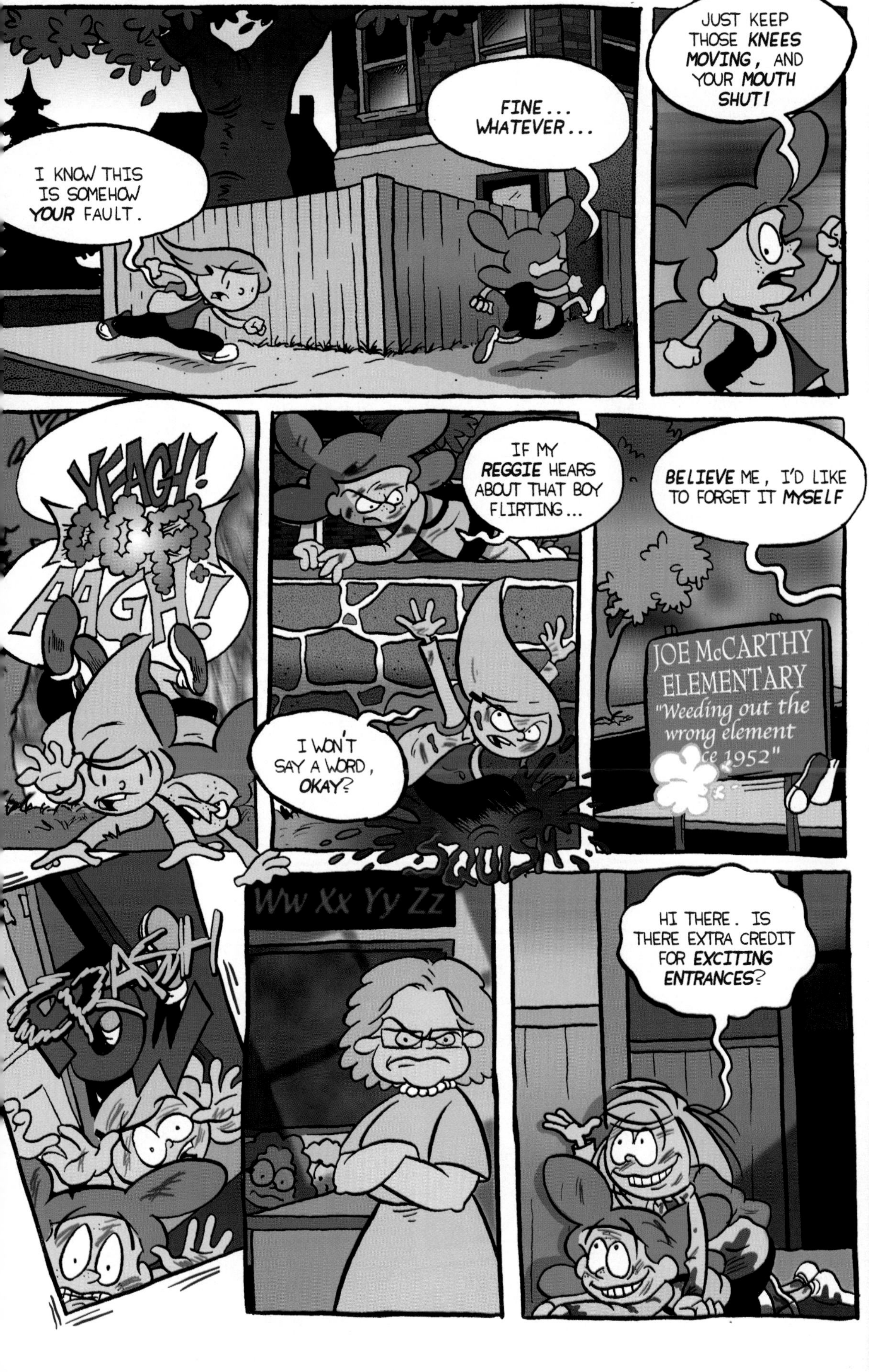
I KNOW THIS IS SOMEHOW YOUR FAULT.
FINE... WHATEVER...
JUST KEEP THOSE KNEES MOVING, AND YOUR MOUTH SHUT!
YEAGH!
AAGH!
IF MY REGGIE HEARS ABOUT THAT BOY FLIRTING...
I WON'T SAY A WORD, OKAY?
BELIEVE ME, I'D LIKE TO FORGET IT MYSELF
JOE McCARTHY ELEMENTARY
"Weeding out the wrong element
ce 1952"
Ww Xx Yy Zz
HI THERE. IS THERE EXTRA CREDIT FOR EXCITING ENTRANCES?

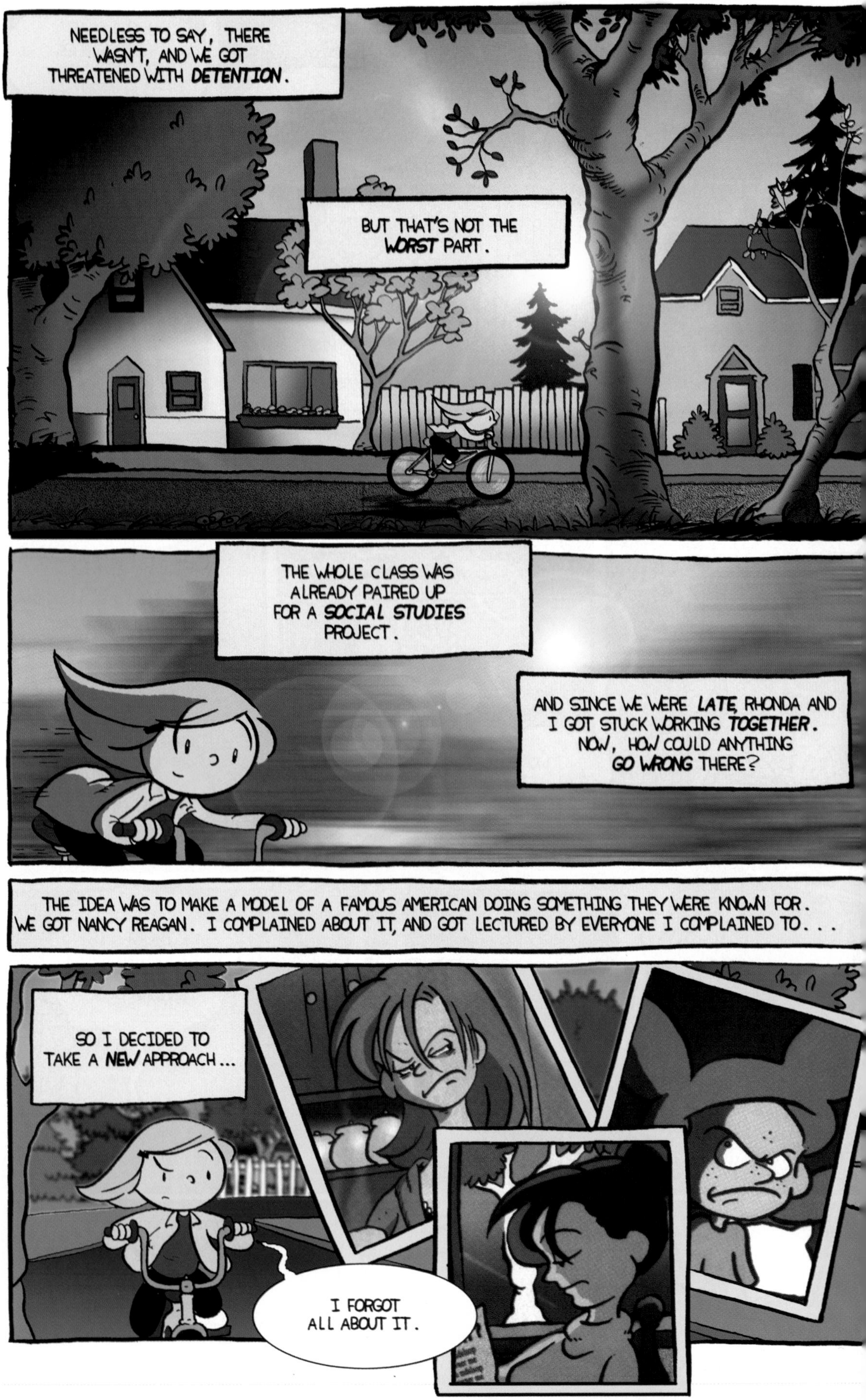
NEEDLESS TO SAY, THERE WASN'T, AND WE GOT THREATENED WITH DETENTION.
BUT THAT'S NOT THE WORST PART.
THE WHOLE CLASS WAS ALREADY PAIRED UP FOR A SOCIAL STUDIES PROJECT.
AND SINCE WE WERE LATE, RHONDA AND I GOT STUCK WORKING TOGETHER. NOW, HOW COULD ANYTHING GO WRONG THERE?
THE IDEA WAS TO MAKE A MODEL OF A FAMOUS AMERICAN DOING SOMETHING THEY WERE KNOWN FOR. WE GOT NANCY REAGAN. I COMPLAINED ABOUT IT, AND GOT LECTURED BY EVERYONE I COMPLAINED TO...
SO I DECIDED TO TAKE A NEW APPROACH...
I FORGOT ALL ABOUT IT.

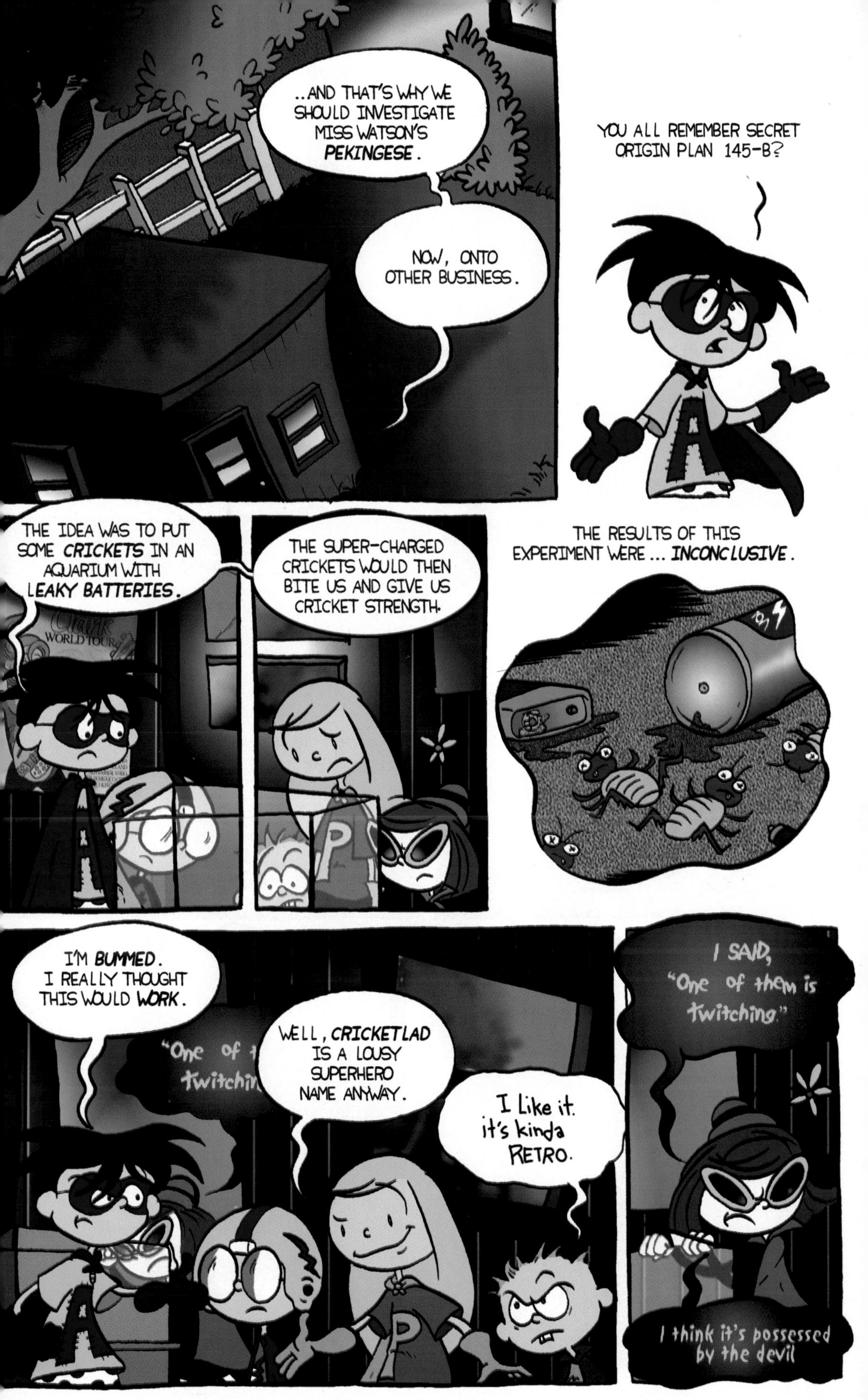

..AND THAT'S WHY WE SHOULD INVESTIGATE MISS WATSON'S **PEKINGESE**.
NOW, ONTO OTHER BUSINESS.
YOU ALL REMEMBER SECRET ORIGIN PLAN 145-B?
THE IDEA WAS TO PUT SOME **CRICKETS** IN AN AQUARIUM WITH **LEAKY BATTERIES**.
WORLD TOUR
THE SUPER-CHARGED CRICKETS WOULD THEN BITE US AND GIVE US CRICKET STRENGTH.
THE RESULTS OF THIS EXPERIMENT WERE ... **INCONCLUSIVE**.
I'M **BUMMED**. I REALLY THOUGHT THIS WOULD **WORK**.
WELL, **CRICKETLAD** IS A LOUSY SUPERHERO NAME ANYWAY.
I Like it. it's kinda RETRO.
I SAID, "One of them is twitching."
I think it's possessed by the devil

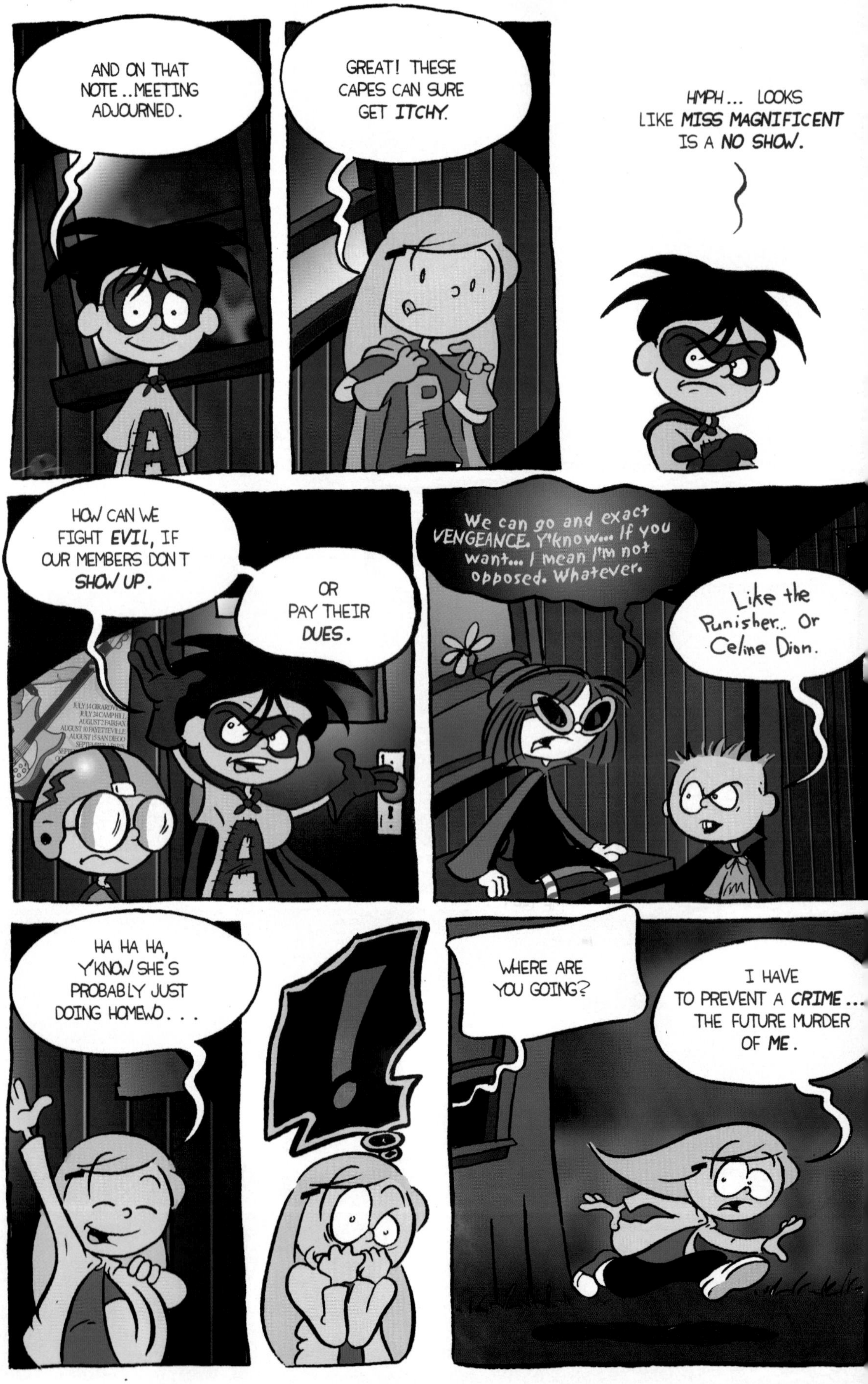
AND ON THAT NOTE ..MEETING ADJOURNED.
GREAT! THESE CAPES CAN SURE GET ITCHY.
HMPH ... LOOKS LIKE MISS MAGNIFICENT IS A NO SHOW.
HOW CAN WE FIGHT EVIL, IF OUR MEMBERS DON'T SHOW UP.
OR PAY THEIR DUES.
We can go and exact VENGEANCE. Y'know... If you want... I mean I'm not opposed. Whatever.
Like the Punisher... Or Celine Dion.
HA HA HA, Y'KNOW SHE'S PROBABLY JUST DOING HOMEWO . . .
!
WHERE ARE YOU GOING?
I HAVE TO PREVENT A CRIME ... THE FUTURE MURDER OF ME.

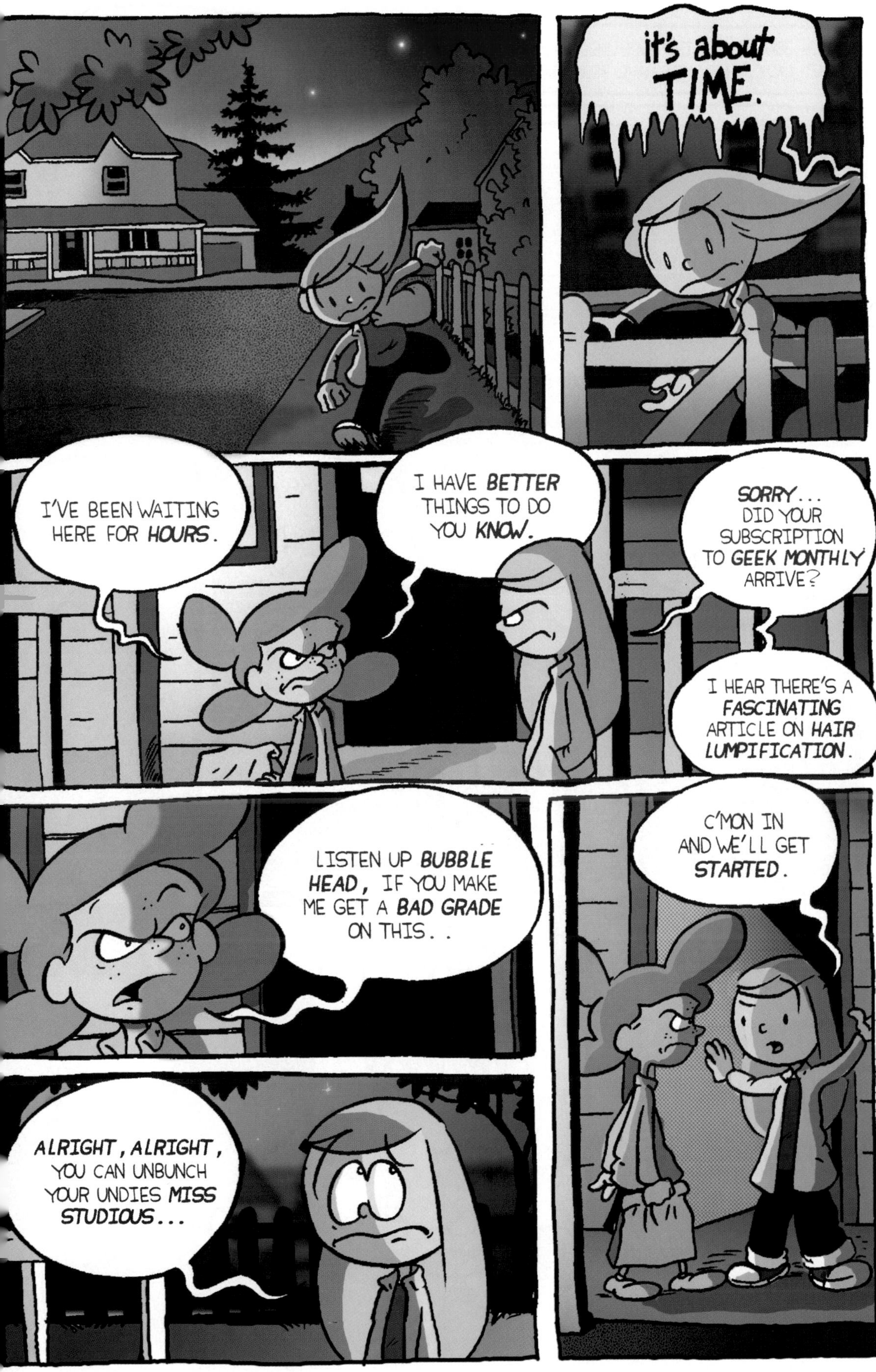
it's about TIME.
I'VE BEEN WAITING HERE FOR HOURS.
I HAVE BETTER THINGS TO DO YOU KNOW.
SORRY... DID YOUR SUBSCRIPTION TO GEEK MONTHLY ARRIVE?
I HEAR THERE'S A FASCINATING ARTICLE ON HAIR LUMPIFICATION.
LISTEN UP BUBBLE HEAD, IF YOU MAKE ME GET A BAD GRADE ON THIS..
ALRIGHT, ALRIGHT, YOU CAN UNBUNCH YOUR UNDIES MISS STUDIOUS...
C'MON IN AND WE'LL GET STARTED.

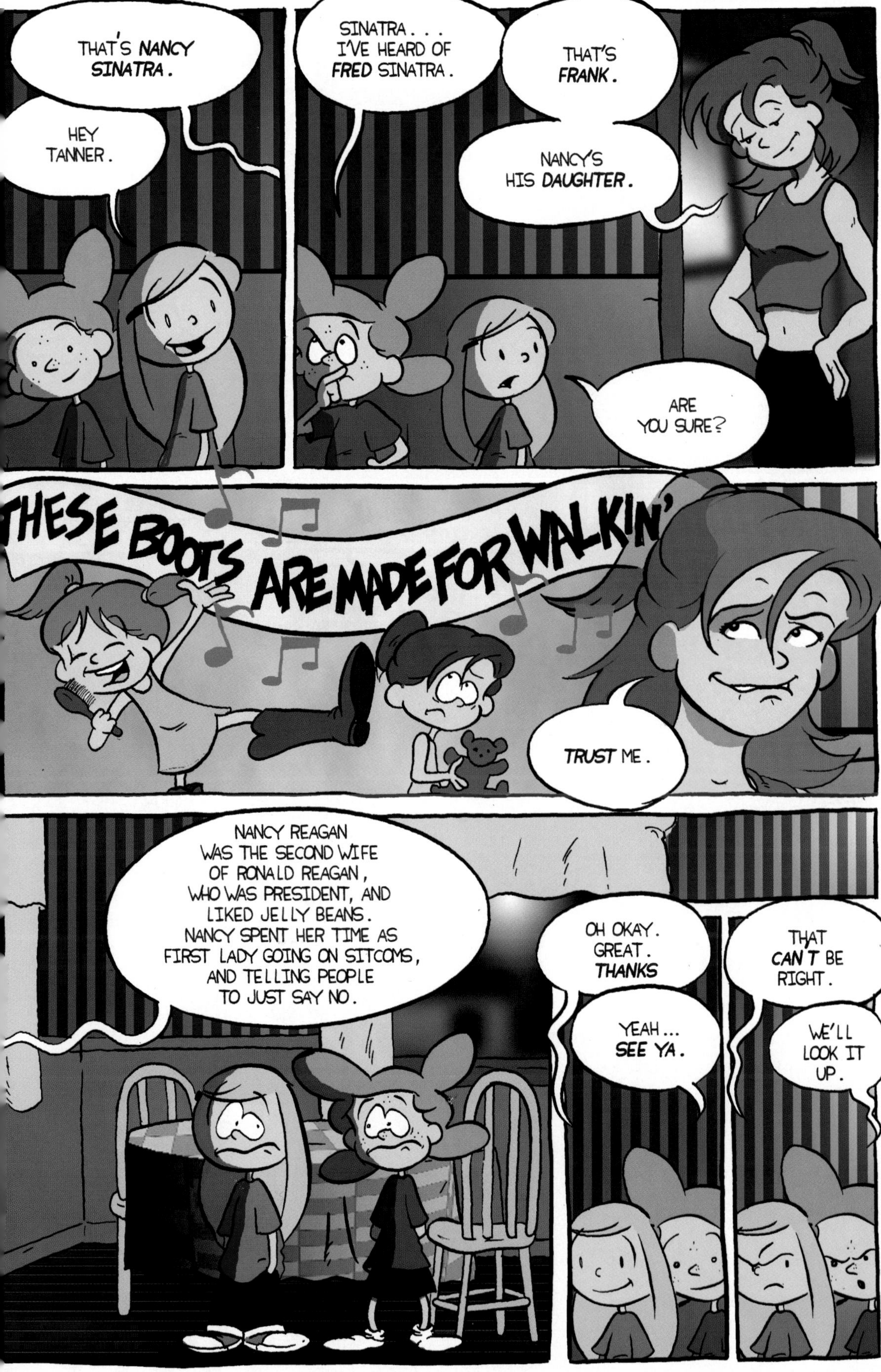
HEY TANNER.
THAT'S NANCY SINATRA.
SINATRA . . . I'VE HEARD OF FRED SINATRA.
THAT'S FRANK.
NANCY'S HIS DAUGHTER.
ARE YOU SURE?
THESE BOOTS ARE MADE FOR WALKIN'
TRUST ME.
NANCY REAGAN WAS THE SECOND WIFE OF RONALD REAGAN, WHO WAS PRESIDENT, AND LIKED JELLY BEANS. NANCY SPENT HER TIME AS FIRST LADY GOING ON SITCOMS, AND TELLING PEOPLE TO JUST SAY NO.
OH OKAY. GREAT. THANKS
YEAH... SEE YA.
THAT CAN'T BE RIGHT.
WE'LL LOOK IT UP.

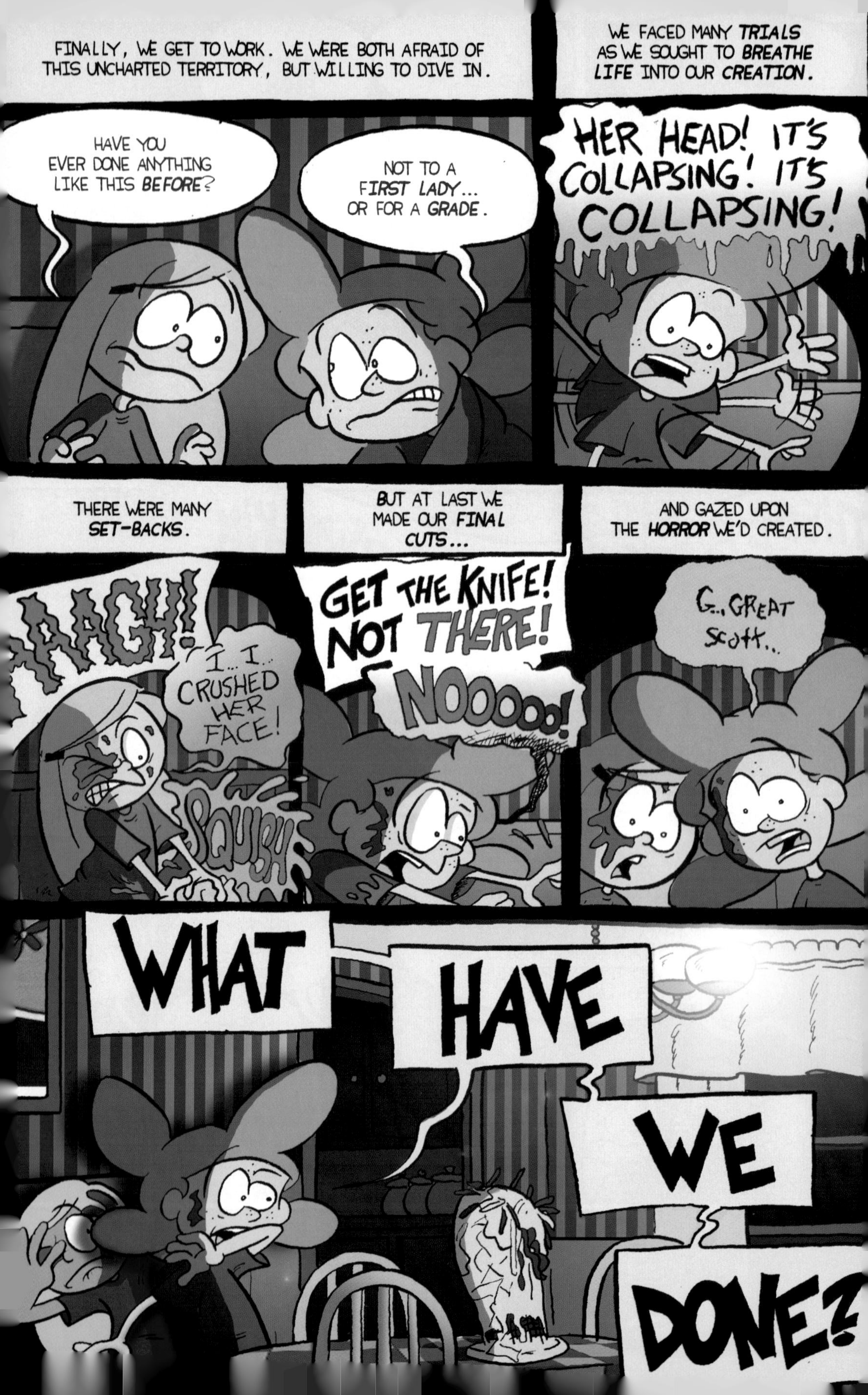
FINALLY, WE GET TO WORK. WE WERE BOTH AFRAID OF THIS UNCHARTED TERRITORY, BUT WILLING TO DIVE IN.
HAVE YOU EVER DONE ANYTHING LIKE THIS BEFORE?
NOT TO A FIRST LADY... OR FOR A GRADE.
WE FACED MANY TRIALS AS WE SOUGHT TO BREATHE LIFE INTO OUR CREATION.
HER HEAD! IT'S COLLAPSING! IT'S COLLAPSING!
THERE WERE MANY SET-BACKS.
AAGH!
I.. I.. CRUSHED HER FACE!
SQUISH
BUT AT LAST WE MADE OUR FINAL CUTS...
GET THE KNIFE! NOT THERE!
NOOOOOO!
AND GAZED UPON THE HORROR WE'D CREATED.
G.. GREAT SCOTT..
WHAT HAVE WE DONE?

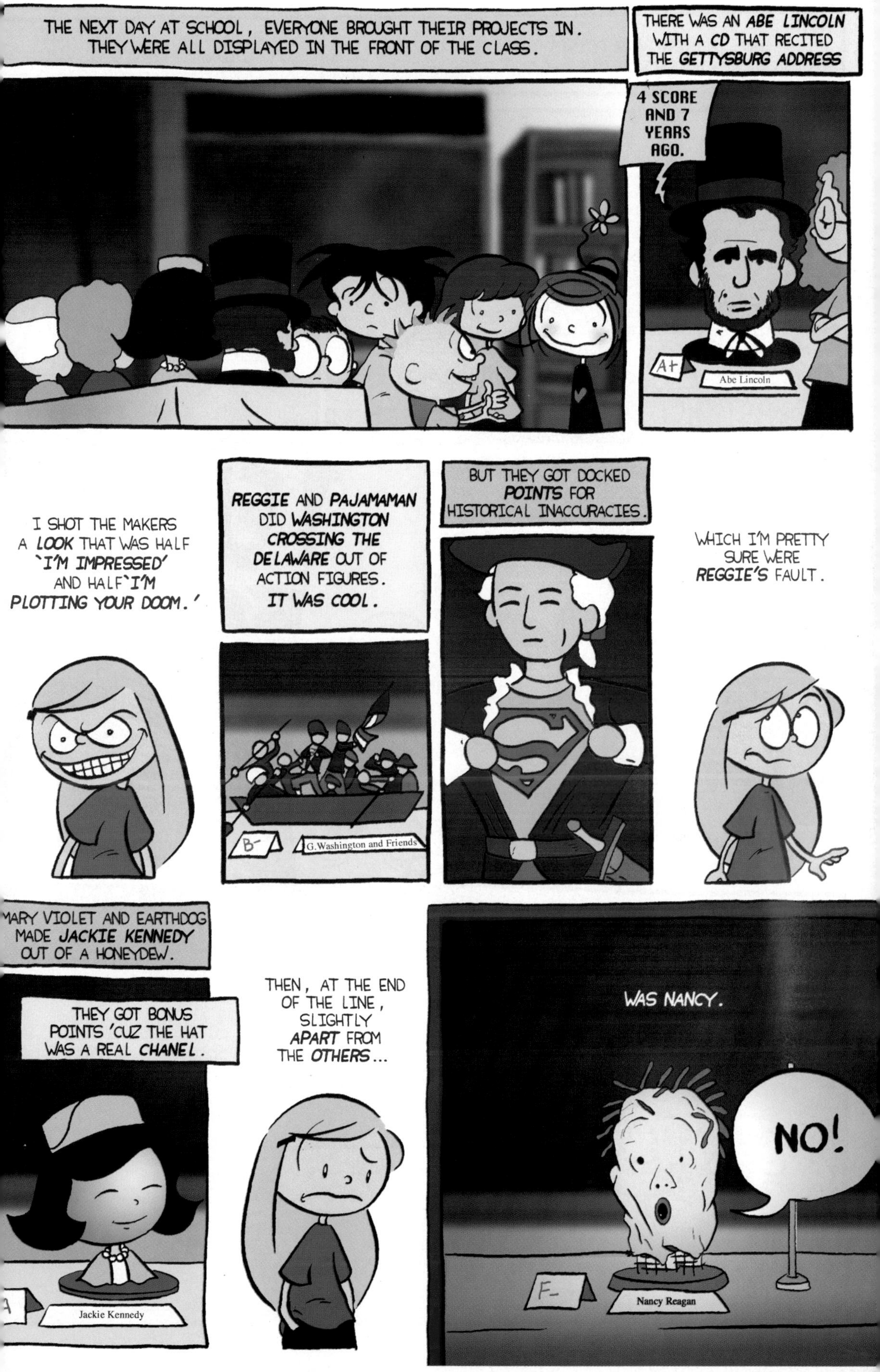
THE NEXT DAY AT SCHOOL, EVERYONE BROUGHT THEIR PROJECTS IN. THEY WERE ALL DISPLAYED IN THE FRONT OF THE CLASS.
THERE WAS AN ABE LINCOLN WITH A CD THAT RECITED THE GETTYSBURG ADDRESS
4 SCORE AND 7 YEARS AGO.
A+
Abe Lincoln
I SHOT THE MAKERS A LOOK THAT WAS HALF 'I'M IMPRESSED' AND HALF 'I'M PLOTTING YOUR DOOM.'
REGGIE AND PAJAMAMAN DID WASHINGTON CROSSING THE DELAWARE OUT OF ACTION FIGURES. IT WAS COOL.
B-
G.Washington and Friends
BUT THEY GOT DOCKED POINTS FOR HISTORICAL INACCURACIES.
WHICH I'M PRETTY SURE WERE REGGIE'S FAULT.
MARY VIOLET AND EARTHDOG MADE JACKIE KENNEDY OUT OF A HONEYDEW.
THEY GOT BONUS POINTS 'CUZ THE HAT WAS A REAL CHANEL.
A
Jackie Kennedy
THEN, AT THE END OF THE LINE, SLIGHTLY APART FROM THE OTHERS...
WAS NANCY.
NO!
F-
Nancy Reagan

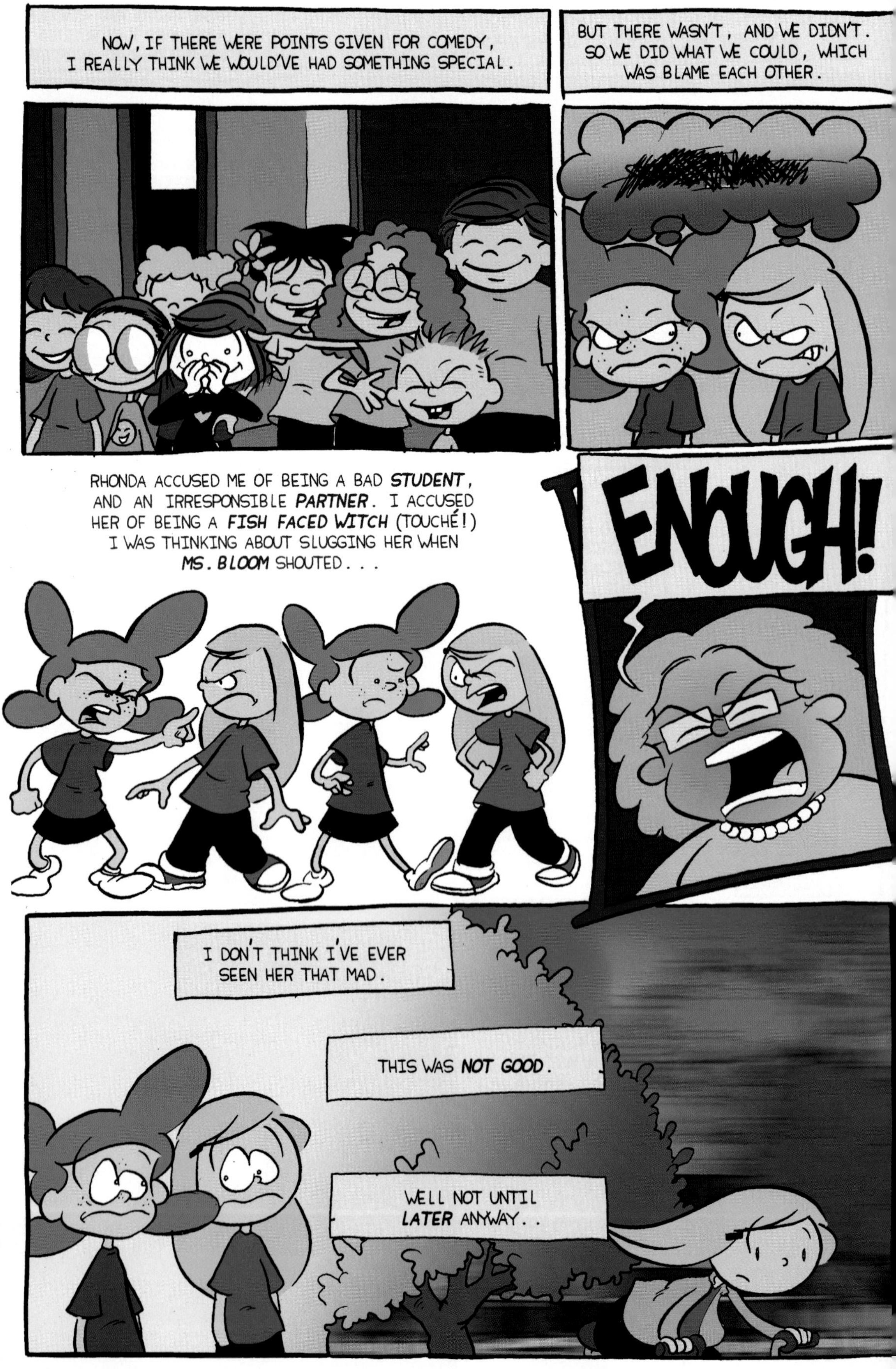
NOW, IF THERE WERE POINTS GIVEN FOR COMEDY, I REALLY THINK WE WOULD'VE HAD SOMETHING SPECIAL.
BUT THERE WASN'T, AND WE DIDN'T. SO WE DID WHAT WE COULD, WHICH WAS BLAME EACH OTHER.
RHONDA ACCUSED ME OF BEING A BAD **STUDENT**, AND AN IRRESPONSIBLE **PARTNER**. I ACCUSED HER OF BEING A **FISH FACED WITCH** (TOUCHÉ!) I WAS THINKING ABOUT SLUGGING HER WHEN **MS. BLOOM** SHOUTED . . .
ENOUGH!
I DON'T THINK I'VE EVER SEEN HER THAT MAD.
THIS WAS **NOT GOOD**.
WELL NOT UNTIL **LATER** ANYWAY. .

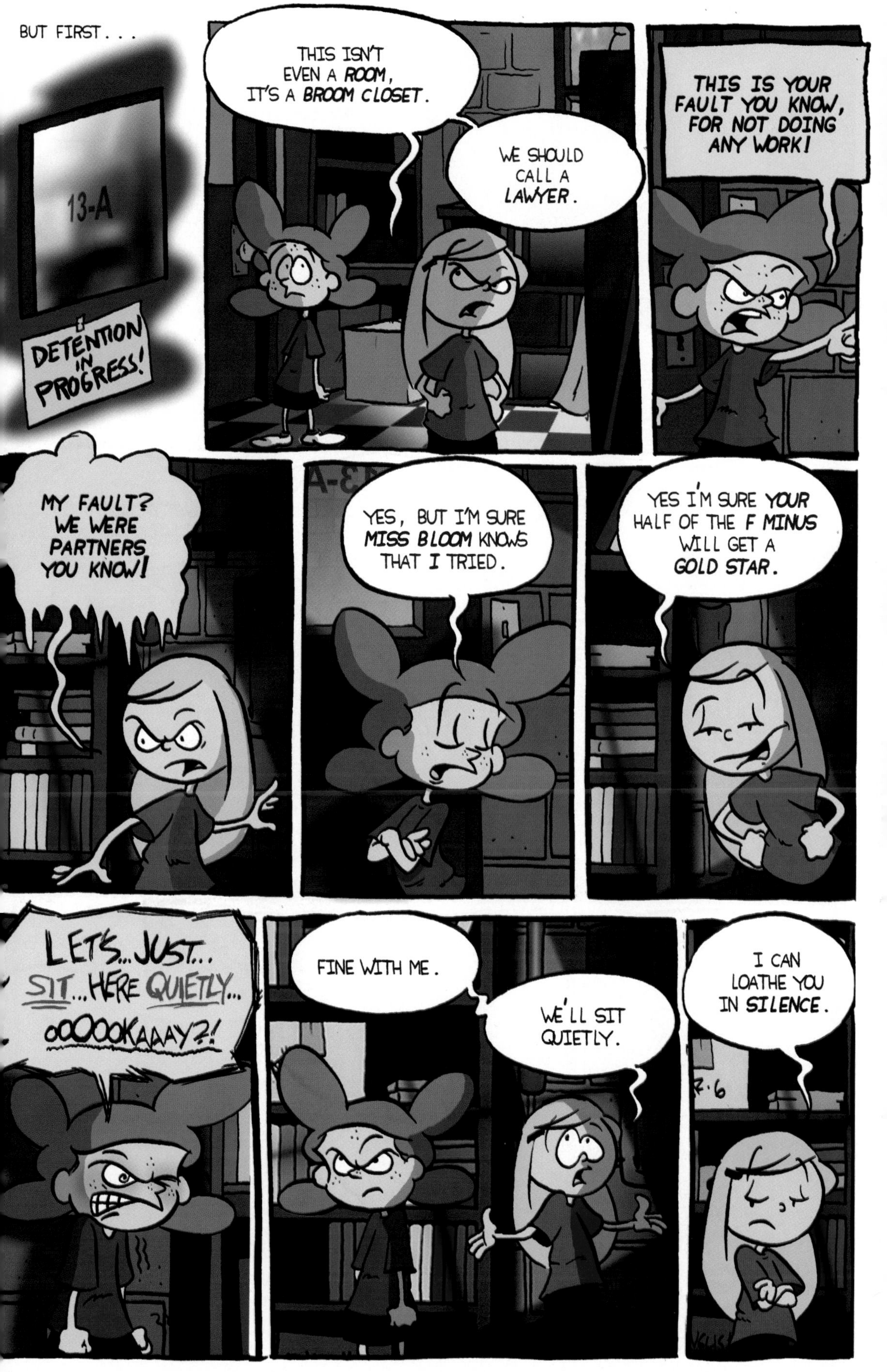
BUT FIRST . . .
13-A
DETENTION IN PROGRESS!
THIS ISN'T EVEN A ROOM, IT'S A BROOM CLOSET.
WE SHOULD CALL A LAWYER.
THIS IS YOUR FAULT YOU KNOW, FOR NOT DOING ANY WORK!
MY FAULT? WE WERE PARTNERS YOU KNOW!
YES, BUT I'M SURE MISS BLOOM KNOWS THAT I TRIED.
YES I'M SURE YOUR HALF OF THE F MINUS WILL GET A GOLD STAR.
LET'S...JUST... SIT...HERE QUIETLY... OOOOOKAAAY?!
FINE WITH ME.
WE'LL SIT QUIETLY.
I CAN LOATHE YOU IN SILENCE.

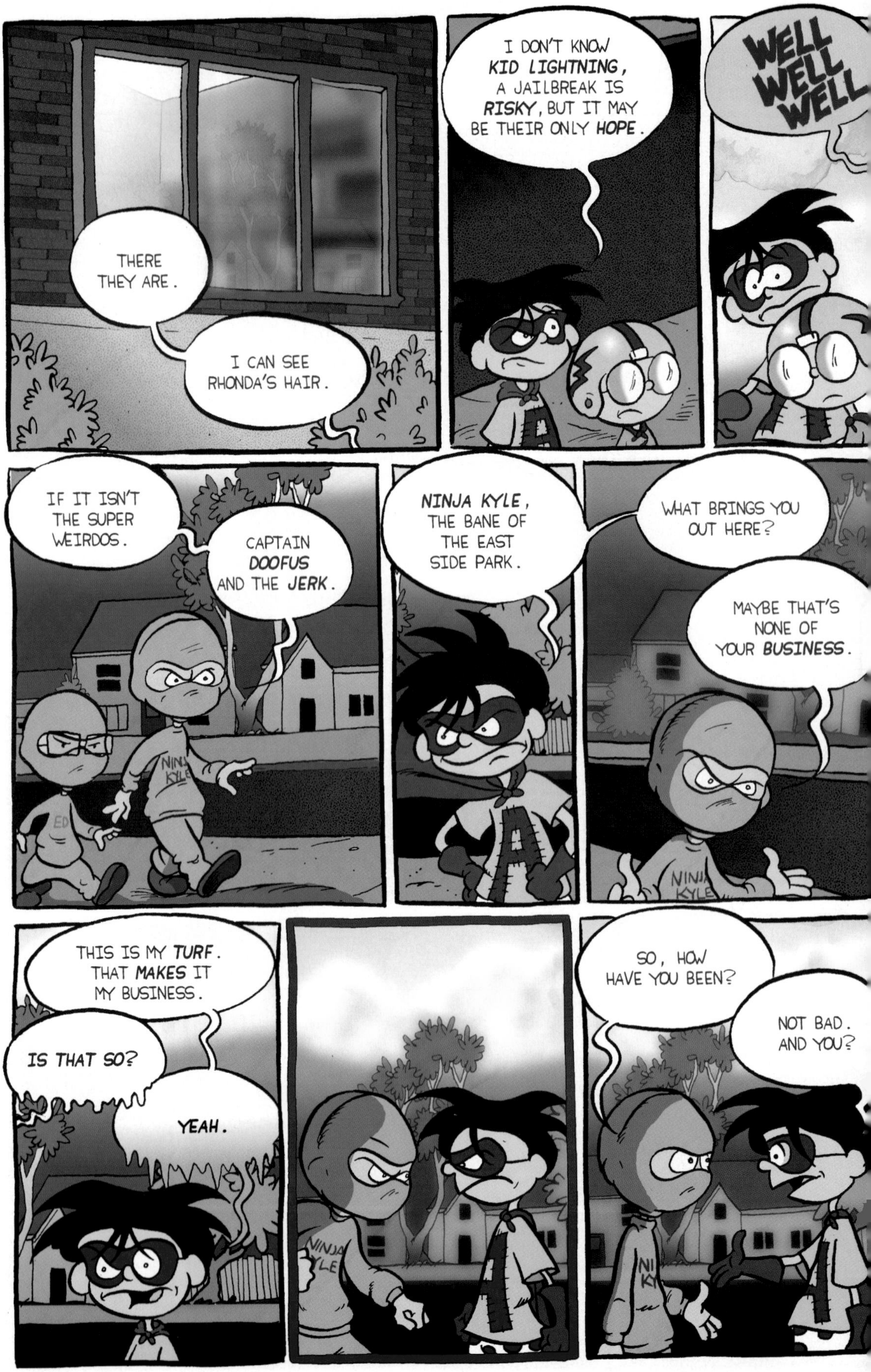
THERE THEY ARE.
I CAN SEE RHONDA'S HAIR.
I DON'T KNOW KID LIGHTNING, A JAILBREAK IS RISKY, BUT IT MAY BE THEIR ONLY HOPE.
WELL WELL WELL
IF IT ISN'T THE SUPER WEIRDOS.
CAPTAIN DOOFUS AND THE JERK.
NINJA KYLE, THE BANE OF THE EAST SIDE PARK.
WHAT BRINGS YOU OUT HERE?
MAYBE THAT'S NONE OF YOUR BUSINESS.
THIS IS MY TURF. THAT MAKES IT MY BUSINESS.
IS THAT SO?
YEAH.
SO, HOW HAVE YOU BEEN?
NOT BAD. AND YOU?

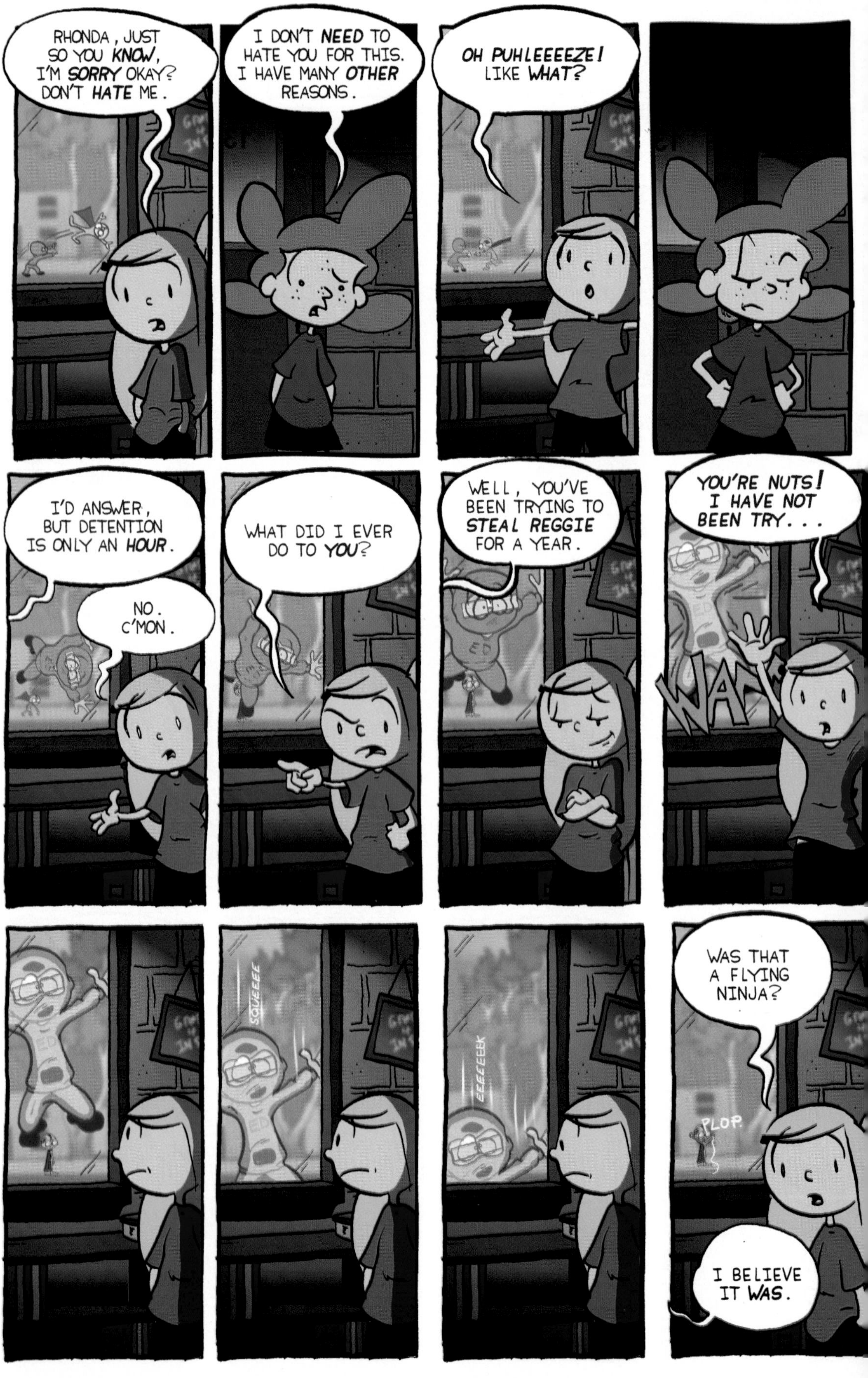
RHONDA, JUST SO YOU KNOW, I'M SORRY OKAY? DON'T HATE ME.
I DON'T NEED TO HATE YOU FOR THIS. I HAVE MANY OTHER REASONS.
OH PUHLEEEEZE! LIKE WHAT?
I'D ANSWER, BUT DETENTION IS ONLY AN HOUR.
NO. C'MON.
WHAT DID I EVER DO TO YOU?
WELL, YOU'VE BEEN TRYING TO STEAL REGGIE FOR A YEAR.
YOU'RE NUTS! I HAVE NOT BEEN TRY. . .
SQUEEEEE
EEEEEEEK
WAS THAT A FLYING NINJA?
PLOP.
I BELIEVE IT WAS.

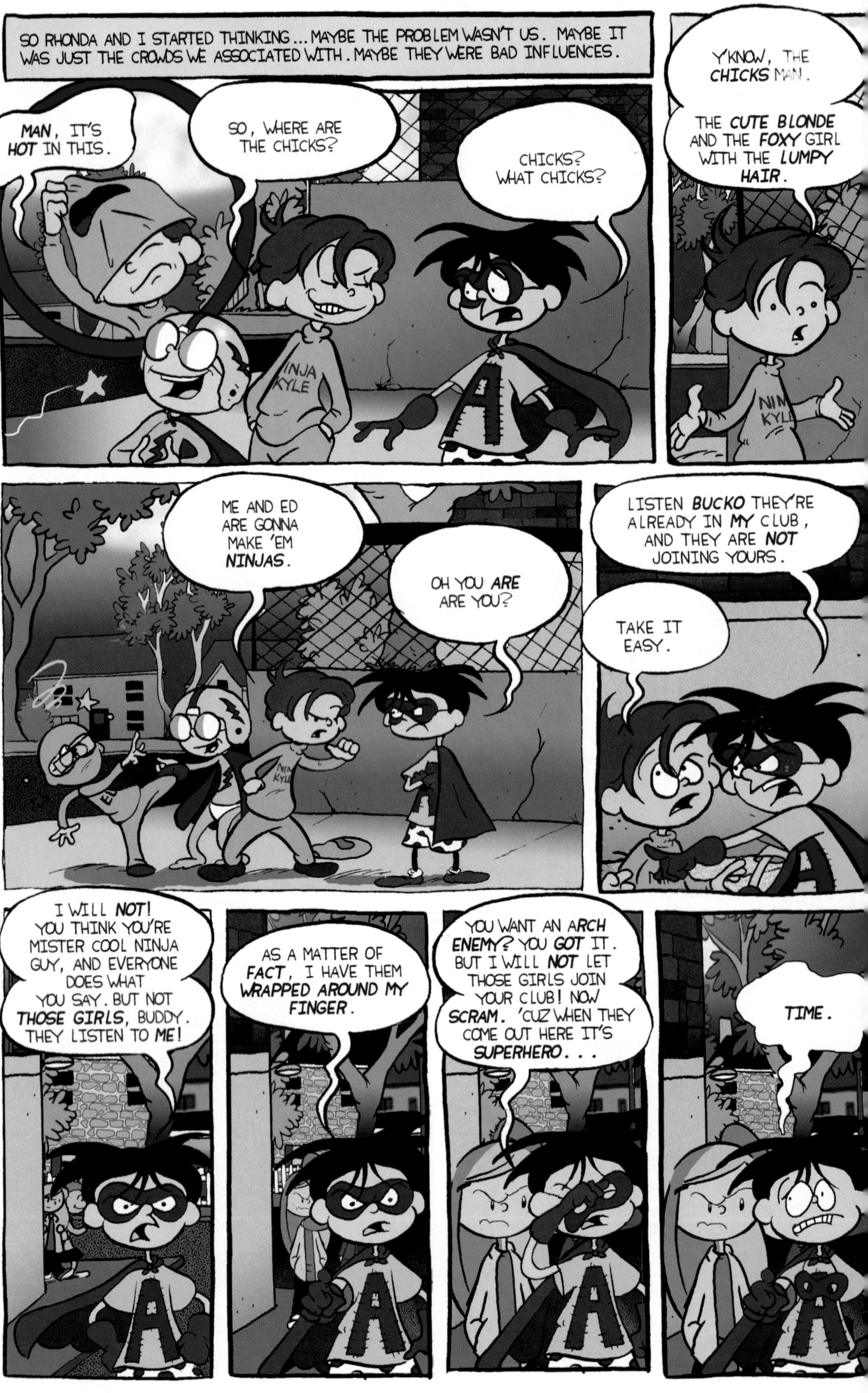
SO RHONDA AND I STARTED THINKING... MAYBE THE PROBLEM WASN'T US. MAYBE IT WAS JUST THE CROWDS WE ASSOCIATED WITH. MAYBE THEY WERE BAD INFLUENCES.
MAN, IT'S HOT IN THIS.
SO, WHERE ARE THE CHICKS?
CHICKS? WHAT CHICKS?
NINJA KYLE
Y'KNOW, THE CHICKS MAN.
THE CUTE BLONDE AND THE FOXY GIRL WITH THE LUMPY HAIR.
ME AND ED ARE GONNA MAKE 'EM NINJAS.
OH YOU ARE ARE YOU?
LISTEN BUCKO THEY'RE ALREADY IN MY CLUB, AND THEY ARE NOT JOINING YOURS.
TAKE IT EASY.
I WILL NOT! YOU THINK YOU'RE MISTER COOL NINJA GUY, AND EVERYONE DOES WHAT YOU SAY. BUT NOT THOSE GIRLS, BUDDY. THEY LISTEN TO ME!
AS A MATTER OF FACT, I HAVE THEM WRAPPED AROUND MY FINGER.
YOU WANT AN ARCH ENEMY? YOU GOT IT. BUT I WILL NOT LET THOSE GIRLS JOIN YOUR CLUB! NOW SCRAM. 'CUZ WHEN THEY COME OUT HERE IT'S SUPERHERO...
TIME.

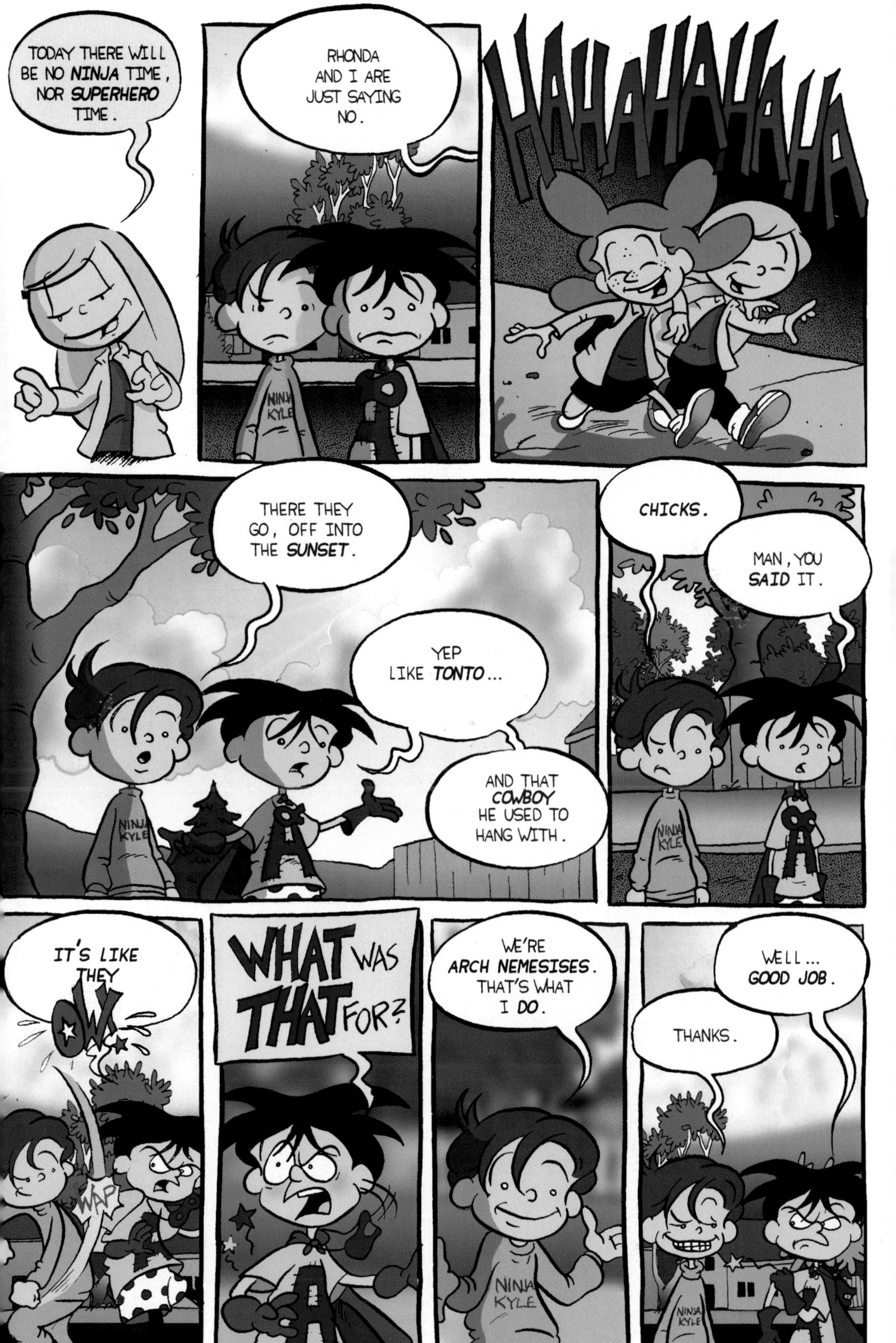
TODAY THERE WILL BE NO NINJA TIME, NOR SUPERHERO TIME.
RHONDA AND I ARE JUST SAYING NO.
HAHAHAHAHAHA
THERE THEY GO, OFF INTO THE SUNSET.
YEP LIKE TONTO...
AND THAT COWBOY HE USED TO HANG WITH.
CHICKS.
MAN, YOU SAID IT.
IT'S LIKE THEY
OW
WAP
WHAT WAS THAT FOR?
WE'RE ARCH NEMESISES. THAT'S WHAT I DO.
WELL... GOOD JOB.
THANKS.

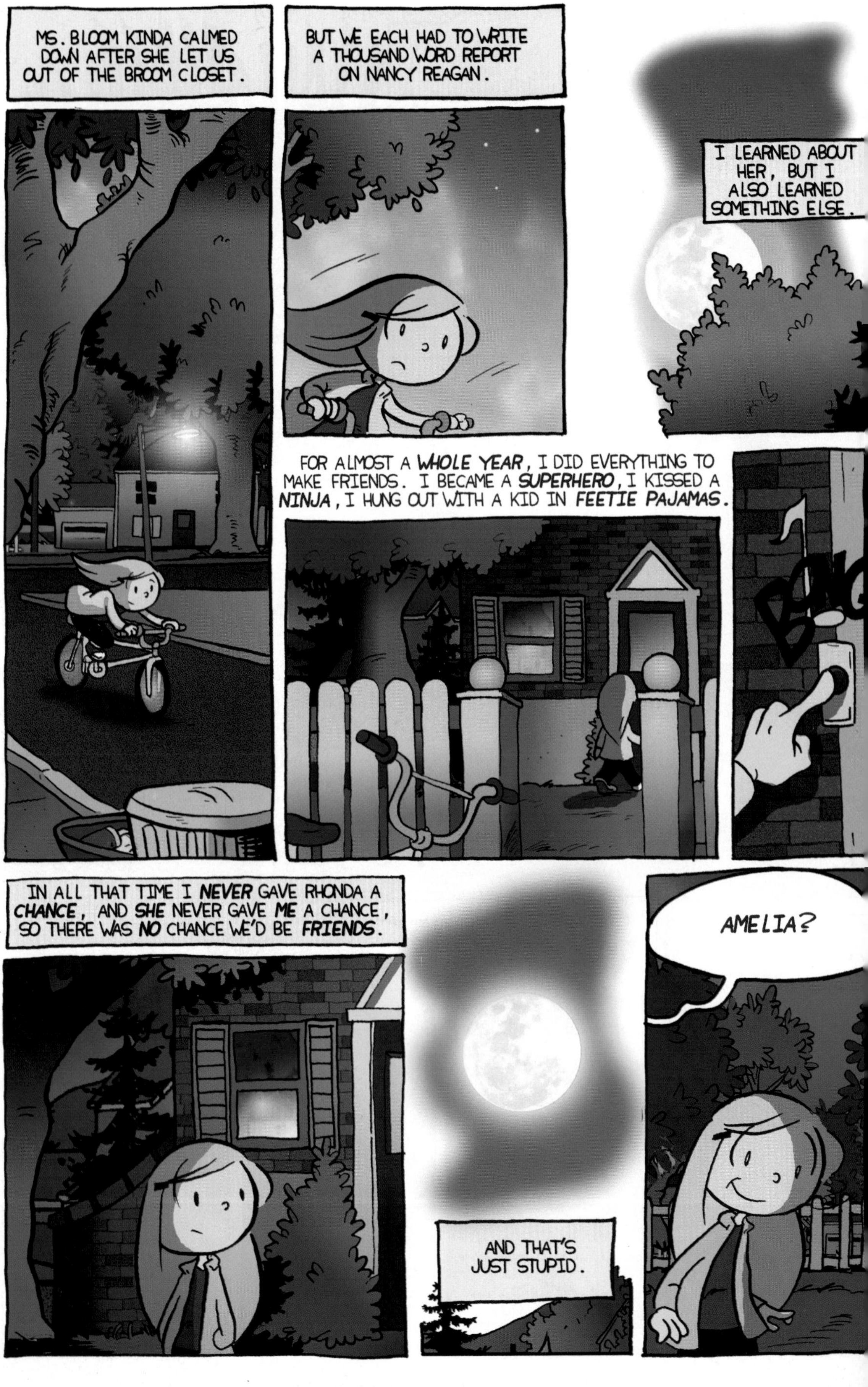
MS. BLOOM KINDA CALMED DOWN AFTER SHE LET US OUT OF THE BROOM CLOSET.
BUT WE EACH HAD TO WRITE A THOUSAND WORD REPORT ON NANCY REAGAN.
I LEARNED ABOUT HER, BUT I ALSO LEARNED SOMETHING ELSE.
FOR ALMOST A WHOLE YEAR, I DID EVERYTHING TO MAKE FRIENDS. I BECAME A SUPERHERO, I KISSED A NINJA, I HUNG OUT WITH A KID IN FEETIE PAJAMAS.
IN ALL THAT TIME I NEVER GAVE RHONDA A CHANCE, AND SHE NEVER GAVE ME A CHANCE, SO THERE WAS NO CHANCE WE'D BE FRIENDS.
AND THAT'S JUST STUPID.
AMELIA?

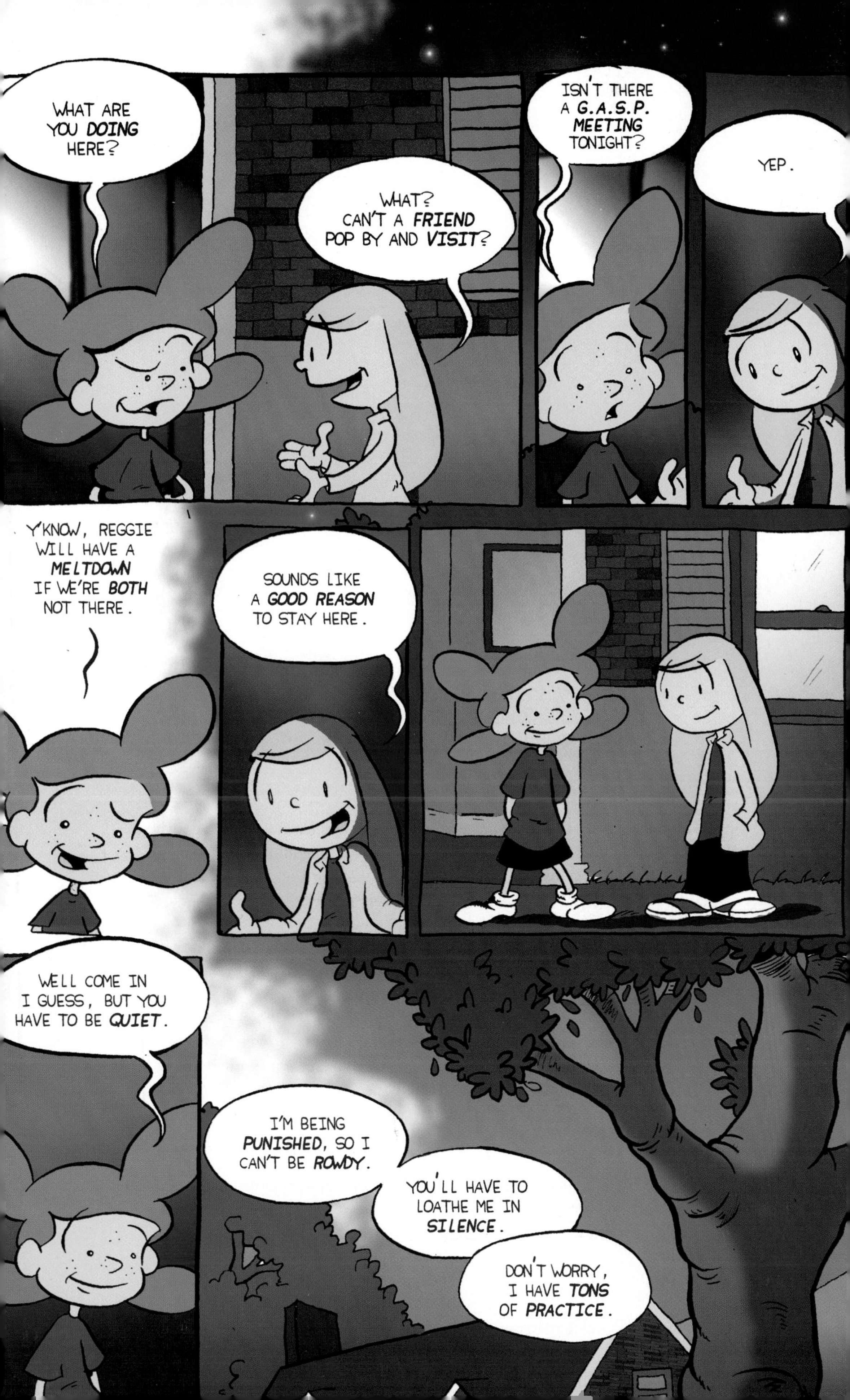
WHAT ARE YOU DOING HERE?
WHAT? CAN'T A FRIEND POP BY AND VISIT?
ISN'T THERE A G.A.S.P. MEETING TONIGHT?
YEP.
Y'KNOW, REGGIE WILL HAVE A MELTDOWN IF WE'RE BOTH NOT THERE.
SOUNDS LIKE A GOOD REASON TO STAY HERE.
WELL COME IN I GUESS, BUT YOU HAVE TO BE QUIET.
I'M BEING PUNISHED, SO I CAN'T BE ROWDY.
YOU'LL HAVE TO LOATHE ME IN SILENCE.
DON'T WORRY, I HAVE TONS OF PRACTICE.

About the Author:

Cartoonist Jimmy Gownley developed a love of comics at an early age when his mother read *Peanuts* collections to him. Not long after, he discovered comic books (via his Dad) and developed a voracious appetite for reading any and all things comic-related.

By the age of 15, Gownley was self-publishing his first book, *Shades of Gray Comics and Stories*. The black & white, slice-of-life series ran 16 issues and enjoyed cult success.

The idea for *Amelia Rules!* came about several years ago while Gownley was still working on *Shades of Gray*. The goal was to create a comic book with comic strip sensibilities that both traditional and non-traditional comic book fans could enjoy. He also wanted to provide good, solid entertainment for kids that didn't talk down to them.

Since it's debut in June 2001, *Amelia Rules!* has become a critical and fan favorite, and has been nominated for several awards, including the *Howard Eugene Day Memorial Prize* and the *Eisner Award*. The first volume of Amelia stories, entitled "The Whole World's Crazy", was released in October 2003, and was named an ALA Notable Book.

31-year-old Gownley lives in Harrisburg, Pennsylvania with his wife Karen, and twin daughters Stella and Anna.